Exploring the Basic Income Guarantee

Series Editor
Karl Widerquist, Georgetown University in Qatar, Doha, Qatar

Basic income is one of the most innovative, powerful, straightforward, and controversial proposals for addressing poverty and growing inequalities. A Basic Income Guarantee (BIG) is designed to be an unconditional, government-insured guarantee that all citizens will have enough income to meet their basic needs. The concept of basic, or guaranteed, income is a form of social provision and this series examines the arguments for and against it from an interdisciplinary perspective with special focus on the economic and social factors. By systematically connecting abstract philosophical debates over competing principles of BIG to the empirical analysis of concrete policy proposals, this series contributes to the fields of economics, politics, social policy, and philosophy and establishes a theoretical framework for interdisciplinary research. It will bring together international and national scholars and activists to provide a comparative look at the main efforts to date to pass unconditional BIG legislation across regions of the globe and will identify commonalities and differences across countries drawing lessons for advancing social policies in general and BIG policies in particular.

More information about this series at
https://link.springer.com/bookseries/14981

Roberto Merrill · Catarina Neves · Bru Laín

Basic Income Experiments

A Critical Examination of Their Goals, Contexts, and Methods

palgrave
macmillan

Roberto Merrill
Departamento de Filosofia
University of Minho
Braga, Portugal

Catarina Neves
University of Minho
Braga, Portugal

Bru Laín
University of Barcelona
Barcelona, Spain

ISSN 2662-3803 ISSN 2662-3811 (electronic)
Exploring the Basic Income Guarantee
ISBN 978-3-030-89119-0 ISBN 978-3-030-89120-6 (eBook)
https://doi.org/10.1007/978-3-030-89120-6

This Palgrave Macmillan imprint is published by the registered company Springer Nature Switzerland AG
The registered company address is: Gewerbestrasse 11, 6330 Cham, Switzerland

Acknowledgements

We would like to thank to all of those who helped us in this book journey. We are extremely indebted for their support and for the humble way with which they provided their opinions and experiences.

We would like to especially thanks to all our eighteen interviewees. Without the valuable and insightful contribution, and revision of the manuscript of each one of them, this book would not have been possible. Thank you to Amy Castro, Caroline Teti, Dirk Haarmann, Djavad Salehi-Isfahani, Fábio Waltenberg, Fernando Freitas, Hyosang Ahn, Jamie Cooke, José Luís de Sales Marques, Lluís Torrens, Maheba Goedeke Tort, Minna Ylikännö, Randall Akee, Roger van Loon, Sarrath Davala, Stacia West, Timo Verläat, and Wayne Lewchuk.

We would also like to thank Will Wojcik Shook, who provided one of the most comprehensive, critical, and insightful content and language spelling review of each part of the manuscript. His review was critical to our iteration on the arguments and conclusions of the book.

Finally, we would like to thank the peer reviewers who analyzed our manuscript proposal, and the Palgrave Macmillan editor team, who was patient, and helpful throughout the process of writing and submitting the book manuscript.

The research involved in this book has received funding from the Foundation for Science and Technology (PTDC/FER-FIL/28078/2017. ref.POCI).

Contents

CHAPTER 1

Introduction

Unconditional basic income (UBI) has in the recent years captured the attention of many academics, policymakers, politicians, businessmen, activists, and all citizens concerned with the common good. This interest has largely been driven through the many contemporary UBI experiments. Such experiments have sparked debate on why a basic income should be implemented and given rise to objections on its desirability and feasibility. Before presenting the goals the book wishes to accomplish, it is important to briefly define and outline UBI and UBI experiments.

1.1 UBI and Conditional Transfers

Modern society often forces individuals to rely on employment for income. When income is not available through employment, welfare state regimes reserve different types of minimum aid schemes for those who have less resources, and less capacity to obtain them. In this situation, the assumption is that people belong to a certain political community governed by a state, which guarantees them the right to survive. However, this is a flawed system which obviously does not do enough to ensure real freedom of opportunity for everyone (Van Parijs 1995).

An unconditional basic income is an income of sufficient amount to guarantee decent living conditions, paid unconditionally in cash to all

R. Merrill et al., *Basic Income Experiments*, Exploring the Basic Income Guarantee, https://doi.org/10.1007/978-3-030-89120-6_1

citizens and legal residents of a political community without taking into account the financial situation of the recipients. Some proposals also include children as beneficiaries of a UBI. UBI should be universal, individual, obligations-free, and ideally it should be of a sufficiently high amount to guarantee all members of the political community a dignified existence and civic participation. Most proposals feature monthly payments, although there are cases in which the distribution may be more spaced (annual) or less (weekly).

In some sections of this book, we will refer to the Negative Income Tax (NIT) experiments which took place in the USA and Canada in the 1970s. So, it is important from the outset to expose the differences and similarities between UBI and NIT. The most important differences are the following: a UBI is paid without a means test, whereas a NIT is means-tested. However, they share a fundamental similarity which is that both are unconditional in the sense of being obligation-free, that is without work requirements. This similarity between UBI and NIT regarding their being obligation-free is what distinguish them from all other conditional cash transfers, which are restricted to those willing to work. By being obligation-free, both policies share the aim of relieving people from what is called the "poverty trap" in a more effective way than conditional cash transfers, since both allow to cumulate the unconditional income with an employment income. It is however accurate to consider some of the case studies explored in this book as NIT experiments, in the sense that the beneficiaries of these experiments are means-tested, such as the experiments in Finland, The Netherlands, Spain, Canada, the Stockton experiment in the USA, and in Brazil. This is the case because it is much easier to test some of the potential benefits of a UBI through a means-tested experiment, since it is much less expensive to do so.

But some of our case studies can be on the contrary considered UBI experiments, the experiments in Namibia, India and Kenya, or the policies that have been tested after implementation, namely the Macau's Wealth Partaking Scheme, the Eastern Band of Cherokee Indian's dividend, or the Iranian cash grants, since these are not means-tested, tend to be obligation-free, individual and universal, or near universal. Nevertheless, even if these examples can be described as UBI experiments, they are not examples of a "pure" UBI, since the amounts received are too small and according to our definition a UBI must be of a sufficient level for a dignified life.

In order to understand the difference between UBI and actual existing social protection schemes (most prominently occurring in Europe), it is important to underline that UBI is not a social aid directed only at those who are poor or have little to no income. So at the outset, UBI immediately eliminates the stigmatizing factor associated with those who are obliged to "live off subsidies", by being universal on the one hand, and obligation-free on the other. On the contrary, a UBI can be supplemented by additional incomes, whether they result from work or not. This raises the objection of granting an income to those who, in theory, do not need it. But this is a manageable objection, because depending on the modes of financing adopted, the UBI allocated to those who are wealthier may later be recovered by taxes through a progressive tax system (Arcarons et al. 2014; Torry 2019; Widerquist and Arndt 2020).

This equal treatment exempts the state from endless discussions about the choice of beneficiaries; moreover, due to its simplicity, it eliminates a substantial part of the bureaucracy. It should be stressed, however, that this does not imply the state's resignation from its social responsibilities. There still needs to be social protection for specific problems (think, for example, of physical, psychological, or other health problems), but it is legitimate to think that they would be less numerous, since the UBI would already equip people the ability to resolve most of them. In our opinion, it is also important to note that, whatever the model adopted, it would have to be ensured that no one who previously received social benefits would see their income diminished as a consequence of the introduction of the UBI, since this would be a regressive measure which would worsen the position of the most disadvantaged in society.

Unconditional basic income can then be considered as a preventive form of social justice that makes the economy less likely to produce unacceptable income inequalities by providing everyone with at least a minimum level of resources. This preventive approach to social justice considers that, on the one hand, private property should not necessarily be condemned, but, on the other, it should be the object of a more equitable distribution in society, as property reinforces the control that individuals can have on their ability to govern themselves. Thus, if one wants to privilege the responsibility of individuals and increase their freedom, it is necessary to be able to simultaneously widen their real possibilities (e.g., not working only out of necessity, being able to refuse jobs that do not correspond to what each one intends, etc.) and to allow individuals to have a greater economic capacity in the exchanges they make with others in different markets (market goods, certainly, but also labor market).

UBI therefore represents a guarantee of greater autonomy in the face of market relations or, at least, of resilience in terms of the disadvantageous terms that others typically may want to impose—thus, it is a response to a demand for "honest reciprocity" among citizens and a fairer access to the distribution of goods and opportunities in society.

Poverty is one of the most serious problems affecting modern society. It is both an ethical problem (how is it possible to allow people to drop below a poverty threshold?) and a social one, hence one needs to look for the best mechanisms available to mitigate it. In fact, this is a problem that states have faced and have been trying to resolve, even before the institution of the modern welfare state. However, this is perhaps a problem that should be seen in a transformative and dynamic way, and it is in this perspective that it is worth considering UBI as a possible solution.

The idea of giving money directly to the poor was put into practice for the first time in England in 1795, in the village of Speenhamland. It was decided to provide all families in Speenhamland with income support that would ensure their livelihood. In England, during the reign of Queen Elizabeth I (1533–1603), other assistance programs for the poor had already existed, but these distinguished between the "poor who deserve help" (the elderly, children, and the disabled) and others, who were forced to work. In 1830, the government decided to re-evaluate Speenhamland's program concluding that it had been a disaster. The conclusion they reached was that the population had grown a lot, wages had decreased and immoral behavior had increased, among other aspects. This government report was widely circulated and helped to create what Bregman (2017) calls "the Speenhamland myth".

The idea that the poor are not responsible enough to receive cash subsidies is still present today. However, the non-paternalistic idea of a direct and unconditional transfer that allows everyone (including the poor) to make their own choices has spread, little by little. For example, starting in the USA in the 1960s and 1970s, personalities as different as Milton Friedman, Richard Nixon, and Martin Luther King defended various versions of a UBI. Their main purpose was to avoid the so-called poverty trap, where the poorest Americans receive support from social assistance and still end up being "trapped" in poverty. The jobs they were able to access were so poorly paid, that in many cases it was (and still is today) preferable not to work and continue to receive social security support, such as some health care, food stamps, and social housing. This situation can cause many families and individuals to be trapped in a situation of poverty, with no prospect of social mobility or personal fulfillment. Since transfers are conditional, these people can be disadvantaged by accepting a job, and they find themselves in a trap from which they cannot escape (Cappi and Delvaux 1990; Redley et al. 1992).

This situation helps illustrate a large part of the problem with conditional transfers and the difficulty they have in alleviating poverty. UBI has the advantage of being a simple, effective, and non-degrading solution to the issue of poverty. It creates a safety net for all citizens without implying any request for social security assistance, since it is universal and unconditional. It allows everyone to look for more satisfactory paths for their life without having to lose that basic safety net. It also enables long-term planning, which is essential for individuals and families to build a healthy and fulfilling life.

Furthermore, one of the best arguments in favor of UBI is that no one knows better than individuals in poverty how to use money to plan and invest in their lives. For a family it may be more important to immediately invest in a house, for another training may be more important. The assumption that social security knows what the poor need better than themselves is absurd, expensive, and ineffective.

Across the developed world, the sustainability of social security has been a recurring issue for several decades. Most developed welfare states (especially European ones) were implemented in their strongest form in the first thirty years after the Second World War, a time when the global economy and demography were much different. Considering the reversal of the demographic pyramid in many of these states, the precariousness of family ties, and the difficulty in maintaining very low unemployment rates, the future viability of these systems may be questioned. The calculation is easy to do: if the system is largely based on workers' contributions, if workers live (and work) longer, and fewer jobs are available, it can be increasingly difficult to raise enough contributions to finance a potentially growing mass of pensioners.

The implementation of a UBI would allow the replacement of a variety of other social programs, if these benefits were less than the amount of a UBI payment. Assuming that this income would be above the poverty line, some benefits would become redundant. This would be the case, for example, with family allowances and minimum income schemes totaling less than the basic income payment. But UBI does not necessarily replace all other forms of social assistance, nor unemployment benefits; in cases where the unemployed have an allowance higher than the UBI, its value can be fixed by the difference between the UBI and the amount of the allowance. Unconditional basic income does not necessitate the withdrawal of other types of social assistance, such as maternal, people with physical or mental disabilities, etc., that is people in situations of greater vulnerability.

A UBI would effectively make it possible to reach all people, including those who have the right to minimum income benefits but do not receive them due to bureaucratic difficulties, stigma associated with these benefits, simple ignorance, or another reason. In fact, all over the world, there are people who could benefit from social support but do not; because they do not register with employment centers or are in fact in a situation of poverty but are ashamed to ask for help or to submit to all the conditions existing in current systems (Skocpol 1991; Korpi and Palme 1998; Warin 2012; Brady and Bostic 2015). Being universal and unconditional, UBI would make it possible to include all of these people in a way conditional transfers never could.

1.2 The Surge in UBI Experiments and Their Limitations

The implementation of a UBI, whether complete or partial in a first phase, would represent a profound change in our social protection system, and several experiments made in various countries can be of great use in realizing and evaluating the potential benefits of this type of income.

Before moving into the methodology of the book and outlining the case studies we will be discussing, it is important to briefly present the ongoing discussions on the distinction between pilots and experiments, and mention some of the key objections and limitations of experimenting with a UBI in real-life contexts.

As mentioned in *The Palgrave International Handbook of Basic Income*:

> Only if a project is testing a genuine Basic Income is it right to call the project a 'Basic Income pilot project'. A project that tests anything else should be called an 'experiment' from which useful lessons might be learnt. (Torry 2019, 10–13)

As we will be discussing in Chapter 2 our case studies consist of basic income pilot projects, experiments, and even policies which have been studied after implementation. We will discuss how these differences impact the results gathered in our book and its conclusions. We will distinguish in the book between the experimental cases, including basic income pilots, experiments, and the non-experimental cases, which include the case studies which are policies. We will highlight these distinctions throughout the book when we consider them relevant for our conclusions. However, for convenience, we will use the expression "basic income experiments" most of the time, as the more generic term to refer to our case studies, also when referring to pilots, NIT experiments, or policies, unless otherwise stated.

Despite the distinction between them, it is possible to briefly identify four of the most common criticisms and limitations addressed to both experiments and pilots.

Firstly, even with positive results from a UBI experiment, popular or political support for the establishment of a permanent and universal basic income will not automatically be won. From the outset, an experiment will be carried out on a small scale—with a city or a group of individuals as the object of experimentation for a limited duration—so the transposition of the experiment's conclusions to a larger and permanent scale will not be linear. But it could, of course, be a starting point.

Likewise, as this topic touches on some of the central points of the way we currently organize ourselves as a society, namely in relation to the role played by paid employment and access to an unconditional income, it is not at all unrealistic to think that, even if the experiments show the viability of a UBI and the advantages vastly outweigh the disadvantages, there will still be opposition to it. Think, for example, of the common criticisms often made to social inclusion income schemes, even though they represent a very small part of the public budget and are allocated in large part to people who are not in a position to have a job. What we can hope for is that, with the implementation of a UBI, the empirical support for this opposition would be diminished, since everyone would receive it, a complete UBI being universal.

A third criticism that can be made of UBI experiments is that they necessarily refer to a UBI model (or a range of models). Thus, while this model is being tested, it will be difficult to move forward with the discussion on alternative models. And in the end, if that experiment is unsuccessful, there is a serious risk that the window of discussion on the implementation of a UBI will close for several years, just as, when a proposal is rejected in a referendum, it does not reappear on the public agenda for a long period.

Finally, another possible criticism of the implementation of a UBI experiment would be to say that, if it is understood as a right, then the UBI should not be subject to this experiment. The institution of public, free, and universal education has not been subjected to any explicit experiment, as well as the institution of a national health services. Being also a political issue, if UBI is seen as a right, then, in theory, it could be applied directly—although the question of its financial feasibility is always an important "detail" to establish.

Such criticisms are mostly related with the highly polarized nature of UBI, and how it touches upon entrenched beliefs, hence becoming a difficult policy to implement, even if evidence is greatly positive. However, experiments and pilots also face limitations because of their design and nature as social experiment. Some of these include the issue of time frame—how can we believe that a 2–3 year experiment will yield robust findings on issues such as employment or community effects?—the issue of where to concentrate our analysis—our research bias might jeopardize data collection on other important variables, hence reducing our overall understanding of the policy—or even how an experiment might bias the results, since participants will know they are being evaluated—can we believe in the behavioral patterns of people receiving a UBI when they are part of a basic income experiment? Several strategies are used to try to mitigate such impacts. However, it is still important to acknowledge most of them and accept that experiments will have inherent limitations, hence the knowledge we can get out of them will always be to a certain extent quite limited.

Despite the legitimacy of the doubts about UBI experiments, the truth is that they allow a clarified analysis of the role that UBI can play. First, by entering the public discussion as something that is in fact being done, many of less reflected criticisms that are made of the UBI could disappear. In addition, this type of experiment allows for a comprehensive public debate in which everyone can clarify their doubts regarding basic income and the impacts it may have on their lives. Also, one of the most prominent criticisms of basic income experiments is the potential inability of testing a policy that is defined (ideally) as universal. Nevertheless, the results from experiments can be used to justify (or reject) its full implementation. These benefits and hurdles of UBI experiments will be discussed throughout the book, in hopes of advancing the ongoing discussion on the role played by them.

1.3 Methodology

This book's main goal is to inform students, researchers, practitioners, and policymakers about the main philosophical, epistemological, and sociological questions stemming from basic income experiments past, present, and future. The book brings together insights and reflections following a set of interviews conducted with people who have been involved in past, current, and future basic income experiments, pilots, and policies. It aims to provide analysis of some of the major elements and factors influencing experiments, as well of some of their most important outputs (understood as results of their own experimental design, their sociological and political basis, and the epistemological status of their results). The main question the book will be asking is: What is the role of basic income experiments, pilots, and policies as political, research, or advocacy tools?

Since the main insights of the book are a direct result of our interviews, the methodology of the book follows a bottom-up strategy. Interviews with pivotal stakeholders involved in data collection and analysis of our case studies were conducted to generate the discussions we present in each chapter. In each interview, key questions on the methodology, political context, and the future of the basic income debate in each context were assembled and supplemented with specific questions pertaining to the case studies. A general script was created (see Exhibit 2 for the general script used in the interviews), and the existing reports, literature, and other relevant resources on each experiment were used to prepare each interview and adapt the general script to each case study.

By adopting a bottom-up strategy, where the relevant stakeholders involved in the experiments are the ones providing insights and information, the overall reflections which will be present in the book's chapters answer both theoretical and empirical challenges.[1] It will thus help compare some of the challenges and strategies of different basic income experiments, according to their research design, but also adding details of their political and social context, the goals of each experiment and the motivations and actions of different stakeholders.

The general underlying question we are trying to answer is: "Why should we have basic income experiments?" However, we do not provide any general theory as an answer on the role experiments can play, but

[1] However, our interpretations of the transcriptions of the opinions and ideas of the stakeholders interviewed are obviously exclusively our responsibility.

rather use the particular and general findings from our case studies to come up with several possible answers to our underlying question.

Besides the discussion on the role experiments can play in our understanding of UBI, and in the general movement for its implementation, we will also focus on more particular questions, namely in the inherent paradox of how most experiments fall short of providing an example of a "pure basic income" as defined in the first section of this introduction. A significant aspect of analyzing experiments is understanding how closely they fulfill this definition.

Alongside the key issues mentioned above, we will also try to provide answers to the following questions:

- What is the impact of the different motivations to conduct basic income experiments in the overall implementation?
- What is the role of the political context when deciding to implement a basic income experiment, throughout the project, but also in ensuring its future?
- Can we draw differences between research on UBI experiments and research on basic income implemented as a policy in each context?
- How is the overall reception to basic income experiments from the different stakeholders?
- What are the main difficulties in conducting a basic income experiment and why?
- What are the main results taken from different basic income experiments, and what changes were most relevant according to the stakeholders involved in the research?
- In what way do basic income experiments generally contribute to the basic income debate?

Other relevant issues might be included, given the insights collected in the interviews.

1.4 Our Interviewees

We conducted 18 interviews over a period of six months. For most case studies, we interviewed only one stakeholder per case study, although in the cases of Utrecht and Maricá we had the opportunity of interviewing two people. We will briefly present our interviewees. During the book, when relevant, we will attribute the insights presented to the interviewee who introduced them to us.

Most of our interviewees are researchers involved in the design, implementation, and/or evaluation of the experiment, pilot, or policy. These is the case in 12 of 18 of our interviewees, namely:

- Minna Ylikännö: Senior Specialist, Ministry of Economic Affairs and Employment. At the time of the experiment in Finland, worked at the Research Unit of Kela as a head of a research team involved in the evaluation of the Finnish basic income experiment.
- Timo Verlaat: from Utrecht University School of Economics is a PhD candidate and one of the researchers involved in the design, implementation, and evaluation of the Utrecht experiment.
- Lluís Torrens: from Barcelona City Council, Director of social innovation at Barcelona city council, and director of the B-MINCOME experiment in Barcelona.
- Wayne Lewchuk: from McMaster University was one of the researchers involved in the Ontario experiment, in Canada.
- Claudia and Dirk Haarmann: They coordinated the Basic Income Grant Coalition Namibia (2004–2009), implemented the BIG Pilot Project in Otjivero (Namibia) and led its impact assessment.
- Sarath Davala: one of the lead researchers involved in the design and implementation of the pilot Project in Madhya Pradesh, in India.
- Stacia West: from University of Tennessee, College of Social Work, Nashville, and Senior Fellow at The University of Pennsylvania, School of Social Policy and Practice. Co-Principal Investigator of SEED—the Stockton Economic Empowerment Demonstration, in California. Co-Founder of the Center for Guaranteed Income Research at The University of Pennsylvania.
- Amy Castro: from The University of Pennsylvania, School of Social Policy and Practice. Co-Principal Investigator of SEED—the Stockton Economic Empowerment Demonstration, in California. Co-Founder of the Center for Guaranteed Income Research at The University of Pennsylvania.
- Fábio Waltenberg: from Universidade Federal Fluminense. Lead researcher responsible for evaluating the results of the *Renda Básica da Cidadania* em Maricá (Brazil).

- Fernando Freitas: from Universidade Federal Fluminense. PhD candidate, and researcher responsible for evaluating the results of the *Renda Básica da Cidadania* em Maricá (Brazil).
- Randall Akee: public policy researcher at the Luskin School of Public Affairs, at University of California, Los Angeles (UCLA). He has worked with the evidence collected in "The Great Smoky Mountains Study of Youth", which was able to analyze the impact of the introduction of the dividend in the Eastern Band of Cherokee Indians.
- Djavad Salehi-Isfahani: Professor of Economics at Virginia Tech and Nonresident Senior Fellow, Brookings Institution.

The remaining six interviewees have distinct roles and influence on basic income experiments, pilots, or projects. Some are part of non-governmental organizations who have supported the UBI movement in their countries or have actively worked toward generating evidence that can be used in the UBI movement worldwide to make a case for basic income. Roger van Loon is the only public servant we interviewed. He works for Utrecht Municipality and was involved in the experiment in the city. Finally, it is worth mentioning that one of our interviewees, José Luís de Sales Marques has not been involved in the wealth partaking scheme implemented in the region. However, he has connection with political representatives and has benefited from the scheme, hence was able to provide important accounts on the scheme implemented in Macau. The six interviewees are:

- Caroline Teti: from GiveDirectly. Director, recipient Advocacy at GiveDirectly who was also involved in the design, implementation, and oversight of UBI experiment in Kenya.
- Hyosang Ahn: executive director of BIKN—Basic Income Korea Network has been following and conducted research on the Youth Basic Income Project in South Korea.
- Jamie Cooke: Head of RSA Scotland has been one of the main advocates for UBI in Scotland. He has written several opinion and research articles on the potential for UBI in Scotland, and was on the research team which conducted the RSA report on basic income in Scotland.
- Maheba Goedeke Tort: from *Mein Grundeinkommen*. Responsible for the conception and research coordination of the Basic Income Pilot Project in Germany.

- Roger van Loon: from Utrecht Municipality is a policy advisor for Utrecht Municipality, which was the main institution behind the experiment in Utrecht. He was responsible for the execution of the final stage of the experiment in Utrecht and its evaluation.
- José Luís de Sales Marques: President of the Institute of European Studies. Member of the Board of Directors at Portuguese School Foundation—Macau. Beneficiary of Macau's wealth partaking scheme has also been president of Macau's City Council.

1.5 The Case Studies

We will now briefly outline the main case studies that will be the focus of this book. Across six months, we interviewed researchers, politicians, and in some cases beneficiaries of fifteen case studies. Several criteria were used to include each of the case studies, namely:

- Their prominence in the basic income debate;
- Available evidence (reports and others);
- Proximity to the ideal type of basic income as defined above.
- Their contemporary nature.

We chose to focus on case studies whose findings are relatively recent, or up-and-coming, as opposed to older experiments, which have already been discussed to a great extent. Therefore, we focused on the contemporary wave of basic income experiments, namely the ones that took place in the first and second decade of the twenty-first century, but also some which are now starting. This means some important cases were excluded, which we will nonetheless discuss occasionally, namely the NIT experiments in USA and Canada in the 1960s and 1970s, but also the Alaska Permanent Fund policy.

Before going into the case studies, it is important to account for a particular limitation of our sample. Our case studies include recent experiments, which are in differing stages of implementation and assessment of their results. Some of the case studies already have final reports on their impacts—such as the ones in Utrecht, Finland, Namibia, Kenya, Madhya Pradesh in India, and South Korea. Barcelona has published the main results of the experiment, and only qualitative data is missing. Maricá's

Renda Básica de Cidadania is still in the analysis phase (due to COVID-19 the research process was delayed). There is also Ontario, where the experiment was cut short, and existing evidence is scant and based on a small and incomplete sample of data. The Eastern Band of Cherokee Indians' Dividend has a lot of information, but since existing evidence was not collected for a study on basic income, relevant data is scarce and at times lacks context. The Stockton Economic Empowerment Demonstration (SEED) project in Stockton has provided preliminary findings, while the Iranian universal subsidy scheme has limited evidence of its impact. Lastly, evidence is very scarce in the case of Macau, since no systematic research has been conducted on the Wealth Partaking Scheme of the region and obviously in Scotland too, since there is no experiment being conducted. Therefore, when discussing evidence, our conclusions will be somewhat imbalanced, being mostly formed by analysis of where there is some evidence on their impacts. To mitigate this gap and to provide a richer discussion, we will relate our conclusions with existing evidence from former experiments, such as the Negative Income Tax experiments in the USA, the MINCOME experiment in Canada, and Alaska' Permanent Fund, when relevant, taking into account their inherent limitations, and the ongoing discussions on their findings. This is why we chose to include a brief presentation of the experiments from the 1960s to 1970s which took place in the USA and Canada, as well as of the Alaska Permanent Fund, although we were not able to interview stakeholders involved in these experiments and thus cannot include them in our case studies.

1.5.1 Experiments from the 1960s to 1970s in the USA and Canada

Between 1969 and 1980, a few UBI experiments were carried out in several locations in the USA and Canada (Moynihan 1973; Lenkowsky 1986; Widerquist 2005; Steensland 2008; Caputo 2012) to study their possible effects in the fight against poverty and incentives for employment. The American experiment of "guaranteed income" was designed to test the effects on employment, education, and the family, as well as the conditions of capital accumulation. The US federal government committed itself to the following four experiments, between 1968 and 1972.

A first experiment took place in New Jersey and Pennsylvania in an urban population (Pechman and Timpane 1975). A second one took place in Gary, Indiana with the objective of evaluating the effects of

UBI in single-parent families. A third was carried out in North Carolina and Iowa to study the impact of such a measure on the rural population. Finally, a fourth experiment, much more significant because of a larger scale, known by the acronym SIME-DIME (Seattle Income Maintenance Experiment-Denver Income Maintenance Experiment), was put into practice in the cities of Seattle and Denver.

Unfortunately, the effects of these experiments were not evaluated as seriously as initially intended, due to insufficient funding. However, according to Evelyn Forget (2011), some statistical data collected revealed a significant, albeit limited, decline in the work effort of the beneficiaries. This decline was generally distributed unevenly among different members of the household. It appears that for those who occupied the position of "head" of the family (i.e., the main breadwinner), the decline in working hours was less than 5%. In the case of the spouse however, the decrease was more significant (25%) and matched by an increase in time spent on domestic and family tasks. In the case of adolescent beneficiaries, mainly male, the reduction in working hours was more pronounced, resulting in prolonging the duration of their studies before entering the workforce.

Forget characterizes the results of this experiment as positive in relation to the increase in the level of education of the beneficiaries. Note that this experiment is presented frequently as a proof that a UBI can be the cause of a large-scale exit from the labor market. However, as demonstrated by a more detailed analysis of the available data, this departure was largely because many adolescents and young adults chose to devote more time to school, which is why this "escape" from work can hardly be seen as negative.

In the 1970s, two other experiments were carried out in Canada. In the province of Manitoba, an experiment took place between 1974 and 1979 in two cities—Winnipeg and Dauphin—known by the acronym MINCOME. In Winnipeg, the experiment was conducted on a small scale and primarily focused on testing the effects on employment by comparing working-age beneficiaries against those not receiving benefits. The results were similar to those of the experiments carried out in the USA (Hum and Simpson 1991, 1993, 2001; Calnitsky and Latner 2017; Calnitsky 2016).

Among the USA and Canadian experiments, the experiment in the city of Dauphin was the only truly comprehensive experiment, incorporating the entire urban and surrounding rural population, about 10,000 people in total. Families and individuals not meeting Canada's low-income threshold received monthly payments equal to 60% of the threshold, its amount being reduced by 50% for every dollar of income from other sources. It should be noted that this income was equivalent to the level of income paid to families that already benefited from social assistance, but it represented a substantial improvement in the income of families not eligible to receive social assistance, which were largely composed of farmers or people with disabilities. Although the statistical evaluation of this experiment is incomplete, Evelyn Forget came to the conclusion that MINCOME brought health benefits to the affected population (Forget 2011).

These North American experiments were carried out with a desire to assess the potential effects on the beneficiaries of UBI payments. However, for budgetary reasons and due to a growing political disinterest in the late 1970s for the concept of UBI as a tool to reduce poverty, it was not possible to fully explore the beneficial effects or possible disadvantages of the experiments. Despite their limitations, they nonetheless provide interesting evidence on the impact a negative income tax can have on working hours, family relations, health and well-being, education, and stigmatization of the recipients of social assistance. We will therefore keep these results in mind and discuss them in the context of our case studies, whenever we think that this might be helpful to understand some of the evidence from our case studies.

1.5.2 Alaska's Permanent Fund

The Alaska Permanent Fund, along with Macau's Wealth Partaking Scheme, is one of the two most successful examples of the widespread attribution of a form of UBI. This income is financed by returns on the investment of profits from the sale of state-owned natural resources (mostly oil). In the late 1960s, the Alaskan state budget received $900 million US dollars because of the allocation of rights to explore for oil fields in Prudhoe Bay, in the northeast of the state. In 1976, the government made the decision to allocate that amount to a public fund, with a portion of the proceeds from that fund distributed annually to Alaskan citizens. The state constitution was amended to stipulate that at least 25% of all revenue generated by the state's exploitation of the natural resources from the soil would be placed in a permanent fund—the Alaska

Permanent Fund—with the objective of generating income to be reinvested in the economy, as well as for the benefit of citizens through an annual dividend.

An ad hoc structure established by state law—the Alaska Permanent Fund Corporation—was responsible for administering and managing the proceeds obtained. Since 1976, the fund's appreciation has been exponential. In 2019, each of the 633,243 beneficiaries received a sum of 1,606 USdollars.[2] The dividend is paid to adults and children, by check or transfer to their bank accounts, although it must comply with several conditions: the residence requirement of at least one year from the date of application to receive the dividend, the condition of regular residence, and the absence, during the previous year, of conviction or imprisonment for a crime. It should be noted that the dividend benefit presupposes an annual voluntary request from each potential beneficiary (for an exhaustive description and assessment of the Alaska Permanent Fund, see Widerquist and Howard 2012).

1.5.3 *Outline of Our Case Studies*

Our case studies will be outlined below. They illustrate examples of UBI experiments which have been implemented locally or nationally. We can distinguish them based on their current implementation status: "Finished"—those that have been implemented, and which have published some form of results, such as the ones which took place in Namibia, India, Iran, Finland, the Netherlands, Canada, and Spain; "Ongoing"—those that are now taking place, or are complete but lack published data at the time of writing this book, such as the ones in Kenya, the USA, Macau, Brazil, and South Korea; and "Planned"—those which are still in development, but will most likely be carried out in the future, such as in Germany and Scotland.

1.5.4 *The Experiments in India*

India has shown great interest in adopting a UBI, as the experiments that took place between 2008 and 2013 demonstrate (which include the project led by SEWA, which took place between 2011 and 2012).

[2] See the official website here: https://pfd.alaska.gov/.

The first one took place in 2008 in New Delhi. The income was distributed to some families who because they were below the threshold of poverty, were already covered by public programs that allowed them to purchase essential products (e.g., rice, cereals, fuel) at subsidized prices. Participants were able to choose between maintaining access to these products at subsidized prices or receiving a cash income. This experiment demonstrated improved eating habits among families that opted for cash payments, while families which chose continued access to price-subsidized products showed no change.

Another experiment began in several villages in the Indian state of Madhya Pradesh in 2012 lasted about 18 months and had the greatest impact. The experiment featured an unconditional monthly cash payment of 200 rupees per adult and 100 rupees per child, benefitting about 6,000 people in total. After 12 months, the amount was increased by 50%. The results of this experiment were statistically evaluated by a team of experts appointed by Self Employed Women's Association (SEWA) which initiated the study. UNICEF funded the project. The evaluation demonstrates that this payment enabled the beneficiaries to satisfy their basic needs, including improving their diet, health, education, or, when applicable, purchase production tools. This experiment has not given empirical support to the common criticism that recipients might "waste" or "misuse" a UBI. This last case is the focus of our interview and discussion in the book. Having been part of the team of researchers of this project in Madhya Pradesh, Sarath Davala (whom we interviewed for this book) and his colleagues (Davala et al. 2015) summarize its results in four dimensions: (1) improvements in access to sanitation, health care, education, nutrition, and school attendance; (2) improvements in social equity, namely through the training of women and members of the castes considered inferior; (3) increased work, with the exception of young people who spent more time enrolled in school; and (4) contributions to the emancipation of individuals, giving them greater control over their lives. Our interview on the Indian experiments and hence our conclusions in the book are based on the experience, insights, and results from the Madhya Pradesh pilot.

1.5.5 *The Experiment in Namibia*

In Namibia between 2008 and 2009, which was the first world-wide pilot in a community, and extended on a lower level through to 2012.

The Namibia Basic Income Grant Coalition (BIG Coalition) designed and implemented this first unconditional cash transfer pilot project in the world. The BIG Coalition's practical aim was to pilot the Namibia Government's NAMTAX (Namibian Tax Consortium) recommendation for a basic income grant in Namibia. Thus, the BIG Coalition regarded this project as the first step toward a BIG for all. The Coalition consisted of four big umbrella bodies in Namibia, namely the Council of Churches (CCN), the National Union of Namibian Workers (NUNW), the Namibian NGO Forum (NINGOF), and the Namibian Network of AIDS Service Organizations (NANASO). The BIG Coalition raised funds from supporters of the idea from all sections of Namibia's society, including individuals, churches, organizations, and donors in other countries. The BIG pilot project ran for a period of 24 months up to December 2009 and extended on a lower level to 2012. The effects of the BIG pilot project were scientifically evaluated for the first year. The research used four complementary methods: a baseline survey in November 2007, subsequent panel surveys in July and November 2008, continuous key informant interviews and detailed case studies of individual living in Otjivero. An international team of experts guided and evaluated the research. The amount paid monthly was the equivalent of 9 euros, which amounted at the time to food poverty line. The amount was granted to 1000 inhabitants of the village of Otjivero. The research team found the following effects: a reduction in the number of malnourished children, an increased rate of education, and the development of new businesses (Haarmann and Haarmann 2007; Osterkamp 2013). As in the Madhya Pradesh pilot, the results indicated that the monthly allowance did not lead beneficiaries to adopt idle behavior. To the contrary, unemployment dropped from 65% to 45% and income through self-employment increased threefold by over 300%. The overall crime rate dropped by 42%.

1.5.6 *The Experiment in Finland*

The experimental project in Finland was the result of a process that begun in 2015, when a new government came to power. After the elections, the government launched a study aimed at establishing a UBI experiment for a two-year period starting in January 2017, with an evaluation to be made in 2019, and mobilizing a budget of 20 million euros. UBI was mainly seen to promote labor market activation in a country that had been facing an economic recession for several years and an unemployment rate at around 8%. The experimental project was carried out through the establishment of a partnership between the Social Insurance Institution of Finland (Kela) and various academic institutions and think tanks. In November 2016, a report was prepared that recommended the experimental introduction of a partial basic income—replacing some of the current subsidies, but without taking the place of other social security benefits. The experiment was limited to 2000 individuals between 25 and 58 years old looking for work and receiving the unemployment benefit paid by Kela. The €560 allowance was not subject to tax and was maintained if individuals found employment during that period. The UBI was only paid to unemployed people who already receiving unemployment benefits. unfortunately, in the middle of the experiment, the Finnish government introduced changes in the benefits' sanctions implemented at the time (e.g., making more severe cuts in the cash grants attributed for those who took longer to find a job).

Despite all these limitations and changes introduced, the experiment was carried on to the end. This even though the refusal to prolong the project was, on several occasions, misinterpreted by some media outlets that mistakenly reported that the experiment had been "cancelled" or "failed".[3] The results of the Finnish pilot project are public and show positive effects (Kangas et al. 2020). The first result to be reported was that the effects on insertion into the labor market were insignificant: the difference between incentives to work in the beneficiaries of the UBI and in the control group was very low. At first glance, it might appear that this signaled some "failure" of the UBI effect. But it seems to us that this result also shows, although for a limited period of two years, that the accusation of UBI detractors regarding the supposed disincentive of work was not empirically verified by this case. Despite the limited nature of this experiment, the beneficiaries showed significant positive results with regard to their physical and mental well-being, levels of confidence (in other people, in institutions, and in relation to their personal future), and feelings of economic security. Beneficiaries also reported lower levels of stress and depression.

[3] See, for example, https://www.theguardian.com/world/2018/apr/23/finland-to-end-basic-income-trial-after-two-years.

1.5.7 *The Experiment in the Netherlands*

The experiment in the Netherlands was carried out in six municipalities and not at a national level. In fact, most national political groups are opposed to the very principle of a UBI. In an economy that approaches full employment, the priority is to encourage work.

Six independent experiments were carried out in six different municipalities. The most complete of those experiments was held in Utrecht. The initiative was called "Weten wat werkt" ("Knowing what works" or "What works") and was considered an alternative to the so-called Participation Act law, which makes the payment of certain subsidies conditional on the fulfillment of certain administrative obligations as well as looking for training or jobs (Groot et al. 2021). This creates a situation fraught with administrative complexity, stress for potential beneficiaries, and which favors strategies of omission to maintain the right to subsidies. The experiment in Utrecht involved the participation of about 750 beneficiaries of the social insertion income, who had consented to participate. Among these 750 beneficiaries, the city officials tested income variations in three groups of individuals for almost two years. In addition, two control groups were also considered.

1. A first group had no obligation to look for a job.
2. A second group continued to have an obligation to look for a job and received one-on-one intensive counseling from a municipality caseworker.
3. A third group continued to have an obligation to look for a job and was allowed to keep a larger share of income when working while receiving the social insertion income.

The results were mostly focused on labor market participation, given the inherent scope of the experiment. No significant differences were found between groups, although the experiment found that some groups (namely distinct in terms of their educational background, or the amount of time they had been unemployed) responded differently to having an obligations-free income or having other social security programs with obligations.

1.5.8 *The Experiment in Ontario*

More than 40 years after the experiment in Manitoba, another Canadian Province tested a UBI model again, although of course falling short of a full UBI, since again, none of the experiments included in our case studies represent a "pure" UBI. In June 2017, the province of Ontario began the first phase of this new experiment, which aimed to test the health, employment, and housing benefits among beneficiaries. This experiment should have lasted three years, covering a total of 4000 participants, from rural and urban areas, to be as comprehensive as possible. However, the new provincial government ended the experiment in July 2018.

Similar to other experiments, the participants had to be unemployed and meet means-tested conditions. To be eligible, participants must have been living on a low income (less than 34,000 Canadian dollars for individuals or 48,000 for couples) or beneficiaries of social assistance programs. In addition to the group of beneficiaries, there was also a control group, which received no income. It should be noted that this experiment applied only to adults of working age—between 18 and 64 years old—thus excluding children and the elderly. However, the project was very ambitious in relation to the aspects that it intended to evaluate. The government's intention was to study how a UBI can help low-income individuals improve their living conditions in the following areas: food security, mental and physical health, use of health services, housing stability, education and training, employment, and participation in the labor market. The evaluation of these criteria was the responsibility of a research group that included a hospital and a university. In parallel, the government would also create a council to follow the project closely, bridging the gap between the research group and the relevant ministries.

The amount to be allocated to all beneficiaries would be 16,989 Canadian dollars per year for individuals and 24,027 Canadian dollars per year for couples, divided into monthly payments. These figures corresponded to about 75% of the poverty line. Other social benefits were maintained, such as those related to the care of minors. Individuals with a disability received an additional 500 Canadian dollars. This income was reduced by 0.5 Canadian dollars for each dollar earned if the individual was working. This was an extremely promising project, but unfortunately it was abruptly stopped in July 2018, with the election of conservative Doug Ford. Since the program was canceled, obtaining complete, reliable results was impossible, to the dismay of investigators who followed the case and to the beneficiaries of the experiment. The payments continued until March 2019. Limited evidence was gathered on the experiment, and interviews with some beneficiaries were conducted afterward.

1.5.9 *The B-MINCOME Experiment in Barcelona*

The 'B-MINCOME' experiment in Barcelona—a minimum guaranteed income combined with active social policies in impoverished urban areas of Barcelona—started in October 2017 and finished at the end of 2019.[4] The project aimed to fight poverty and social exclusion and was headed by the Department of Planning and Innovation of the Barcelona City Council's Area of Social Rights, funded partially with funds from the European Union's Urban Innovative Actions program.

The project comprised of 24 months of implementation, followed by 12 months of evaluation. It targeted 1,000 vulnerable households (and it paid members of these households individually) in ten neighborhoods and was designed to test the policy combining a monetary transfer—Municipal Inclusion Support or SMI—with four active policies of social and labor inclusion in the areas of training and employment, entrepreneurship in social and the cooperative economy, housing reforms for refurbishing and renting rooms, and a community participation program (Laín 2019). Therefore, while there were some participants that received a guaranteed income with no obligations, the experiment did not exclusively test the impact of an unconditional grant, but different cash transfer modalities through ten different treatment groups. Moreover, since it targeted vulnerable groups, it was also not universal in the sense mentioned in the definition of a "pure basic income", although it targeted individuals.

The experiment measured and assessed results in areas such as material deprivation and well-being, finance, employment, health, children, and the community. The results available show that participation in B-MINCOME had a positive effect in all dimensions studied, with no significant differences between groups. However, in some outputs analyzed, the conditional group recorded slightly better results than the other groups, which is attributed in the report to the "fact that people obliged to take part in the active policies strengthen their social relations, group cohesion, individual and collective confidence and trust, their social

[4] See more info at the B-MINCOME website at: https://ajuntament.barcelona.cat/bmincome/en/.

and communication skills, and many more" (Laín 2019, 21). The fact that most households included in the experiment were quite vulnerable might have increased this overall effect. The most plausible explanation for these results is that the beneficiaries are among the least well-off members of society, with hardly any social interactions, so the activation policies provided them with an opportunity to feel more socially integrated. These results mainly remind us that a UBI must be accompanied by strong inclusive social policies to have the most effective results. In the employment dimension, the experiment found some disincentive to work, which was more significant in conditional groups, and was explained by the lock-in effect hypothesis that having to comply with conditional measures might reduce the time available to look for a job.

1.5.10 The GiveDirectly Experiments in Kenya

Some private organizations, namely non-profit organizations, have tried to implement UBI experiments using crowdfunding campaigns. In this field, organizations such as the Belgian Eight, the Brazilian ReCivitas, the German *Mein Grundeinkommen*, the Indian Cashrelief, and the American GiveDirectly stand out. The latter is probably the best known, covers the largest group of individuals, and focuses on East Africa, particularly Kenya, where it is testing a UBI in several villages and communities. This project follows two trends that are observed more and more frequently. On the one hand, the fact that development and support policies in countries and for populations in situations of extreme poverty increasingly provide income instead of aid in the form of goods. On the other hand, the fact that many UBI advocates, tired of the inaction of public authorities, opt for a do-it-yourself approach (Pel and Backhaus 2016).

The stated objective of GiveDirectly is to combat extreme poverty, which is why it focuses on individuals considered most in need, based on official statistics from the countries concerned (currently in nine African countries and also in the USA). Local missions also assist in verifying, based on criteria such as house size and access to sanitation, among others, who is eligible to be included in the program. The experiment started at the end of 2017 and the funding was mostly guaranteed through private donations. This experiment includes 295 villages in rural Kenya, divided into four groups, covering a total of about 26,000 recipients, in addition to a randomized control group[5]:

- The experiment on a long-term basic income: 44 villages (4,966 people) with recipients receiving roughly 0.75 US dollar per adult per day, delivered monthly for 12 years. Our interview was mostly focused on the experiment which is still ongoing, and its differences with the control group, and in particular cases with the other two treatment groups.
- A short-term basic income: 80 villages (7,333 people) with recipients receiving the same monthly amount, but only for 2 years.
- A lump sum: 71 villages (8,548 people) with recipients receiving the same amount as the short-term basic income group (in net present value), but all up front as a "lump sum".
- A control group: 100 villages that did not receive cash transfers.

Results are still being collected, particularly in the long-term basic income program, which is ongoing. However, some qualitative data has already been collected, and some findings on well-being, health, and investments in education already show that the policy has had positive impacts in the villages where the long-term basic income has been implemented. Initial results also seem to indicate a significant increase in community engagement.

1.5.11 The Experiments in the USA: Stockton Economic Empowerment Demonstration (SEED)

Interest in implementing a UBI in the USA can be traced back to the first negative income tax experiments implemented in the 1960s in some states (see above). However, after the controversial results of these programs were released, the policy was not implemented and the push for UBI decreased significantly. Recently, interest in UBI has returned in the USA, not only because of the work of civic society organizations, but also due to an increase in prominent public figures who have actively spoken in favor of a UBI—Elon Musk and Mark Zuckerberg, and Democratic presidential

[5] Give Directly website: https://www.givedirectly.org/ubi-study/ (2021).

candidate Andrew Yang and his "Freedom Dividend", to name a few—as an answer to the possible consequences of automation.

In February 2019, Stockton's then-mayor Michael D. Tubbs launched the first mayor-led guaranteed income—The Stockton Economic Empowerment Demonstration (SEED)—where 125 randomly selected residents received 500 US dollars per month for 24 months with no strings attached, namely no work requirements. SEED's preliminary findings show improvements in mental health and increased well-being. Participants reported experiencing more financial security, which encouraged more entrepreneurial activity, and increased self-determination and goal setting. It also enabled more people to find full-time employment (Baker and Martin-West 2020).[6] The SEED project catalyzed a nation-wide movement—"Mayors for Guaranteed Income" (MGI) which includes several additional experiments taking place in the USA, all fueled by mayors in different cities. While the SEED project was fully funded through philanthropic means several of the new experiments at MGI are being publicly funded. Since then, the MGI research initiative[7] has been created, with a commitment to "a centralized, independent research and evaluation infrastructure that ensures future advocacy is rooted in both anecdotal and data-based evidence" (Baker and Martin-West 2020). Using the same core instrumentation across all of the MGI cities will allow the creation of a centralized database on guaranteed income at the conclusion of all of experiments taking place in the USA, which will provide aggregated quantitative and qualitative data.

1.5.12 *The Eastern Band of Cherokee Indians' Dividend (USA)*

In 1997, the Eastern Band of Cherokee Indians in North Carolina opened a casino located on tribal land and used part of its revenue to distribute an obligations-free annual sum to every tribal member. Depending on each

[6] SEED project website—summary of key findings: https://www.stocktondemonstration.org/#summary-of-key-findings (2021).

[7] The research center at University of Pennsylvania has not only been one of the organizations in charge of the designing and evaluation of the SEED Project in Stockton, but it is also one of the partners of the MIG initiative following the outburst of unconditional cash grants in the US. The commitments, goals, and progress of the initiative can be found both in its "Learning agenda document" (Baker and Martin-West 2020) but also in the main website of the initiative: https://www.mayorsforagi.org/about (July, 2021).

years' revenues, the amount of money received by each member averages between 4,000 and 6,000 US dollars (Marinescu 2019).

In 1992, before the dividend had been implemented, a longitudinal study named "The Great Smoky Mountains Study of Youth (GSMS)" was implemented, focusing on children and adolescents' mental health in North Carolina. The design of the experiment, combined with the implementation of the casino revenue policy in 1997, allowed for an almost "natural" experiment on the impact of basic income. The study allowed for a comparison of children's and adolescents' mental health, and also issues related with familial relationships. Available data, though limited, shows members who receive the casino dividend do not stop working; children experience improved education (as much as one extra year for the poorest Cherokee households), tend to commit less crime, and have improved mental health and decreased rates of alcohol and drug addiction (Marinescu 2019).

1.5.13 *Macau's Wealth Partaking Scheme*

The Macao Special Administrative Region of the People's Republic of China, which has been under the control of the People's Republic of China since December 1999, provides one of the most prominent examples of a UBI, distributed annually, alongside the *Alaska Permanent Fund*. This income is financed through profits from the region's casino industry.

In 2008, the Macao Special Administrative Region announced the creation of a Wealth Partaking Scheme, which pays a sum to each of its permanent and non permanent residents. This payment is made by public authorities with the aim of sharing the fruits of economic development with residents, especially those related to casino games, which make up almost 40% of Macau's GDP. During the 2007–2008 financial crisis, it was also used as a way to combat the effects of the crisis on the population, justifying an increase in the amount paid. Since its creation, the annual amounts paid vary from year to year: 5,000 *patacas* (533 euros) for permanent residents and 3,000 (320) for non-permanent residents in 2008, values that reached, respectively, 10,000 (1067 euros) and 6,000 *patacas* (640 euros) in 2018.

The examples of Macau and Alaska are both atypical, as they are directly linked to a source of national wealth that few countries can claim today. Both also are distributed annually to a limited number of beneficiaries and in variable modest amounts, by western standards. The allocation of income on an annual rather than monthly basis raises other issues, especially regarding consumption and financial security, which must be taken into account. Despite the policy's duration, very little data has been gathered on its impacts at the individual or group level.

1.5.14 Renda Básica Da cidadania—the Local Currency Policy in Maricá, Brazil

In 2013, Maricá's mayor, Washington Quaquá, decided to move toward implementing a guaranteed income in the city. The policy was funded with oil revenues and was part of a broader program to foster engagement and a "social economy", which also included a community bank—Banco Mumbuca. The policy has been changed and expanded since its inception, and the current structure has been fixed since December 2019. Besides being one of the largest basic income schemes in the world, including 42,000 people (out of the 165,000 inhabitants of Maricá), one of its most distinctive features is the fact that the basic income is granted in a local digital currency—*mumbuca*—administered by the community bank.

The beneficiaries of the *mumbuca* basic income must have lived in Maricá for at least three years and belong to households earning less than three times Brazil's minimum monthly income of approximately 169 euros as of March 2021. Hence, in the eligible household, one person is deemed the household holder of the local *mumbuca* card (usually the mother) and the value wired to the card is defined according to the number of people of the household. Hence, at the rate of 130 *mumbucas*, a household with 5 people receives 650 *mumbucas*.

Initially, each individual received a monthly payment equivalent to 20 euros paid in *mumbucas*. In response to the COVID-19 pandemic, the value of the benefit was more than doubled to 300 *mumbucas* (46 euros) in April 2020.[8] This value is planned to be adjusted and set at 170 *mumbucas* (26 euros) per month in November 2021, more than 95% of the individual poverty line. The policy may be expanded, possibly to account all the residents of Maricá soon. However, it is currently still a

[8] Maricá's basic income website—https://www.maricabasicincome.com/en/about-the-study#what-is-the-program (2021).

targeted program, although the amount is unconditional in the sense of being obligation-free.

In July 2019, an international, interdisciplinary research team of social scientists from the Jain Family Institute in New York City and the Universidade Federal Fluminense of Brazil got together to design and implement a large-scale study of the program, combining quantitative and qualitative methods to examine the effects of the program on Maricá's citizens and economy. Results are expected to be published in late 2021.

1.5.15 *Youth Basic Income Policy in South Korea*

The Youth Basic Income project was first piloted when the provincial governor of Gyeonggi, Lee Jae-myung, was the mayor of Seongnam City. Lee Jae-myung made the expansion of his Youth Dividend program part of his winning electoral manifesto in the 2018 local elections. After winning the governor's seat, he expanded the project to cover the entire province of Gyeonggi in April 2019.

Under the Youth Basic Income project, every 24-year-old registered resident (for at least three consecutive years or ten years in total) of Gyeonggi Province is paid KRW 250,000 every quarter, in a local currency (approximately 182 euros every quarter, that is 727 euros per year). Around 175,000 people are eligible for the basic income policy which is financed by the Gyeonggi Provincial government. The basic income is therefore not universal, and not completely unconditional, since it is paid in local currency (as in Maricá, Brazil). It is also rather limited, since people only receive the amount while they are 24 years old.

Several surveys have been conducted to assess the impact of the policy on happiness, health, diet, awareness, and attitudes (trust in others, society, and institutions, self-determination, welfare, basic income, etc.), and also on relevant indicators of local economic activity. Existing evidence shows that there are improvements in the overall satisfaction with life, perception of work values, and level of happiness among participants. Perception and attitudes toward basic income also changed positively, with an increase in "dream capital[9]", and positive impacts in recipients' motivation to work (Yoo et al. 2019).

1.5.16 *Iran's Universal Subsidy Policy*

As in the case of the Alaska Permanent Fund, Iran also launched a basic income partially based on the revenues from oil reserves. However, contrary to the former, Iran's UBI was established to substitute and otherwise compensate the population for the withdrawal of price subsidies which had been in place for several years. Hence, in 2010, Iran launched a program to reform its system of price subsidies. Initially, subsidies were partially cut, with parallel increases in prices, namely of fuel products. The net proceeds were partly used to finance the cash transfer policy. In later stages, subsidies were continuously cut, raising prices, and funding compensatory transfers, until all subsidies were eliminated (Tabatabai 2012). The monthly transfer amounted to 29% of the median household income or about 1.22 euros extra per household member per day. Because of its design, it amounted to a truly unconditional and universal policy. It was also one of the most generous basic incomes, larger, relative to the cost of living, than the ones granted in the Alaska or Macau schemes.

There is limited evidence available on the impacts of this scheme. However, some results seem to highlight no significant impacts on overall labor supply, meaning that people continued working despite the cash transfer. Researchers even found that women and self-employed men worked more with the cash transfer (Salehi-Isfahani Mostafavi-Dehzooei 2016). Moreover, there seems to have been an impact in poverty alleviation (particularly in rural areas), although data is limited, and also changes in consumption patterns, partly because of the increased prices on certain items, namely fuel and electricity, but also bread flour (Tabatabai 2012).

[9] Dream capital was a particular term for the Youth Basic Income Project in South Korea, since it was considered as one of the key outcomes that should be studied, when assessing the impacts of the policy. As mentioned in one of the reports on the policy's findings, "Dreams now serve as the capital for young generations. The ability to dream functions as "capital" because the ability itself is treated as an important resource and its integrated into the social process. (…)" This was measured using a particular scale, which included four elements, namely "imagination, hope, optimism and resilience" (Yoo et al. 2019, 35–36).

1.5.17 *Basic Income Pilot Project in Germany*

In late 2020, a joint study was launched by the German Institute for Economic Research (DIW Berlin) and the *Mein Grundeinkommen* association (a non-profit organization). It features other partners, namely The University of Cologne and The University of Vienna. The study plans to pay 122 participants 1,200 euros per month unconditionally over a period of three years. Applications were accepted from August 2020 until November 2020, and individuals only needed to be residents of Germany and at least 18 years of age to be eligible.[10] Despite being associated with Berlin, the project does not have any geographical focus within Germany. The experiment was rolled out in June 2021.

The project's goals are quite ambitious, ranging from assessing the impact on variables related to health, work, the Digital Revolution, social cohesion, politics, and consumption. It is being funded through monthly donations from over 180,000 private individuals, which will be used to pay the basic incomes.

1.5.18 *The Basic Income Debate in Scotland*

The debate on UBI in Scotland has been one of the most intense and promising worldwide. Since at least 2015, through the efforts of several non-profit organizations, particularly the *Royal Society for Arts* (RSA) in Scotland, multiple conferences have been held and some reports published on the possibilities and models for implementing a basic income in Scotland.

At least two important reports are worth mentioning. One is the RSA's report, released in 2019 and titled "A Basic Income for Scotland". This report discusses the possible political strategies and models for a basic income experiment in the country. The report favors "saturation type" studies,[11] to be conducted in several locations in Scotland and other places in the UK, while also developing a basic income in Scotland (Painter, et al. 2019). The second report was released in June

[10] Basic Income Pilot Project website—https://www.pilotprojekt-grundeinkommen.de/english#: (2021).

[11] "Saturation Studies" are a method used in social science experiments, usually opposed to the RCT—Randomized Control Trials methodology. They do not randomize participants, but rather select a particular context where everyone will be in the treatment group (hence being called "saturation" sites).

2020 and resulted from the work of the Citizens' Basic Income Feasibility Study Steering Group, a group created through the collaboration of local government and public health and supported by the Scottish government. This feasibility report developed a proposed model for a large-scale experiment in Scotland, designed to assess the policy's impacts on poverty and unemployment, health, and financial well-being, as well as the social security system (Citizens' Basic Income Feasibility Study Steering Group 2020). The report not only demonstrates the possibility of conducting an experiment and proposes a model, but also encourages national and local authorities to commit themselves to implementing a basic income, although it recognizes the challenges of doing so considering Scotland's political context.

Despite the debate and reports, an experiment has not yet been implemented in the UK. Recent developments such as movements encouraging experiments in other places (e.g., Wales and Sheffield) and the renewed public support of the Scottish national government for basic income might lead to the implementation of an experiment in the near-term, or possibly even the introduction of UBI as a local or national policy. In the most recent elections in 2021, the Scottish National Party Government committed to basic income as the long-term goal, with minimum income guarantee as a policy for the coming Parliament. Moreover, four out of five of the major party leaders supported basic income with a solid majority in Parliament. Such developments show the increasing support for basic income in Scotland, and the possibility for such a policy to be implemented in the country.

1.6 The Outline of the Book

As mentioned above, this book aims to contribute to the ongoing discussions on the role UBI experiments play in contributing to knowledge of basic income, and how they foster advocacy movements worldwide. Through the interviews conducted on the fifteen case studies, we wish to provide a comprehensive landscape of learning, pitfalls, existing evidence, strategies, and recommendations for those engaging in experimentation, assessing results, or even those curious to know more about UBI experiments and their overall impacts. To do so, the book is divided into three main parts, beside the introduction.

Part one attempts to answer the question "*what have we learned from the interviews?*". It provides a comprehensive assessment of the interviews' main insights and connects them to ongoing discussions in the literature. It maps out how our interviews contribute to discussions on the evidence from basic income experiments conducted so far. Part one is divided into two main chapters. Chapter 2 discusses the role played by the social, political, and economic contexts as well as the methodology in the design and implementation of our fifteen case studies. How has the context and the methodology shaped the evidence? In which ways can we define them as basic income experiments? What limitations in the roll-out of experiments resulted from both the methodological decisions and the political context of each of our fifteen case studies? Chapter 3 discusses the main evidence from our case studies and asks two fundamental questions which have been debated in the literature on experiments: Do we know enough already to implement a full-scale UBI? If so, what can the role played by basic income experiments regarding the moral desirability of implementing a full-scale UBI be?

Part two builds on the discussion in part one. While part one focuses on recurrent questions already discussed in the literature, which were highlighted in our interviews, part two aims to build on and advance the existing knowledge on what UBI experiments can tell us. It is divided into three main chapters. Chapter 4 discusses the decisions behind conducting a basic income experiment, raising questions on whether moral or instrumental values are behind the decision to support a UBI experiment, or even whether a top-down or a bottom-up movement might influence those decisions. Chapter 5 discusses existing evidence again, but focuses on two questions: What impacts are new or have not received significant attention in the worldwide basic income debate? And how are results interpreted locally and worldwide, and what factors might be influencing these interpretations? Chapter 6 raises some of the most fundamental questions emerging from our interviews, particularly the question of how to move from experimentation to policy implementation and then whether to prioritize continued experimentation or political lobbying. This chapter not only discusses the role of UBI experiments in general, but also surveys existing issues such as the possibility of political instrumentation of basic income, namely as a populist policy.

Part three endeavors to accomplish two main objectives. The first is to provide input and answers to discussions and questions raised throughout the book, namely the role of UBI experiments in making the case for a full-scale UBI and returning to the paradox between experiments and the definition of a "pure basic income" as defined earlier. Moreover, we provide our normative view on many debates and challenges discussed throughout parts one and two of the book. Part three is composed of one chapter, divided in three sections. The first section asks if we still have questions regarding the necessity of conducting basic income experiments. The second section provides a comprehensive analysis of some of the key normative discussions surrounding both the political and methodological contexts of our case studies, the interpretation of evidence, and the role UBI experiments can currently play in the worldwide discussion on UBI. The third section addresses the issue of external shocks, such as COVID-19, as potential catalyzers of UBI experiments, or even as policy. The book closes with a final conclusion and a summary of the key discussions and findings of all three sections.

References

Arcarons, Jordi, Daniel Raventós, and Lluís Torrens. "Feasibility of Financing a Basic Income." *Basic Income Studies* 9, no. 1–2 (2014): 79–93.

Baker, Amy Castro, and Stacia Martin-West. Learning Agenda. The Center for Guaranteed Income Research. The University of Pennsylvania School of Social Policy and Practice, 2020.

Bonno, Pel, and Julia Backhaus. "Just Do It! Shifting Dimensions of Social Innovation in Basic Income." Interpretive Policy Analysis Conference. Hull (UK), 2016.

Brady, David, and Amie Bostic. "Paradoxes of Social Policy: Welfare Transfers, Relative Poverty, and Redistribution Preferences." *American Sociological Review* 80, no. 2 (2015): 268–298.

Bregman, Rutger. *Utopia for Realists: And How We Can Get There*. London: Bloomsbury Publishing, 2017.

Calnistsky, David. "'More Normal than Welfare'": The Mincome Experiment, Stigma and Community Experience." *Canadian Sociological Association/La Société Canadienne de Sociologie* 53, no. 1 (2016): 26–71.

Calnitsky, David, and Jonathan Latner. "Basic Income in a Small Town: Understanding the Elusive Effects on Work." *Social Problems* 64, no. 3 (2017): 373–397.

Cappi, Riccardo, and Bernard Delvaux. "Les allocataires sociaux confrontés aux pièges financiers." IRES, 1990: Louvain.

Caputo, Richard K. "United States of America: GAI Almost in the 1970s But Downhill Thereafter." In *Basic Income Guarantee and Politics: International Experiences and Perspectives on the Viability of Income Guarantee*, Richard K. Caputo (ed.), 265–281. New York: Palgrave Macmillan, 2012.

Citizens' Basic Income Feasibility Study Steering Group. Assessing the Feasibility of Citizens' Basic Income Pilots in Scotland: Final Report. Citizens' Basic Income Feasibility Study Steering Group, 2020.

Davala, Sarath, Renana Jhabvala, Guy Standing, and Soumya Kapoor Mehta. *Basic Income. A Transformative Policy for India*. London/New York: Bloomsbury, 2015.

Forget, Evelyn. "The Town with No Poverty: The Health Effects of a Canadian Guaranteed Annual Income Field Experiment." *Canadian Public Policy* 37, no. 3 (2011): 283–305.

Groot, Loek, Stephanie Rosenkranz, Mark Sanders, and Timo Verlaat. "Experimenting with Basic Income Inspired Experiments." *Ethical Perspectives* 28, no. 1 (2021): 53–61.

Haarmann, Claudia, and Dirk Haarmann. "From Survival to Decent Employment: Basic Income Security in Namibia." *Basic Income Studies* 2, no. 1 (2007): 1–7.

Hum, Derek, and Wayne Simpson. *Income Maintenance, Work Effort, and the Canadian Mincome Experiment*. Ottawa: Economic Council of Canada, 1991.

Hum, Derek, and Wayne Simpson. "Economic Response to a Guaranteed Annual Income: Experience from Canada and the United States." *Journal of Labor Economics* 11, no. 1 (1993): 263–296.

Hum, Derek, and Wayne Simpson. "A Guaranteed Annual Income? From Mincome to the Millenium." *Policy Options Politiques* 22, no. 1 (2001): 78–82.

Kangas, Olli, Signe Jauhiainen, Miska Simanainen, and Minna Ylikännö. *Suomen perustulokokeilun arviointi*. Finland: KELA, 2020.

Korpi, Walter, and Joakim Palme. "The Paradox of Redistribution and Strategies of Equality: Welfare State Institutions, Inequality, and Poverty in the Western Countries." *American Sociological Review* 63, no. 5 (1998): 661–687.

Laín, Bru. "Report on the Preliminary Results of the B-MINCOME Project (2017–2018)." *Ajuntament de Barcelona*. 2019. Available at: https://ajuntament.barcelona.cat/dretssocials/sites/default/files/arxius-documents/results_bmincome_eng.pdf

Lenkowsky, Leslie. *Politics, Economics, and Welfare Reform: The Failure of the Negative Income Tax in Britain and the United States*. New York: University Press of America, 1986.

Marinescu, Ioana. "Summary: Universal Basic Income." *Wharton PPI B-School for Public Policy Seminar. Summary: Universal Basic Income*. Philadelphia, PA: University of Pennsylvania Scholarly Commons, 2019, 3–4.

Moynihan, Daniel Patrick. *The Politics of a Guaranteed Income: The Nixon Administration and the Family Assistance Plan*. New York: Random House, 1973.

Osterkamp, Rigmar. "The Basic Income Grant Pilot Project in Namibia: A Critical Assessment." *Basic Income Studies* 8, no. 1 (2013): 71–91.

Painter, Anthony, Jamie Cooke, Ian Burbidge, and Aima Ahmed. *A Basic Income for Scotland*. London: RSA, 2019.

Pechman, Joseph A., and Michael Timpane. "Work Incentives and Income Guarantees." Brookings Panel on Social Experimentation. Washington, DC: Brookings Institution, 1975.

Redley, Marcus, Simon James, James Simon, and Bill Jordan. *Trapped in Poverty? Labour-Market Decisions in Low-Income Households*. London: Routledge, 1992.

Salehi-Isfahani, Djavad, and Mohammad H. Mostafavi-Dehzooei. "Cash Transfers and Labor Supply: Evidence from a Large-Scale Program in Iran." *Journal of Development Economics*, 2016: 1–45.

Skocpol, Theda. "Targeting within Universalism: Politically Viable Policies to Combat Poverty in the United States". In *The Urban Underclass*, Christopher Jencks and Paul E. Peterson (eds.), 441–436. Washington, DC: The Brookings Institution, 1991.

Steensland, Brian. *The Failed Welfare Revolution: America's Struggle over Guaranteed Income Policy*. Princeton: Princeton University Press, 2008.

Tabatabai, Hamid. "From Price Subsidies to Basic Income: The Iran Model and its Lessons." In *Exporting the Alaska Model: Adapting the Permanent Fund Dividend for Reform around the World*, Karl Widerquist and Michael Howard (eds.). New York: Palgrave Macmillan, 2012.

Torry, Malcom (ed.). *The Palgrave International Handbook of Basic Income*. London: Palgrave Macmillan, 2019.

Van Parijs, Philippe. *Real Freedom for All*. Oxford: Oxford University Press, 1995.

Warin, Philippe. "Non-Demand for Social Rights: A New Challenge for Social Action in France." *Journal of Poverty and Social Justice* 20, no. 1 (2012): 41–55.

Widerquist, Karl. "A Failure to Communicate: What (If Anything) Can We Learn from the Negative Income Tax Experiments?" *Journal of Socio-Economics* 34, no. 1 (2005): 49–81.

Widerquist, Karl, and Georg Arndt. "The Cost of Basic Income in the United Kingdom: A Microsimulation Analysis." BasicIncome.org. 2020. Available at: https://basicincome.org/wp-content/uploads/2020/07/Cost-of-BI-in-the-UK-A-Microsimulation-ForPosting.pdf

Widerquist, Karl, and Michael Howard. *Alaska's Permanent Fund Dividend: Examining Its Suitability as a Model*. New York: Palgrave Macmillan US, 2012.

Yoo, Young Seong, Jeong Wonho, Rhie Kwanhyung, Yun Sungjin, and Ma Jooyoung. *Analysis of the Effects of the Youth Basic Income Policy in Gyeonggi Province: Comparison of the Ex-Ante and Ex-Post Survey*—Gyeonggi: Gyeonggi Research Institute—Policy Study, 2019.

PART I

What We Have Learned from the Interviews

The fifteen interviews conducted in the process of creating this book provide a rich overview of some of the key basic income experiments conducted (or in the process of being implemented) in the last few years. Not surprisingly, the insights gathered while interviewing the stakeholders amount to a set of different conclusions in several dimensions of basic income experiments and pilots, but also of basic income as a policy. In this first part of the book, we will map out the main conclusions and lessons taken from the interviews, connecting them to the general and ongoing debate on basic income experiments. This requires one brief comment, regarding the nature of our sample, and how it can impact some our conclusions.

Our interviews cover a rich and representative group of recent basic income experiments. The main criteria used was the selection of stakeholders with knowledgeability, which usually meant people who have been directly engaged with the experiments, such as researchers or politicians. This means that in certain experiments we might have interviewed researchers involved in the designing and/or evaluation of the experiment, while in others we interviewed a civil servant, or someone involved in the implementation of the experiment. The latter cases were much less common. In the Scottish case, we interviewed the head of RSA Scotland, an advocate involved in the basic income movement there, while we interviewed both a civil servant and one of the researchers involved in the experiment in Utrecht. In Macau, particularly, we were only able to interview a beneficiary of the policy. Nonetheless, there is still a degree of variability in the stakeholders interviewed (e.g., which stage of the research process they were involved in) which introduces a fair degree of differences in perception, analysis, and discussion of the basic income experiments. Moreover, in the majority of cases where researchers were interviewed, we found some degree of difference in their roles, which can also contribute to distinct differences in their perceptions. The diversity of our case studies (and their various contexts, constructions, aims, etc.) presents us with a challenge, but also an opportunity. On the one hand, it makes comparisons more difficult and results are perhaps less transferable to other contexts. On the other, if these different cases display similar results it can strengthen the case for a UBI and potentially increase transferability and applicability of results to other contexts. If similar results are repeatedly observed in vastly different contexts, it makes the conclusion drawn from these results more robust and increases the legitimacy of applying these results to other contexts. Physical and mental health and well-being readily spring to mind.

Part one is divided into two main chapters.

Chapter 2 will introduce general lessons from the interviews, mapping out key conclusions in terms of context of and methodologies implemented to evaluate results in each case study. It will start by discussing the main conclusion from the interviews: how each of our case studies differ tremendously—in terms of their main characteristics, and their general goals and details. This leads to a discussion of how our case studies can be construed as basic income experiments, pilots, or policies (or not). From there, we will raise key questions on the methodological decisions, either in terms of design model, type of evidence collected, and even the way ethical criteria can sometimes be taken into account. This discussion leads us to conclusions on the role the sociopolitical context plays in any basic income experiment and can therefore have tremendous impacts on how experiments are conducted, implemented, and perceived. The chapter closes with key conclusions from the interviews related to the implications of methodological decisions and context, specifically the limited comparability and scalability that basic income experiments offer so far.

Chapter 3 starts with the assumption of the possibility for scalability and comparability and tries to identify whether basic income experiments and pilots offer some common ground, namely in terms of knowledge of their impacts, and how they relate to basic income as a concept as outlined in the introduction. By analyzing existing evidence, it is clear how the problem of limited comparability can partly be solved by examining the qualitative and quantitative evidence (together?), and by relating it with the theoretical discussion on the impact of basic income. This should help the reader to understand our general perception and interpretation of all the interviews: we already know much about the possible impacts of implementing a basic income, namely in terms of well-being or health, even if we still have significant gaps in our understanding of the effects of basic income on labor market participation or community effects in general. Chapter 3 closes by asking what the role of basic income experiments as an instrument for advocacy, policymaking, or as a research tool can be. As a key question of the book, we received many answers from the stakeholders we interviewed, which are worth mentioning and connecting to the ongoing debate in the literature.

CHAPTER 2

The Goal, Context, and Methods Behind Our Case Studies

The constellation of basic income experiments implemented in the last few decades is impressive. One may be dazzled not only by their numbers, but also their differing methodologies, objectives, and contexts where they have been implemented. And such a rich sample could yield the possibility to aggregate conclusions and generalize findings. But there is more than meets the eye in such a universe.

One of the first lessons from the interviews was how different each case was, and therefore, how distinctively unique some of their conclusions could be. We are not, for now, stating any conclusive opinion regarding the possibility of generalizing any findings. It is simply an acknowledgment of the fact that many of these experiments result from different groups, political parties, individuals, and are influenced by very distinct contexts. There is a degree of influence from the existing international debate on basic income, and from certain organizations like Basic Income Earth Network (BIEN) particularly in some experiments in developing contexts, but in many cases this role is not significant.

One of the characteristics that makes the case studies so different is their geographical location. Our fifteen cases represent fifteen different realities. We have several case studies which were designed to compare conditional and unconditional policies in Europe, like in Utrecht and Finland. We also have large-scale pilots implemented to evaluate the

R. Merrill et al., *Basic Income Experiments*, Exploring the Basic Income Guarantee,
https://doi.org/10.1007/978-3-030-89120-6_2

impacts of a basic income in impoverished and rural areas in both India and Africa. Finally, we have policies that have been implemented in administrative regions and cities, with different levels of affluence, namely in Macau and South Korea but also in Maricá, in the Rio de Janeiro region of Brazil. The geographical differences are important, not only in terms of the evidence and impacts, but also in terms of goals and political and social framing. The different countries, regions, or cities naturally have different social assistance mechanisms, if applicable, and experience different needs from their target groups. These often-striking differences affect how each experiment, pilot, or policy is set up, which obviously impacts the types of results which will be assessed.

As developed in our introduction, our case studies consist of:

- Five cases that are policies, most of which have been studied—Iran's universal subsidy scheme, Maricá's *Renda Básica de Cidadania*, South Korea's Youth Basic Income Project, Macau's Wealth Partaking Scheme, and the Eastern Band of Cherokee Indians' Dividend in North Carolina.
- Nine which fall within the category of experiments and pilots—the Namibian Pilot, the Madhya Pradesh case in India, the GiveDirectly experiment in Kenya, Finland's Basic Income Experiment, the Utrecht "What Works" experiment in the Netherlands, the B-MINCOME experiment in Barcelona, the SEED project in Stockton, California, the experiment in Ontario, Canada, and finally the recent basic income experiment in Germany.
- One is a planned study for an experiment or policy—in Scotland.

As might be clear from the outline above, our case studies are not only different in terms of their geographical location. They reflect two distinct pairs of realities: on the one hand, the dichotomy between having an experiment or pilot, or having a policy: we have some case studies which illustrate policies that have been implemented for some years, like in Brazil, Macau, and South Korea, whereas the other case studies are experiments or pilots, designed to test either a basic income, or some feature of what a basic income is. On the other, the distinction between basic income pilots, and experiments: as mentioned in the introduction, "pilot projects" aim to test a UBI. Therefore, they usually attribute a monthly amount to every individual in each context, unconditionally. Namibia or the experiments in India, for example, are pilot projects. Basic income experiments are usually not aiming to test a genuine UBI, as we define it in our introduction. Rather, they focus on testing particular features of a basic income. Hence, we might have an experiment that grants money unconditionally, but targets their beneficiaries. Most of our case studies fall into this second category of basic income experiments. We will examine the former conclusion first, before comparing each case study to the definition of basic income as presented in the introduction. However, and as mentioned in the Introduction, regarding these differences between plots and experiments, we will use these two terms indistinctly to facilitate the reading of the book.

2.1 What Goals Are Behind Our Case Studies?

When discussing basic income experiments, we may tend to overlook the fact that some existing examples are not experiments at all, but rather policies. Among our case studies, five were policies: Maricá's *Renda Básica de Cidadania*, the Eastern Band of Cherokee Indians' Dividend, Iran's universal subsidy policy, Macau's Wealth Partaking Scheme, and the Youth Basic Income Project in South Korea.

After years of conflict and policies that left many Native Americans secluded on very constricted pieces of land, many Native American tribes began building and operating casinos, which were then regulated by a US federal law in 1988. The law regulated gaming activity, but also how profits should be used to promote tribal government operations and economic development to "provide for the general welfare of the Indian tribe and its members".[1] From then on, tribes started using casino profits to fund many infrastructure projects, such as schools or hospitals, but some also decided to distribute a percentage of the profits to their members. This was the case in the Eastern Band of Cherokee Indians. As mentioned in the introduction, since there was a long-term social experiment underway to study the mental health of the children in the tribe and the surrounding communities, this became a "natural" experiment for basic income when the wealth partaking scheme was introduced by the tribe (in 1997). As such, the Eastern Band of Cherokee Indians' Dividend is a tribal government policy and not a basic income experiment. It

[1] Full text for the Indian Gaming Regulatory Act available at: https://www.nigc.gov/general-counsel/indian-gaming-regulatory-act (June, 2021).

is unconditional and universal within the members of the tribe—which means that only people who are considered as tribal members are eligible to receive the grant, regardless of their residence.[2]

Macau's Wealth Partaking Scheme is also quite similar, since it is also funded through the profits from the casino industry established in the region. It is paid unconditionally and annually to both residents and non-residents. Though the amounts differ between the two groups and from year to year, they can generally be considered quite modest. It has not specifically been the focus of research, so there is limited evidence on its impacts. It also is a governmental policy and not a social experiment.

The other two case studies which are also policies are different. Maricá's *Renda Básica de Cidadania* is a local policy, targeting some of the most vulnerable members of the city. It is also geared toward promoting the local economy, and therefore a local currency—the *mumbuca*—was created, alongside a community bank. Since it was created, it has increased in amount and has been extended to more people, beyond the poorest members of the community. Our interviewees informed us of progress to make it a more universal policy, with plans in place to expand it to every resident of Maricá. Since 2019, a research team has been studying the policy to understand its impacts in a range of outcomes, including well-being, employment, consumption patterns, and media attention. Research is ongoing, with a field study in the city.[3] It is not an experiment and can properly be considered a mostly unconditional

[2] As discussed during the interview, such definition—of those who are part of the tribe or not—is a particular aspect of the tribal government's mandate. The criteria include blood relations, which means that if people marry and have children with people of a different ethnicity, they reduce the likelihood of the children belonging to the tribe, by blood relatedness. It is also a criterion that is quite different from the ones in the other case studies that represent policies: in Macau and Maricá Brazil the cash grant is attributed to residents (in Macau to both permanent and non-permanent ones). Hence, the main eligibility criterion is geographical: whether people live or not in the city or region. In the Eastern Band of Cherokee Indians' Dividend, the criterion is related with tribal membership, as defined by blood heritage, which means that people living in different locations, outside the tribe, might still receive the unconditional cash grant. Such a difference might be explained by the mandate of the tribal government, and the initial decision to establish the cash grant, namely that of contributing to the general welfare of tribal members.

[3] To know more about the study of the Maricá's *Renda Básica de Cidadania*, there is a website of the study with relevant information, namely the context of basic income in the country, the development of the policy in Maricá, and the study's main deadlines. Available at: https://www.maricabasicincome.com/en/about-the-study (June, 2021).

(conditional only in the sense of being paid in a local currency, hence the money must be used in local stores) transfer. It is still a targeted policy, despite its progress toward universality within the city.

The Youth Basic Income Project in South Korea started off as a pilot project in Seongnam City. It was a basic income targeted toward every 24-year-old in the city. It has since progressed to a provincial program, since the mayor of Seongnam City, Lee Jae-myung, became the Governor of Gyeonggi Province. It is an unconditional cash transfer, but targets only a small segment of the province's population: those aged 24 years old. Like Maricá, it is also paid in a local currency, and therefore is also unconditional, except that the money needs to be used in provincial stores.

Finally, Iran's universal subsidy scheme is also a very distinct case. Instead of starting off as a policy implemented aiming to solve issues of poverty or distributing revenues, it was rather designed to compensate citizens for the removal of subsidies on commodities like gas, bread, and electricity. The government at the time wished to eliminate the subsidies, but understood this should be done in steps, considering the popular outrage that eliminating the subsidies altogether might generate. Hence, it implemented a plan to phase out the subsidies, while substituting them, for a period, with an unconditional cash grant. Funded by oil reserves, this generated the implementation of a large-scale unconditional and universal cash grant in the country.

Although the five cases all represent established policies, they are funded and implemented in very different ways, and in very different contexts, which makes comparing them a difficult challenge. For example, amounts attributed in the examples of the policies on the Eastern Band of Cherokee Indians reserve and in Macau depend on casino revenues and in the latter case also in resident status in Macau, whereas in the policy in Maricá or in the province of South Korea the money is set by local and provincial governments. Moreover, Macau's Wealth Partaking Scheme has not been researched to understand how it has impacted recipients, whereas we have some evidence from the other four cases, although it is limited, especially in the Iran's universal subsidy scheme and the Eastern Band of Cherokee Indians' Dividend. But most importantly, it means that in these cases the goal of the policies implemented was not to *test if and how a basic income works*. At most, in the cases where researchers are now involved, this is an ad hoc question, which in no way, or in a very limited way has influenced the policy.

The remaining nine cases (labeled as experiments and pilots), excluding the debate and discussions in Scotland, have certain differences in design and context, which also necessarily impact results. In some of our case studies, such as the ones in Utrecht and Finland, the goal seems to be "scientific" in nature. Within these existing welfare states, their governments wanted to understand how introducing unconditional cash transfers and comparing them with existing conditional ones could improve labor market activation or social inclusion. This was very clear in some of the interviews.

For example, in the Finnish case, judgments on the experiment's success (or not) made by the researchers we interviewed, the central government, and also local and international media was a matter of (i) whether unconditional cash transfers were more successful in increasing labor market take-up for long-term unemployed people than conditional cash transfers (and this was especially relevant for the government's and media's judgment) and (ii) whether the experiment was scientifically robust (especially important for the research institute who was responsible for the experiments).

Also, in Utrecht, the experiment was labeled "What Works" specifically because it focused on analyzing what might work best in promoting labor market activation. Hence, the focus was purely scientific, although with the hopes of informing political decision, namely through the municipality's involvement in the experiment. The research team focused on understanding whether attributing an unconditional cash transfer to the long-term unemployed could fare better than existing conditional cash grants in promoting labor market activation.

The experiment in Barcelona—B-MINCOME—was also geared toward analyzing how unconditional cash transfers might compare with various conditional cash grants in terms of enhancing social inclusion, alongside aiming to understand the role cash grants play in solving systemic poverty. Hence, the design of the experiment features several treatment and control groups, testing how cash grants with different activation policies—from volunteering, to counseling, to training—both compulsory and non-compulsory, contributed to social inclusion.

In the remaining five cases, the experiments seemed to be more geared toward advocacy and to serve as instruments for a potential future implementation of basic income as a policy, even when research purposes were also involved. The pilot in Namibia seems to have been partly the result of the government's acknowledgment of the need to understand how basic income could work in their context, but it was nonetheless implemented by a cluster of different organizations supporting basic income—the BIG Coalition—churches, unions, NGOs and AIDS service organizations. After the central government discussed the issue of basic income, it pushed for a pilot, arguing for evidence as a necessary tool to help them decide how to implement a basic income nationally. Hence, our interviewee from the Namibian experiment highlighted how the experiment was mostly designed and implemented as a policy, and not so much as an experiment, since the goal was to figure it out *how it could work, what could work best and why* to then roll it out nation-wide.

In India, there was a clear goal of promoting a change in policies, namely food and commodity subsidies, which were seen as a bureaucratic hazard and a source of ongoing systemic inefficiencies, according to the leading research of the Madhya Pradesh experiment that we interviewed, Sarath Davala. Hence, several cash transfer experiments were implemented. One of those, which was the focus of our interview, was a pilot implemented in 2012 in Madhya Pradesh by the Self-Employed Women's Association (SEWA),[4] a women's trade union who worked in the region. In our interview, it was clear how SEWA was also initially skeptical about the impacts of basic income, but believed it was important to understand how different policies could work in the rural contexts in India, namely, to improve lives in the communities. Hence, as in the case of Namibia, the pilot wanted to understand *how basic income could work and what impacts could it have* for those receiving it.

The goals were similar in Kenya, as well. The project was the initiative of an American non-profit organization—GiveDirectly—who wished to understand the impact basic income could have in the global South and contribute to a discussion of its function as an alternative to existing aid and development mechanisms in these regions. Contrary to the cases of the rural villages in Namibia and the pilot in India however, it also wanted to test different design models of unconditional cash transfers: hence it tested lump-sum grants, unconditional short-term grants, and finally, the longest running basic income pilot to date, with one of the control groups planned for 12 years (started in 2016, scheduled to end in 2027). Give Directly chose to focus on understanding *how basic income works, what impacts it can have* but also *what might work best.*

[4] For more information about SEWA: https://sewabharat.org/sewas-pioneering-studies-on-basic-income-show-transformative-results/.

Our case studies also include three more recent experiments. The first is the Stockton Economic Empowerment Demonstration experiment (SEED), which was launched in 2019 and whose initial results have just been released (West et al. 2021). Besides being a local government initiative and a personal political commitment of former-mayor Tubbs, the experiment has become a source for community engagement, which was a goal for the experiment from the onset, as both Stacia West and Amy Castro from the SEED experiment pointed out. Hence, not only was there a concern for the design of the experiment, and with what it could reveal about basic income, but also about how it could foster community engagement by using basic income as a tool for individual and collective empowerment. This was clear when considering how the community was involved in designing the experiment and choosing some of the outcomes that would be targeted by the research, and even available in almost "real-time". For example, our two researchers from the SEED experiment explained how the community believed the research on consumption patterns was not only important but should also be made available during the span of the experiment, and not only in the final report. Hence, this outcome, which was of no particular interest for the research team as our interviewees pointed out, was analyzed and made available throughout the experiment's running time. Moreover, the SEED project catalyzed a nation-wide movement—"Mayors for Guaranteed Income", which includes finished and ongoing experiments taking place in the country. The movement's goal is both scientific, namely through the partnership with the Center for Guaranteed Income Research at the University of Pennsylvania, but also political, in the sense of promoting the local and nation-wide debate on basic income (Baker and Martin-West 2020).

The second is the Ontario experiment, whose goal was to understand the impact an unconditional cash grant could have in the lives of low-income individuals in Ontario. It was therefore focused on some of the challenges faced by local government, namely systemic poverty, but also growing precariousness. It was not so much a project focused on community engagement around basic income, but rather focused on understanding whether an unconditional cash transfer could be more successful in mitigating or altogether solving some of the pressing social challenges in Ontario, not only for research purposes, but also to inform political processes. It is therefore closer in terms of its aims to the experiments that took place in Utrecht, Finland, and Barcelona, even if the observed outcomes of the first two mentioned cases were rather narrower than the ones considered in Ontario (which included labor market participation, but also housing stability, food security, mental and physical health, education and training, among others). Unfortunately, since the experiment was canceled after one year, there was not much information on its impacts.

The more recent pilot in Germany is, alongside the SEED project in the USA, a relevant case of community engagement. It resulted from years of experiment with basic income, namely through the work of *Mein Grundeinkommen,* which raffled off hundreds of basic incomes funded through an ongoing crowdfunding campaign[5] contributing to the national debate on basic income. Like the SEED project, it also aims to promote the discussion of basic income, while simultaneously collecting evidence on its impacts on a broad range of outcomes on well-being, work, and social cohesion. This is because of the project's legacy and clear considering its design: everyone in Germany was eligible to participate, and the crowdfunding campaign that was necessary to fund it was also a way to promote engagement on basic income. As Maheba Goedeke Tort told us, the project has no particular "agenda", in the sense that it is not aiming to understand a very narrow set of outcomes (e.g., how unconditional cash transfer could improve labor activation). Rather, it focuses on understanding how introducing an unconditional cash transfer could affect people's lives in Germany. In doing so, the organizers of the crowdfunding campaign hope to increase the engagement around basic income, while at the same time they hope to answer what *Mein Grundeinkommen* considers to be the many unanswered questions German people still have on basic income.

The Finnish and Utrecht experiments aimed to evaluate how unconditional transfers are effective than existing social assistance mechanisms in enabling particular outcomes considered relevant by those implementing them (namely central and local governments). Lastly, the Barcelona case also compared unconditional and conditional cash transfers with compulsory and non-compulsory activation policies.

The nine case studies that can be considered pilots or experiments reflect their different contexts, but also the different goals the experiments adjacent to the concept of basic income can have. Such differences

[5] *Mein Grundeinkommen* website: https://www.mein-grundeinkommen.de/.

in goals are a reflection of their context, a topic that will be salient in this book. Such a discussion will include an analysis of different hypotheses.

For one, some of our case studies seem to be more focused on *how basic income works*, such as the cases in Namibia, Madhya Pradesh India, and Kenya. Such a goal might be partly explained by the fact they are geared not only toward understanding the impacts of a basic income, but perhaps understanding how it could function and be implemented, especially considering that such contexts have insufficient or non-existent social assistance mechanisms. It might also be an instrumental reason: the fact that the poverty line in many of these countries or rural communities is so low, and existing social assistance mechanisms are limited or non-existent, makes the implementation of a basic income pilot much cheaper. Logistically, it is also easier than in contexts where the interplay between experiments and welfare policies and tax systems can make for a rather complex experiment. Hence, the context—poor and with insufficient social assistance mechanisms—might help explain the pilot's objectives.

Another set of case studies focused on understanding *what the broad impacts of implementing a basic income are*. These were common to the SEED project in the USA, the pilot project in Germany and the prematurely canceled experiment in Ontario, Canada. A first hypothesis could be to say that they all share a common ambition to empower local and national movements around basic income. If that was the case, the organization behind the experiments could help explain its goal (e.g., non-profit organizations, focused in the basic income debate). Such goals obscure other important considerations in each case. It's true that both the German project and the SEED project in California share the goal of encouraging the movement on basic income. However, in Germany, it is a nation-wide movement, whereas the SEED project bolsters local movements (city level), even if those can also contribute to a nation-wide movement. Moreover, the SEED experiment is a mayor-led initiative, funded with public and private funding, whereas the case in Germany is a non-profit organization initiative with private funding only. This reveals an important difference in Germany, the goal is very broad, since it is focused on promoting the debate in the country and providing answers to some of the most common doubts from the population regarding the impacts of basic income. In the SEED project, the experiment was geared toward understanding the impacts of basic income in people's lives, broadly speaking, but was also focused on understanding how it could help solve some poverty and social inclusion challenges in the city. As a mayor-led initiative, it is normal that the experiment's goals will also fit within the challenges of the city and the political agenda of the politician or coalition behind it.

Finally, some experiments were focused on understanding *what impacts an unconditional cash transfer can have if compared with conditional cash transfers?* These were the cases of Utrecht, Finland, and Barcelona. They are quite different among themselves: Finland was a nation-wide experiment, focused on the unemployed. The goal was to test how basic income (in the form of an unconditional cash grant, granted to the unemployed, which was not withdraw if they could find a job) could be better in labor market activation than existing unemployment benefits where beneficiaries have to comply with a given set of conditions. In Utrecht, the goal was also to analyze what might work better in labor market activation of the long-term unemployed, but the policy was never framed as basic income. Rather, it was framed as an experiment to test how having an unconditional cash transfer (while unemployed) could be better or not than existing conditional mechanisms to promote labor market activation. Finally, the Barcelona case also wanted to test unconditional and conditional cash transfers to understand what could be better in promoting social inclusion (which included labor market participation, but also volunteering, participating in community gatherings or in training). However, they were not only interested in what is the best—conditional or unconditional—but how different activation policies (e.g., volunteer, training, counseling), when available or not, and also when mandatory or not, can be better or worse in promoting social inclusion. It was therefore more focused on understanding which policies might work best, rather than simply answering the question of whether unconditional cash transfers are better than conditional ones or not.

As discussed, these different goals will mean we might have case studies that were the result of scientific motivations or advocacy ones, but most of them will fall in between—where both scientific motivations and advocacy go hand in hand. As discussed, the cases in the "advocacy" group also exhibit strong scientific motivations, as in the SEED project and German pilot's cases, but one can take precedence over the other, which might help explain the design of the experiment or pilot or how its results are interpreted later on. Therefore, considering a motivational spectrum rather than a full-on dichotomy might be more useful when discussing whether our case studies are fully scientific experiments, or rather tools for advocacy.

2.2 Can We Really Call Them UBI Experiments?

Besides the different goals and the differences between our experimental and non-experimental case studies, another important distinction in our case studies is their ability to function as proxies for unconditional basic income. Returning to the definition presented in the introduction, a UBI should be universal, individual, obligation-free, and ideally it should be of a sufficient amount to guarantee each member of the political community a dignified existence and her civic participation in society. None of the fifteen case studies fully meets all the conditions listed in our definition of what an unconditional basic income is, presented above and in the introduction.

Two out the five cases which represent a policy rather than an experiment lack universality. In Maricá's *Renda Básica de Cidadania* only people below a certain income threshold are eligible to receive the basic income in the local currency, *mumbucas*. They have to belong to a household earning less than three times Brazil's minimum monthly income of 1100 Brazilian reais (which is approximately 200 US dollars or 169 euros as of March 2021). It's also not individual, since it is granted to only one person of the household (usually women). The value is granted unconditionally, although being paid in local currency limits the places where people can spend their *mumbucas*. In this case, it has to be used only to buy products and services in local stores who joined the program (which most have according to our interview). Moreover, it is important to consider that Maricá's *Renda Básica de Cidadania* is probably not enough to guarantee a "dignified existence" to everyone in Maricá, though its value is set significantly above Brazil's poverty line (178 Brazilian reais),[6] it's still far from an "average salary". Nevertheless, it still has a significant impact in many of the eligible households and is closer to the goals of unconditional basic income presented above than if it was set at a lower level. The Youth Basic Income Project in South Korea also lacks universality, since it is targeted at only people aged 24 in the province of Gyeonggi. One must also argue that the amount is low (727 euros per year). This is not an amount that ensures a dignified life in South Korea.

[6] To know more about Maricá's *Renda Básica de Cidadania*, and the current study: https://www.maricabasicincome.com/en/about-the-study (June, 2021).

The other three cases are unconditional and universal. Iran's universal subsidy scheme is paid to every Iranian citizen, since it was framed as compensation for previously existent commodities subsidies (e.g., food and energy). Its goal was to provide compensation for withdrawing subsidies, and not as a means to incentivize or restrict given behaviors or actions (e.g., encourage work or decrease consumption of certain products), therefore it was implemented as an unconditional cash transfer. The scheme provided monthly payments, up to 29% of the median household income, hence falling short of providing enough to guarantee decent living conditions, according to the definition we provided on what an unconditional basic income is. Nonetheless, the Iranian scheme is higher than other similar schemes, namely the Alaska Permanent Fund, which is also financed through the profits of oil reserves. Macau's Wealth Partaking Scheme and the Eastern Band of Cherokee Indians' Dividend are both universal, provided those eligible for payments applied to receive them, according to the criteria defined in each. In Macau, recall that the amount is paid to permanent and non-permanent residents (the former receive more than the latter). It's paid annually and individually. The value is set accordingly to the profits of the casino industry; however, they tend to be of a modest amount, which does not fit the conditions of enabling decent living to each recipient. The same happens in the Eastern Band of Cherokee Indians' Dividend, where every tribal member is eligible to receive it, hence being an individual and unconditional cash grant paid annually. Since it is also financed by the casino industry's profits, the amount varies year to year. Moreover, because the number of eligible tribal residents varies (due to deaths or marriages outside the tribe, as Randall Akee told us in our interview) the yearly amount is also affected by this variable. Hence, in this case also, the amount is not necessarily high enough to meet the threshold of enabling a dignified existence.

The remaining nine case studies—once again excluding the Scottish case since there is no experiment there yet—exhibit varying degrees of "noncompliance" with the definition of unconditional basic income we consider in this book. In many cases, the instances of noncompliance have to do with the fact that experiments and pilots are not policies, and therefore are limited in time or budget (although policies might be limited in budget, too). Therefore, they cannot fully comply with at least the universal criteria and possibly the "amount-ensuring-a-dignified-existence" criterion included in our definition. Also, the methodological decisions might imply the need for a control group, within a given region, hence compromising the universal nature of the policy. Take the case of the SEED project in the USA, where budget constraints limited the number of people that could receive the unconditional cash grant. Hence, the amount was granted unconditionally, but only to 125 randomly selected residents, so it did not meet the universal criterion. There was also an income threshold, defined with help from the community, which was selected to avoid taxation of basic income (e.g., if granted a basic income, higher income residents could have their basic income significantly taxed). Moreover, the amount (500 US dollars) is also below the level that could be considered allowing a life with dignity. Meanwhile, two separate factors forced the GiveDirectly experiment in Kenya away from being considered a truly unconditional basic income. First, the experiment targeted poor, rural villages, and excluded children for budgetary reasons since it was financed through private donations. Second, it employed the use of a control and separate experimental groups (two years, lump sum, and 12 years). Hence, despite being unconditional, the experiment is not to be universal, due to the decisions to use a control group and target poorer regions and households. The more recent pilot in Germany is also limited in terms of the number of people who will be granted a basic income—122 participants—mostly because of budget constraints since it also is financed through private donations. Therefore, it is also unconditional, but not universal. It will grant each participant 1,200 euros, and although it lies below German's minimum monthly income, it is nonetheless a more significant amount than other experiments that took place in Europe.

The Namibian and Madhya Pradesh pilots are the closest matches to our definition of unconditional basic income. In Madhya Pradesh, everyone was granted the unconditional cash grant, including the entire members of the village, namely both rich and poor members, but also children (although the amount granted to children was lower). However, the amount was not sufficient to guarantee decent living conditions. Nonetheless, its unconditional and universal nature is closer to the definition of unconditional basic income considered in this book. The Namibian pilot was a saturation study, hence there was no control group. However, the experiment had budget constraints, considering it was financed through a national and international crowdfunding campaign (although as our interviewee responsible for the Namibian experiment mentioned, the amount raised was much higher than what the organizers were expecting). Therefore, the researchers chose a place where a small amount could make a huge difference. But besides the budget constraints, the experiment was also framed because of political agendas. As our interviewee responsible for the Namibian experiment argued, they chose a place where there was "extreme poverty" also because it was considered that if the experiment could work in such a context, it would also work in other contexts in the country. Despite these limitations, since it was a saturation study, the experiment was also closer to the definition of unconditional basic income used in this book. It was both unconditional, universal, and individual (with mothers receiving the children's amount). But again, the amount was not sufficient to guarantee decent living conditions, according to our definition, although it made a significant difference in such a context.

Finally, the remaining case studies illustrate examples where the experiment's goal was not necessarily to test *how a basic income works* or *how it could be rolled out nationally* but rather how unconditional cash transfers could be better or worse in solving particular problems or achieving certain goals, which are now attributed to conditional cash transfers. In Barcelona, the experiment had a clear focus on not only testing the role an unconditional cash transfer could have in the empowerment of the poor, but also to compare it with different activation policies. In this sense, the methodology chosen compromised the basic income definition, by granting priority to a given aspect—most often conditionality—instead of looking to fulfill all the characteristics of what a basic income is, in theory. Moreover, the experiment was targeted toward people from a poor neighborhood in Barcelona. According to one of the leading researchers from the B-MINCOME experiment, this was a decision right from the onset. They wanted to assess the impact of unconditional and conditional cash grants linked with activation policies and knew that political support would require targeting people "in need" instead of people in a middle class, for example. Hence, the experiment ended up being framed as assessing social inclusion in a particularly poor neighborhood of Barcelona, with different treatment and control groups; it was not universal, and only for some groups was it unconditional. The amount was not sufficient to guarantee decent living conditions to fit into the standard of what an unconditional basic income should be. Also in Utrecht, Finland, and Ontario too, the experiments targeted particular segments of the population. While in the B-MINCOME experiment in Barcelona this seems to have been both a political compromise and a strategic decision, considering the goal of the policy, in these last three cases, the latter is more prevalent. In Ontario, for example, the experiment was looking to understand how an unconditional cash transfer could help solve challenges within the community, namely inequality, but more particularly relieving the working poor and the precariat. This cash transfer was unconditional but, although significant (almost 75% of the poverty line), also targeted particular groups, namely poorer members of the city, including the working poor. Hence, this experiment also was not universal, given that it was targeted in order to understand the impact of an unconditional cash transfer on particular challenges. In Finland too, although being named and advertised as a basic income, the experiment targeted only unemployed jobseekers, since its goal was to understand if an unconditional cash transfer could be more effective than existing conditional cash transfers in promoting labor market activation. It was also a modest amount, given the living costs in Finland. Finally, Utrecht too had similar goals: to understand if unconditional transfers are more effective in labor market activation, hence only unemployed people were targeted. However, and contrary to the Finnish experiment, both of our interviewees from the Utrecht experiment highlighted many times how neither researchers nor politicians ever wanted to test or frame their experiment as a basic income. It was always framed as and considered an experiment designed to explore how some changes in the current social assistance system could improve labor activation rates.

Considering the degree of variability in each of the case studies, and whether or not they fit within our definition of basic income, it's possible to ask: Can they really be called UBI experiments?

There is a lot of variability in our case studies, which shows how the concept of basic income is quite flexible. In our fifteen cases, we see instances of targeting (where only some members receive the cash grant), limiting its universal nature. Also, all our case studies fall short in the amount they grant to individuals, either being much lower than the poverty line, or higher, but still far from being sufficient to guarantee decent living conditions. We also see how some cases are not individual cash grants, but rather attributed to households, sometimes covering children, others excluding them altogether. Therefore, it seems researchers, advocates, and politicians have stretched the concept of unconditional basic income to a point where we might lose sight of what it is supposed to be: a universal, unconditional, individual cash transfer that should allow a life with dignity.

In a sense, this could lead to comparisons of policies, experiments, and pilots with very little similarity between each other. Although there is a threat of this happening in our own discussion, we believe the case studies assessed share the most striking characteristic of what a basic income is: being unconditional, in the sense of being obligation-free, that is with "no strings attached", since their beneficiaries do not have to be available on the labor market to receive it. Indeed, all of them, to some degree, have provided money "no strings attached" to their target groups. It is in this dimension we consider them to be the most comparable, and the most similar to what a basic income means at its core. Nonetheless, when relevant, we will discuss how the inherent limitations of not complying with one or more characteristics of unconditional basic income, according to our definition, might influence our take on the results or the methods employed.

The discussion of whether we can call these case studies UBI experiments or not is relevant beyond our own methodology in comparing these cases. On the one hand, it points toward the *conundrum* faced by the basic income movement: there is an underlying assumption of what basic income is and what it can do. These include issues like the happiness claim, the job participation claim, or even the women's emancipation claim (Widerquist 2018, 99–129). Many of these claims have been theoretically settled and do not necessarily need empirical proof (e.g., how basic income can help solve material poverty). Other are still without robust empirical proof (e.g., whether basic income leads to inflation, or to increase entrepreneurial activity). In the latter case, Widerquist rightly points out how some of these claims might nonetheless be untestable (2018). But as mentioned above, basic income experiments, pilots, and policies often differ in one or several dimensions to what basic income is in our definition. This amounts to a problem: we are using "flawed" basic incomes experiments, pilots, and policies to test claims based on an "idealized" or "pure" definition of the policy. This limitation is relevant for our discussion of our case studies, but perhaps particularly when we discuss the roles basic income experiments or pilots can or cannot play as instruments for advocacy, policymaking, or research.

Apart from the paradoxical nature of testing basic income using limited examples of what a basic income could be, increased use (and misuse) of the term can also be seen as a signal of the movement's growth. Consider how the policy has become appealing for politicians. In the Utrecht case, for example, the branding of the experiment as basic income apparently resulted from the statement of one politician, which was then amplified all over Europe, despite both of our interviewees from the Utrecht experiment arguing this was never intended to happen. The Scottish case is another example of how attractive basic income can be for politicians. There is no experiment currently scheduled to happen, but both the basic income movement in the country, namely the Royal Society for the encouragement of Arts, Manufactures, and Commerce (RSA) and the government of Scotland have both studied the concept, which, resulted in an RSA report (Painter et al. 2019) on basic income, and also a government-sponsored feasibility report on the road toward a basic income (Citizens' Basic Income Feasibility Study Steering Group 2020). In our interview, it was clear how the role the government of Scotland has played in the discussion of basic income was considered important, namely due to the recognition they could harness (inter)nationally as experts on the cutting edge of the basic income debate. On the other hand, the researchers of the SEED experiment pointed out that the use of "guaranteed income" in recent experiments in the USA (namely in the SEED one) was an attempt to overcome this challenges, by using different concepts to distinguish between the experimental cash grant—a guaranteed income, where the amount offered in the experiment does not meet basic needs, but rather it meets the definition of unconditional recurring cash—and what a UBI is. Finally, South Korea offers another interesting case displaying the movement's progress. The surge in the discussion there has led to political parties publicly endorsing or discussing basic income. Although one could see this as a positive outcome for the advocacy movement, it has also led one of the conservative parties to endorse some means-tested policies framed as basic income, as Hyosang Ahn, one of the leading advocates for basic income in South Korea, mentioned in our interview. This is a clear case where the term "basic income" is appropriated for political gain. We will return to the discussion on the role basic income experiments can play in the political debate, and in turn, how the political debate influences the possibility of launching a basic income experiment, and how the concept might be used as a populistic tool in Chapter 6.

Before examining some of the conclusions gathered from the interviews related to the context and methods employed, it is important to sum up the differences among our fifteen case studies, outlined above. The first, mentioned in the introduction to part one, is a difference resulting from our own methodology. As mentioned, the differences in the type of stakeholder interviewed, and their profiles, should be kept in mind when discussing some of our conclusions. This might mean that some conclusions could have also been found in some cases, which are not highlighted, because the stakeholder we interviewed might have had other concerns, or opinions or even perspective on the experiment. However, we will also use secondary sources, such as the published results of our case studies or articles on the experiments and pilots, in order to add relevant information to our case studies.

There are also inherent differences which are not a result of our methodology but emerge due to the differences among our case studies.

The first is a difference in geographical context. We have case studies in wealthier countries—the USA, Finland, the Netherlands, Germany, Canada, and Spain. Even among them, there are differences in terms of welfare state mechanisms (between the USA and the rest, or between Finland and the Netherlands, Germany, and Spain). We also have case studies from the global South, namely Brazil, Namibia, India, and Kenya. These represent distinct cases, where the social assistance mechanisms might be deficient or non-existent, but also where needs, consumption, and labor patterns are distinct. At the same time, there also may be kinship and community links which are markedly different from the ones in some of the cities in Western contexts. We also have cases which are very particular, such as Macau Wealth Partaking Scheme, the Eastern Band of Cherokee Indians' Dividend, or the Iranian universal subsidy scheme, either because of how they are funded or because of their goal.

Another important distinction lies in the dichotomy between non-policies and policies. Moreover, within the non-policies category, we have pilots (e.g., Namibia, Madhya Pradesh, and Kenya) and those closer to experiments (e.g., Utrecht, Finland, and Barcelona). As discussed, these are a result of the goals behind each one of them: in the former, they were mostly focused on testing how a basic income could work whereas in the latter cases, the goal was to understand how unconditional transfers might be more effective than conditional ones in solving challenges. As we will discuss in Sect. 2.3 (and in Chapter 4) this is partly due to the fact that in less affluent countries a pilot is easier to conduct the amount granted unconditionally can be lower, which reduces budget constraints, and the lack of welfare states makes the designing of the pilot easier). It is also related with the role of the welfare state: existing social assistance mechanisms, underpinning strong contribution ethics, and existing political agendas might influence the goals of the experiments and pilots.

As mentioned in the introduction, for convenience, we will use the term UBI experiments, which includes both experiments and pilots, but also the non-experimental cases that have been evaluated.

A final distinction is in the degree of separation between our case studies with the concept of unconditional basic income, as defined in the introduction. It's critical to keep this distinction in mind since it will allow us to return to the initial question on the role that basic income experiments and pilots can play as research, advocacy, or political tool. As mentioned, we will consider as the key similarity of our case studies the fact that they all included unconditional cash grants (in their pilot or experiment, or as policy), but we will also highlight, when relevant, the similarities or differences of each model with every single characteristic of basic income, as defined in our introduction.

It is important to keep all these differences in mind, since it necessarily means that results, for example, will be eschewed to certain outcomes, given the case studies' particular goals. It also means that the aftermaths of various experiments and pilots, particularly, might also be quite different. Maybe in some cases political adoption was never looked after, while in others this was a clear objective, and hence if it does not happen, the basic income movement might be considerably frustrated with the consequences from the experiment. Hence, the degrees of variability in our case studies, insofar as they are representative of what is generally considered "basic income policies" or "basic income pilots" or "basic income experiments", should be taken into account in our conclusions as an inherent limitation of our analysis, and in general of our understanding of the impacts of basic income.

2.3 The Role Played by Methodological Decisions

The discussion on which methodology is best—a randomized control trial (RCT), saturation study, or a combination of both—is an ongoing debate in the social sciences experiments field (Cartwright 2007, Cartwright and Hardie 2012). As explained by Karl Widerquist, an RCT is a "test designed to isolate the effects of the factors being studied by using randomization as a method to control as much as possible for all other factors that might influence the relevant outcomes". Researchers do so by randomly selecting two sufficiently large groups that differ as little as possible from each other and from the wider population. They give the treatment to one group only (the experimental group) and observe whether that group differs in relevant ways from the other group (the control group) (Widerquist 2018, 21). A saturation study, in contrast, "involves identifying two relevant communities, such as two small towns, and giving the treatment to everyone in one community and not to people in the other" Widerquist (2018, 22). Since basic income experiments and pilots can be considered social science experiments, it is not surprising that our interviews also reflected many of the underlying arguments associated with this discussion.

As mentioned, and to wrap-up, our case studies consist of:

- Five cases that are policies—Iran's universal subsidy scheme, Maricá's *Renda Básica de Cidadania*, South Korea's Youth Basic Income Project, Macau's Wealth Partaking Scheme, and the Eastern Band of Cherokee Indians' Dividend.
- Nine which fall within the category of experiments and pilots—Finland's Basic Income Experiment, the Utrecht "What Works" experiment in the Netherlands, the Namibian pilot, the Madhya Pradesh case in India, the GiveDirectly experiments in Kenya, the B-MINCOME experiment in Barcelona, the SEED project in Stockton, California, the experiment in Ontario, Canada, and finally the more recent UBI experiment in Germany.
- One is a planned study for an experiment or policy—in Scotland.

Of the five policy cases, four of them have been the object of research and will therefore be included in our discussion and conclusions on the role of the methodology. The remaining case—Macau—will be excluded for lack of evidence. The Scottish case has some relevant insights on the role of methodology, considering the existing conversation between advocates from RSA Scotland and the government research team on which methodology could be implemented in a possible experiment in Scotland, if they decide to conduct it in the near future. The nine remaining case studies are categorized as experiments and pilots and have associated discussions and decisions pertaining to their data collection and analysis that will be included in our analysis.

What have we found? There is a clear preference for the use of RCTs as a methodology to assess results (in experiments and pilots). Seven out of nine of our case studies in this category used this method. This seems to imply a concern with understanding the causal impacts of basic income, as opposed to simply observing particular correlations. A parallel discussion is the need for a control group—again to assess causal links between basic income and particular outcomes. Interestingly enough in the case where a saturation study was chosen, Namibia, the control group was rejected due to ethical concerns: it was judged ethically problematic to survey a control group, considering the extreme poverty in which many households lived.

The use of RCTs seems to overlap with a second concern related with the type of data collected. In many cases where an RCT was used, and there was a significant concern with conducting a rigorous scientific experiment, quantitative data was privileged, even if some qualitative data was gathered (which at times, it was not). This was the case in Finland and Utrecht, where quantitative data was the key variables, namely the ones related to labor market activation.

It is also important to consider that in the four policy cases where we have research data—Maricá's *Renda Básica de Cidadania*, the Youth Basic Income Project in South Korea, Iran's universal subsidy scheme, and the Eastern Band of Cherokee Indians' Dividend—decisions on which methodology was used were more limited, since they were policies, and not designed as experiments. However, they do provide interesting case studies on this account. For example, in the case of Maricá's *Renda Básica de Cidadania*, the research team has been developing a methodology that includes both quantitative and qualitative methods to help understand the impact of the program in the city. Although randomization of participants to account for causality was not possible, they have instead focused on implementing large-scale surveys and interviewing both community representatives and a small sample of participants and non-participants. They are also studying the possible inflationary impacts of the local currency. These strategies have been chosen to account for the possible role of basic income in the city, not only in terms of individuals' behaviors and lives, but also in terms of the larger community surrounding the city of Maricá. The Youth Basic Income Project in South Korea is using surveys targeting the young recipients of the basic income and also of relevant local economic stakeholders to understand the perception and some impacts of the policy. The researchers of this project have included an ad hoc control group when assessing the survey results, which demonstrates a worry with the attribution of the impacts of the policy. Iran's universal subsidy scheme has used administrative data, which has only some particular information on labor market participation and income, and hence our understanding of the impacts of the policy are rather limited. The use of such data was a compromise, given that the initial decision to use surveys was met with backlash from a lot of segments of the population, who refused to fill them out.[7] Another interesting case is the Eastern Band of Cherokee Indians' Dividend. Since the wealth partaking scheme was introduced in the middle of a longitudinal study on children's mental health, the data offers a sort of "natural experiment" to understand the role a basic income, even a modest one, can play in issues of children's mental health. Effects on parents could also be examined, since indicators of stress, alcohol and drug consumption and labor are available. Since the experiment targeted mental health, the data collected was in no way tailored to some of the questions pertaining to a basic income. There are therefore significant gaps in our understanding of the impact of the policy in a range of issues (e.g., were people happier with the unconditional cash grant? Did parents enroll in school or training, or change their occupations? Did the unconditional cash grant lead parents and children to be more involved in the community, for example, in volunteer work?). Because this is a policy, and due to the longitudinal study it offers one of the best windows into how a broader UBI policy might function, even if we could not grasp the full impact of it on numerous variables.

Returning to the discussion on the choices behind the methodology employed in some of the basic income experiments and pilots, there is a range of possible explanations behind some of these decisions. From the interviews, we can advance some possible scenarios explaining the differences in terms of methodology, and some limitations that resulted from these decisions.

It's notable that some of the experiments that focused mostly on quantitative data, and used an RCT, have considerably narrower objectives. Most of our nine experimental case studies—including experiments and pilots—collected both quantitative and some qualitative data. However, cases like Utrecht and Finland were much more focused on gathering quantitative rather than qualitative data. Interestingly, these are the two cases with narrower objectives since both were designed to shed light on

[7] In our interview, we did not have much detail on why there was backlash against filling in the surveys on the impacts of the policy. It seems it could be partly resistance to more bureaucracy, and partly resistance towards anything that could impact the cash grant that was being granted, given that people consider it a right since the subsidies were withdrawn.

the impact of unconditional cash grants or of decreasing conditionality within existing social assistance mechanisms on labor market activation. This was clear from interviews with both the researchers from the experiments and also the civil servant from the municipality of Utrecht. In the Finnish case, the main goal was to test labor activation and participation overall, even though some other variables, such as issues of trust, happiness, and welfare were also examined. It is therefore not surprising that the focus of the analysis and methodology was quantitative—labor market participation rates before, during, and after the experiment—and that an important concern was causality—how those changes could be attributed (or not) to an unconditional cash grant or a decrease in conditionality of existing programs.

Of course, one can argue that the choice between an RCT or a saturation study is simply a matter of objective. As one of the key stakeholders of the basic income discussion in Scotland told us: the choice between an RCT or a saturation study might just be a decision based on the goal of the experiment. If one wishes to know large-scale impacts, such as those on aggregate labor demand, an RCT might be the best option, despite its limitations. Whereas small-scale saturation studies might be the adequate methodological choice if one is especially interested in the stories behind the beneficiaries of basic income and also on the role played by community effects.

Besides the nature of objectives pursued by each experiment—which could favor one methodology over another—the interviews also highlighted some of the possible downsides of using an RCT. Despite their obvious advantage in providing the closest we can get to a "natural experiment", many of the interviewees revealed that RCTs provided little information on community effects and the narratives behind the evidence collected, particularly where the objective and focus of the analysis was mostly quantitative. We therefore lack knowledge on why immigrants and single mothers seemed to work more than other groups when granted the cash grant in Finland, for example. Or why did people in Utrecht with fewer qualifications or lower levels of formal education tend to fair better in finding work when granted unconditional benefits, as compared with other groups? This was also the case in Barcelona, where one of the leading researchers of the experiment that we interviewed, Lluís Torrens, acknowledged that one of the key lessons of the pilot for him was the importance of deepening the ethnographic analysis in order to explore the relationship between much of the evidence collected. This would be important to understand how some of the quantitative data (e.g., increases or decreases in labor market activation) could be connected with or even better explained by the qualitative data reported by the families involved.

It seems that in the discussion of methodology—RCT or saturation—and the type of data to be collected—qualitative, quantitative, or both—there are underlying limitations to how social experiments tend to be conducted (Standing 2019). Great focus is given to robustness of data collection and analysis for certain qualitative variables, which at times leaves little room for qualitative data collection and analysis. This in turn reduces the possibility of exploring the relationship between quantitative and qualitative data, increasing the gaps in the narrative of basic income's potential impacts. Of course, this can be a symptom of the experiments' emphasis, like in Utrecht and Finland, where the focus was clear, and these discussions were perhaps not of interest. It can also be a limitation resulting from potentially scattered objectives of basic income experiments—which often look for answers and impacts of the policy in a range of outputs: from welfare, education, labor participation, or community empowerment. In a way, complexity might be detrimental to a deeper analysis of what UBI's impacts could be in a given set of variables. This is partly Karl Widerquist's argument when encouraging stakeholders involved in experiments to focus as much as possible on the bottom line. Widerquist writes that "although the public discussion varies enormously over time and place, the desire for an answer to the big questions is ubiquitous, and so I suggest focusing on what I call the bottom line: an overall evaluation of UBI as a long-term, national policy" (Widerquist 2018, 12).

Given these limitations of social experiments, there is also the possibility of simply acknowledging that a singular experiment will not be able to tell us everything we, basic income advocates, and society in general, wish to know. The questions on narratives and the interpretation of the evidence might provide avenues for further research, opening up the debate and helping improve our knowledge on each experiment and on UBI in general. In many ways this has already happened. Take the NIT or MINCOME experiments, which have since inspired several notable papers reviving discussion or reviewing collected evidence (see the introduction, where we discuss experiments from the 1960s to 1970s in North America) (Forget 2011; Widerquist 2005; Calnitsky 2016). Rather than having a stance on what works best, the interviews seem to instead highlight the need to fit the methodology to the experiment and not the other way around. When possible, unanswered questions should be identified, either to define new research projects or employ new methodologies to answer some of them.

Another important conclusion stemmed from the fact that in some experiments there was a clear balancing of what were seen as competing interests at the time. On the one side, scientific rigor was essential to allow the possibility of uncovering strong causal links. On the other, ethical criteria were also considered, either from the perspective of the researchers or from the communities themselves, regarding their potential perception of the experiments. It can even be stated that at least two of our case studies valued ethics and/or community acceptance over scientific rigor, or at least balanced out both criteria when designing and implementing the experiments. In Namibia, the decision to forego use of a control group was purely ethical. This was a deliberate decision by the research team, which concluded that a control group would not add much value in the understanding of the impacts of the pilot. One of the research team members we interviewed told us that he considered a control group redundant, especially since in the surrounding areas and Namibia's total poverty did not decrease during the time of the pilot. The SEED experiment changed some design features of its RCT methodology after engaging with the community regarding the experiment's design. In this case, the fact that the team co-constructed the design with the community that would participate in the experiment had a degree of influence on the community's response to the policy. This too was deliberate, namely because of the experiment's aspiration to trigger social change and empower the community, but also concerning community trust in the process. We do not intend to advance any normative judgment on these cases, but both reflect instances where, contrary to more typical experiments such as in Finland, Utrecht, or Barcelona, there is a clear acknowledgment of the role and influence of the context—from either researchers or the community—in how the experiment plays out. This also does not mean altogether forfeiting ambitions of conducting a rigorous experiment. In Stockton, the community influence in the design happened alongside a decision to have two control groups, but the data of—one of them was left largely untampered with. Even in cases like the Finnish experiment, where scientific rigor was prioritized, events like the decision of the government to introduce changes in social assistance mechanisms heavily influenced the overall outcome of the experiment. Social experiments do not occur in a vacuum and are not lab experiments isolated from any outside influence. Hence, our case studies illustrate instances of changes in the experiments' methodology and in what we are defining as "scientific robustness" (linked to untampered causation), either because of actions of different players, which happened in the case of Finland, or more often in our case studies as a deliberate attempt of researchers, where social change or ethical considerations were privileged, like in the cases of Namibia or Stockton.

Before discussing the context's influence, we will sum up the main questions regarding the role of the methodological decisions on the outcome of basic income experiments raised by the interviews. The first is the number of variables determining methodological choices. Scientific concerns, ethical issues, or the goal of the experiment are all determinant factors weighing in decisions between RCTs and saturation studies. Even the academic background of the research teams might influence these decisions, which have a tremendous impact on our knowledge of UBI, particularly whether or not they prioritize quantitative or qualitative data, and the ethnographic evidence contained in the information collected. Whether this is simply a matter of needing more research or a common limitation of UBI experiments and pilots conducted thus far is a discussion for later in our analysis.

A second important question is the role of ethical judgments when deciding upon the methodology of the experiment. Many times, scientific rigor and ethical judgments are seen as a trade-off, where choosing one implies compromise to the other (Munro 2014). But solving this conundrum might simply be a matter of more clearly determining the goal of experiments and discussing how the interplay between scientific methodology and ethical considerations should be taken into account, or not, when designing and implementing the experiment. One final question to consider in this regard is what role a broader set of stakeholders involved in the experiment, beyond researchers, and those in charge of funding or implementing the experiment, should have when it comes to defining the design and goal of the experiment.

2.4 The Role of the Context: UBI Experiments Do Not Occur in a Vacuum

Our fifteen interviews highlighted the role the political and social context played in framing the UBI experiments implemented, namely their goals or which populations or communities should be involved. The political and financial contexts (particularly budget constraints) combined to produce great variability in our case studies: from pilots approaching universality and unconditionality to specific experiments combining various conditional and unconditional measures targeting groups.

The role of the broader context where our case studies took place was one of the most prominent features of nearly all the interviews, albeit in different ways. In some, the key question was the role of the political context in the framing of the experiment's outcome. In others, the welfare and existing social assistance mechanisms and attitudes toward them seemed to have an underlying importance. The role of the basic income movement (either at a national or international level) seemed to be a very relevant contextual background in some of the case studies. In many ways, these variables influenced each other, with public attitudes toward welfare influencing the role of the political context in the framing of the case study, or the role of the national basic income movement and how it pushed the political forces into a pilot, experiment or policy resembling UBI.

It's important to highlight how all the case studies acknowledged the issue of context, and in many ways the inevitability of its influence in some aspect of how the basic income experiment took place. The importance of context has fueled discussion concerning social experiments generally, but particularly in the basic income movement, where some have argued for the need of more "objective" experiments, namely microsimulation studies where political actors or media could not tamper with or misinterpret results (Noguera and De Wispelaere 2006). In these cases, the context's role is considered a significant downside of basic income experiments due to its role in tampering with causality (as in the Finnish experiment) or because of how results can be manipulated or misinterpreted by the media, given their usually long list of either boring or complicated caveats, explaining their designs—what is considered, how a sample was defined—but also their limitations (Widerquist 2005). We will now examine some of the dimensions of our case studies influenced by the context to understand which questions, limitations, and discussions on this issue were raised during the interviews.

One of the first issues discussed was the type of force behind the decision to implement a basic income experiment or pilot. All eight of the basic income experimental case studies resulted from a top-down movement, in the sense that a government, party, or international organization with power, resources, and influence decided to design and implement the experiment or pilot. Of course, this makes sense since often only local or central governments, or NGOs in developmental contexts, have the necessary capabilities to implement a pilot or experiment. In a sense, it demonstrates that the political context is essential in all these cases; in most contexts it was only through political action they were organized in the first place.

However, in many of these cases, the role of the basic income movement as a social movement or coalition, which we categorize as a bottom-up force, has also played an important role. Indeed, it was clear from the interviews how the basic income movement influenced the political decision to implement an experiment or pilot. In Barcelona, the movement has been growing in the last few decades and was therefore largely responsible for putting basic income on the agenda of Barcelona's local government. In fact, the implementation and research team hired included important figures from the basic income movement in Spain. In Namibia, the role of the international movement on basic income played a considerable role. When the majority of the BIEN conference in Cape Town (2006) opposed the idea of a BIG pilot project to show the benefit of a BIG, the Namibian Coalition felt that there was a sense of urgency to move the BIG debate toward concrete implementation in the developing context. One of the researchers involved in the Namibian pilot, Guy Standing, was also part of the experiment in Madhya Pradesh, and was a proeminent figure in the international debate on basic income. In this case, the experience and international debates on the results from the Namibian pilot played a significant role in the decision to do the same in some provinces in India. In a way, this can be said of all the cases, even those where experiments seemed to be implemented as a fully top-down decision, like in Finland or Utrecht. Even in these cases, we can credit the basic income movement for its role in framing the debate, introducing relevant vocabulary, and generally bringing the debate into the public consciousness. Surely this is different from making the decision to conduct an experiment or pilot, and therefore, it's difficult to isolate the precise role the basic income movement played in the case studies analyzed. However, it seems as though in developing contexts, the role of the international and national basic income advocacy movements was more prevalent. In other contexts, where welfare states with strong political support are present, the basic income movement seems to have been important in adding the topic to the agenda, though the decision behind the experiment seems to be purely political.

This conclusion leads us to a second discussion on the role of the political context when it comes to implementing experiments or pilots. There are at least three critical moments where this influence is significantly felt: the decision to implement an experiment/pilot (covered in the discussion above), its design and planning and lastly, in discussion and analysis of the evidence and outcomes.

The design phase of any experiment is critical. As mentioned above, it is where methodological decisions take place, which will determine available evidence. In many cases, researchers consider issues of scientific rigor to define the main elements of the experiment/pilot—its model, type of data collected, beneficiaries targeted and control group procedures, among others. Beyond considerations of how ethical judgments can be taken into account, because the decision to implement is made by a political force or authority, it can also be heavily influenced by political agendas or objectives. Take the cases of Utrecht and Finland, where the experiments' goals coincided with the goal of both local and central governments in testing certain changes in social assistance mechanisms to understand how those changes could impact labor activation. For some in the basic income movement this was disappointing, particularly in the Finnish case, partly because it failed to comply with some of the key characteristics of what a "pure basic income" could be, but also because of its focus on labor activation. When the decision to implement an experiment or pilot comes from a political authority, it should not be a surprise that its framing coincides with the political agenda of those conducting it.

The examples of Barcelona and Namibia also provide interesting, although different, accounts of the political context's role in the framing of experiments or pilots. In Barcelona, for example, the local government included a diverse coalition of political forces. The choice of the experiment's target beneficiaries and the sampling process was a scientific decision, considering the goals of the experiment, in testing how several conditional and unconditional cash grant mechanisms promote social inclusion. But this decision was also political, considering the general perception in the political forces of the local government, that money should only be given to those deemed most in need. This was both an ideological position, and an attempt to avoid political backlash. In Namibia, where the pilot was implemented by a coalition of civil society organizations, the political context was extremely relevant, since one of the inherent goals was to test UBI's impacts and attempt to influence politicians to implement a nation-wide policy afterwards. Therefore, the research team decided to choose a village where the socioeconomic conditions were dire, almost a "worst case scenario", to provide evidence to politicians and the public of how UBI could have positive impacts even in the most extreme situations. Our interview regarding the Finnish case hinted at how the choice of beneficiaries also seemed to be a political decision. Testing how an unconditional cash grant could work better in labor activation than existing conditional unemployed benefits was a political decision to disburse money to a problem considered relevant by the community and politician—persistent long-term unemployment. Hence, instead of testing a basic income for the working poor, for example, or in the general population, the experiment focused on long-term unemployed, but contrary to what happened when people received unemployment benefits, they continued receiving the money even if they found a job (hence resembling what a UBI could be, inasmuch people would receive it, regardless of their employment status).

A final account for what seems to be an upcoming discussion, which we will begin to explore in Chapter 3 and discuss more at length in Chapter 4, is the role of political agendas in implementing or manipulating basic income experiments, pilots, and policies. In both Ontario and in the implementation of Maricá's *Renda Básica de Cidadania*, the decision to experiment with or implement a basic income seems to have resulted only from the decision of a government, or a mayor in the case of Maricá. No movement or political negotiation appears to have been at play in these decisions, despite the significant movement for basic income in Brazil, or the historical negative income tax experiments in Canada. Both examples showcase a genuine concern in testing out a new policy to solve socioeconomic issues. However, in both cases our interviews considered the possibility of basic income being used as an electoral tool or being influenced by electoral calculations. In the case of Ontario, this seemed to be even more obvious. Our interviewee who was involved in the research of the Ontario experiment discussed how the liberal government only decided to implement its experiment approximately twelve months prior to elections. Considering the party's position in the polls at the time (which was low) and the momentum basic income was enjoying in the country (which was quite significant), it seems the pilot was at least partly a move by the liberal government to maintain power. It might also have been a move to put pressure on their political opponents, the conservative party, who even ended up pledging to continue the experiment if they won elections (although they broke this promise later on after winning). In the Madhya Pradesh and South Korean cases too, it seems political parties are now waking up to the possibility of basic income as an attractive political banner. The former mayor of Seongnam, Lee Jae-myung, realized the potential of basic income after having implemented the youth project in the city. By pledging to expand the policy to the entire province, we might speculate this was a ploy used to propel himself to electoral victory as the governor of Gyeonggi. In Madhya Pradesh too, our interviewee, Sarath Davala who was one of the leading researchers of the experiment, mentioned how unconditional cash transfers, and through it basic income as well, have become more popular. This has happened, not only since the experiment took place, but also since a more recent unconditional transfer targeting rural farmers was implemented in the country. This transfer was first implemented in the southern state of Telangana, and it was later extended to the entire country by the federal Government, targeting rural farmers.

The third aspect where the political or social context can play a significant role is in the aftermath of the experiment or pilot, where evidence is discussed and the decision of whether or not to implement a UBI takes place. None of our eight case studies which were experiments or pilots led to a full national or provincial implementation of an actual policy. In cases like Finland, the fact that the unconditional cash grant did not seem to lead to higher labor activation rates meant that no serious discussion among political agents to implement a basic income would take place. It seems that the political agenda and climate at the end of a basic income experiment or pilot will also be determinant in its aftermath, and in a way responsible for how the evidence might or might not be construed as positive and supporting a move toward full-scale policy implementation in that context.

Therefore, as the discussion above demonstrates, the debate on the context's role in a basic income experiment, pilot, or policy is linked with their goal(s). The distinction between the two—policies and non-policies—and the role played by the type of stakeholders who oppose or are in favor of basic income seems to explain many of the disagreements over basic income experiments, pilots, and even policies. This was certainly a key takeaway from our interviews and again seems to fit with Widerquist's diagnosis of the lack of connection between basic income experiments and the bottom-line questions (Widerquist 2018, 12).

In all our case studies, particularly those which are basic income experiments or pilots, we found the existence of key stakeholders—namely research teams, basic income advocacy movements (national, but also international), basic income scholars, political actors, and communities—who often represent competing interests surrounding both the basic income and experimental debates. These differing interests do not perfectly coincide most times, leading to disagreement or frustration with the outlook of the experiment, or from the basic income movement, or even from communities involved. It can also jeopardize not only the success of an experiment or pilot (and how it is interpreted) but perhaps it is a decisive factor to explain why experiments or pilots have not yet succeeded in paving the way for the implementation of a UBI at any administrative level. In the Namibian pilot, despite plentiful positive results, the research team was disappointed that basic income was not implemented by the BIG Coalition chairperson, who was appointed by the Namibian President as the First Minister for Poverty Erradication. This represents a failure for an experiment that aimed to roll-out a nation-wide basic income. In this case, one could say the research team had an interest in knowing the impacts of basic income and advocating for policy implementation. The BIG Coalition was interested in understanding its effects to see if it could then be applied nation-wide. Meanwhile, the government seemed uninterested in the policy despite the experiment and despite appointing the BIG Coalition Chairperson as a Minister. In the Finnish case, the interest of the government—assessing alternative methods of promoting labor activation—differed tremendously from the aspirations and goals of the basic income movement in the country and in Europe, who wished to see a full-fledged policy implemented and test its impacts beyond labor intake. This was also the case in Barcelona, where the experiment's goal was to test certain social activation policies' effectiveness in promoting inclusion of marginalized groups. This is relatively far from the discussion on how basic income could help empower citizens and promote their overall freedom. Hence, often it may even be that the social and political movements might have interests in implementing a basic income experiment which are not fully aligned with those of the broader basic income movement, of researchers or advocates. This misalignment results in unmet and frustrated expectations from different actors—advocates, politicians, researchers, or even society in general—on what they expected could result from a basic income experiment or pilot.

Acknowledging that basic income experiments and pilots face competing interests and goals should help lower expectations as to what they can teach us. When designing an experiment or pilot, or discussing its observed results, we as advocates, researchers, communities, and general public should strive to be more realistic in what we expect to get out of an experiment or pilot's impact report. The background of all our experimental case studies includes different stakeholders—politicians, researchers, advocates, and communities—who compete, albeit with different degrees of influence, in terms of the goals they would like to experiment with or policy to implement. Moreover, not only do such goals have to be harmonized in only one single experiment or pilot, but they also have to be juggled against budgeting and time frame challenges, and the inherent limitations of social science experiments. This usually means that key questions that different stakeholders would like to see answered will most likely either not be or will receive a very limited reply, probably rigged with caveats that make it difficult to obtain a decisive answer. Such challenges in aligning expectations and goals, and in extracting the necessary information to satisfy interested stakeholders, should also temper expectations about what the consequences of a basic income experiment or pilot can be. Such a complex context will hardly lead to a smooth transition from experiment or pilot toward nation-wide basic income policy.

So, what conclusions can we take from the interviews about the ongoing debates on the role of the methodology and the discussion of the context surrounding basic income experiments?

The first conclusion is the obvious role played by methodological decisions and the context where experiments/pilots take place. Moreover, in our case studies, the context—the researchers' ambitions and the political agenda, among others—heavily determined the methodological decisions, beyond the simple use of scientific criteria to define the design of an experiment. The context is therefore one of the most relevant variables in how basic income experiments play out and should not be disregarded.

A second conclusion is the potential misalignment of interests among stakeholders. The most fundamental reason why a certain political outcome or design feature of a basic income experiment is not well received by a given group of stakeholders is due to the fact they have aspirations and interests that differ from the ones governing the basic income experiment's implementation. Better understanding the key players involved, including their interests, motivations, influences, and others can help temper expectations, limit misinterpretations of results, and enable more realistic perceptions on the (un)successful nature of a particular experiment/pilot (or even a policy, for that matter). Moreover, doing so can help understand which role—scientific, advocative, political, or all of them—experiments play in particular contexts.

A third conclusion is how experiments, pilots, and policies are inherently limited in their comparability and scalability. This acknowledgment circles back to the beginning of our chapter, namely the discussion on how many of our case studies, which are usually framed as examples of "basic income experiments, policies or pilots" are quite different from the definition of basic income used in this book and presented in the introduction. This is either because they were not framed as such (by targeting specific groups, for example) or because they were not interested in testing the basic income per se. Because contexts and goals are specific, to a point where some experiments are not even framed as basic income at all, their potential as comparable case studies become very limited. How could we compare the Utrecht experiment, where an unconditional cash transfer was used to test labor activation, with the Namibian pilot, which tested how a UBI could affect malnutrition and children's education? Even disregarding the obvious geographical differences, can the Finnish experiment, where an unconditional cash transfer was given to the long-term unemployed to test its effect on labor activation, be compared with the B-MINCOME experiment in Barcelona, where unconditional benefits alongside different activation policies were used to test their effectiveness in social inclusion? Such different social and political contexts, but also methodological decisions and most importantly specific goals, allow for what seems to be very limited possibilities of comparability among our case studies. This makes the question of *what does the evidence tell us* quite difficult to answer, though we will attempt to do so next chapter.

Besides the challenge of limited comparability, basic income experiments, pilots, and policies also face the challenge of limited scalability. This is partly a result of the methodologies employed in social science experiments, which in themselves are very hard to scale to larger contexts. The main issue, however, is the difficulty in generalizing findings; even in RCTs (testing basic income or other policies) researchers are not prone to generalize their findings because of the role played by issues such as community effects (see Widerquist 2018, Chapter 4 for a discussion on community effects). Hence, basic income experiments/pilots are then stuck between the challenge to generalize and the alternative route of only fitting the findings to a given context. If one is required to situate findings partially in their context, UBI as a policy proposal will always be at least partially dependent on basic income experiments or pilots, in other places, for different people, in different countries. This might lead to a surge in basic income experiments and pilots, which might be perceived as positive, but might also result in misdirection and lack of focus, where instead of moving toward implementing UBI, advocates or politicians continue discussing basic income experiments and their findings, or arguing for experiments and pilots, instead of pushing for and moving toward a national program. We can therefore become trapped in a place where experiments are effectively stalling mechanisms, instead of advocacy tools to promote basic income as a policy. Limited scalability and comparability should therefore propel us to our main question: *What is the role of basic income experiments: a political, research, or advocacy tool?*

References

Baker, Amy Castro, and Stacia Martin-West. Learning Agenda. The Center for Guaranteed Income Research The University of Pennsylvania School of Social Policy and Practice, 2020.

Calnistsky, David. "'More Normal than Welfare': The Mincome Experiment, Stigma and Community Experience." *Canadian Sociological Association/La Société Canadienne de Sociologie* 53, no. 1 (2016): 26–71.

Cartwright, Nancy. "Are RCTs the Gold Standard?" *BioSocieties* 2 (2007): 11–20.

Cartwright, Nancy, and Jeremy Hardie. *Evidence-Based Policy: A Practical Guide to Doing It Better*. New York: Oxford University Press, 2012.

Citizens' Basic Income Feasibility Study Steering Group. Assessing the Feasibility of Citizens' Basic Income Pilots in Scotland: Final Report. Citizens' Basic Income Feasibility Study Steering Group, 2020.

Forget, Evelyn. "The Town with No Poverty: The Health Effects of a Canadian Guaranteed Annual Income Field Experiment." *Canadian Public Policy* 37, no. 3 (2011): 283–305.

Munro, Eileen. "Evidence-based policy." In *Philosophy of Social Science: A New Introduction*, Eleonora Montuschi and Nancy Cartwright (eds.), 48–67. Oxford: Oxford University Press, 2014.

Noguera, José A., and Jurgen De Wispelaere. "A Plea for the Use of Laboratory Experiments in Basic Income Research." *Basic Income Studies*1, no. 2 (2006): 1–6.

Painter, Anthony, Jamie Cooke, Ian Burbidge and Aima Ahmed. *A Basic Income for Scotland*. London: RSA, 2019.

Standing, Guy. *Piloting Basic Income as Common Dividends*. London: Progressive Economic Forum, 2019.

West, Stacia, Amy Castro Baker, Sukhi Samra, and Erin Coltrera. Preliminary analysis: SEED's first year. Stockton Economic Empowerment Demonstration, 2021.

Widerquist, Karl. "A Failure to Communicate: What (if Anything) Can We Learn From the Negative Income Tax Experiments?" *Journal of Socio-Economics* 34, no. 1 (2005): 1–51.

Widerquist, Karl. *A Critical Analysis of Basic Income Experiments for Researchers, Policymakers and Citizens*. Cham, Switzerland: Palgrave Macmillan, 2018.

CHAPTER 3

What Do Our Case Studies Tell Us?

Our interviews provided a rich set of information confirming many of the existing perspectives and debates in the discussion and literature on basic income experiments, pilots, and policies. As mentioned above, we are faced with what seems to be a paradox. We are using case studies, which sometimes bear little resemblance to the formal definition we are using in this book of what an unconditional basic income is, as examples to discuss many aspects pertaining to the debate on basic income. For our discussion on the impacts of our case studies, it is important to keep in mind how our case studies differ from this definition. One particular aspect is how most of our case studies offer very modest cash grants, some of which fall below national thresholds of poverty (e.g., Eastern Band of Cherokee Indians' Dividend national, or the South Korea Youth program), others near subsistence levels (e.g., Utrecht or Barcelona). In some of the pilot projects, the amounts granted were also quite modest, but considering the rural contexts of extreme poverty, they could sometimes be considered almost as "seed capital" to start a business, as one of the project Directors from the GiveDirectly experiment told us. Nonetheless, such modest amounts will necessarily have different impacts than what a UBI (whose value should allow for a life with dignity, as mentioned in our introduction) could allow. Impacts on the labor market, educational choices, or consumption patterns would most likely be quite different. Most of

R. Merrill et al., *Basic Income Experiments*, Exploring the Basic Income Guarantee, https://doi.org/10.1007/978-3-030-89120-6_3

our case studies are also targeted—to marginalized or very poor groups. Their decisions on what to do when granted a basic income (e.g., where to spend the money, find or quit a job) will probably be quite different from other members of society (e.g., more affluent members could afford to save the money, or spend it on positional goods, or make long-term decisions). Besides sometimes barely resembling what a basic income is according to our definition, our case studies also share little among themselves, posing an initial question of whether they are a representative sample for us to draw conclusions from.

Chapter 2 also highlighted the role methodology and context play in influencing the implementation and outcome of these experiments and pilots. Together with the already obvious concerns of how some of these cases often do not resemble UBI at all, we are left with what are common questions in the literature on basic income experiments and pilots: Are they comparable? Or is it possible to scale them up? Can we draw common conclusions on the impacts observed in these case studies?

If limited comparability is a significant issue in this debate, we can ask whether evidence on existing cases is relevant to our perceptions and to the theoretical discussions of the potential impacts of UBI. This is the issue we will now turn to.

3.1 Do We Already Know Enough?

If we put aside the initial concerns of comparability between cases, our interviews are illuminating in the sense of what they tell us about each of their impacts. In every interview, the amount of data collected—quantitative and qualitative—provided rich and often robust evidence of impacts on poverty, malnutrition, or well-being. Of course, the effects' magnitude differs; some experiments perceived minor increases in paid working hours of participants, while others observed nothing of the sort. In some contexts, community empowerment was surprisingly evident, with initiatives created by citizens due to the pilots implemented, while in others it seemed only a minor effect or was not observed. It's undeniable how much evidence has been collected on the (mostly positive) impacts of cash grants for many of these variables and how unconditional cash transfers magnify some of them (Birnbaum and De Wispelaere 2016; World Bank Group 2020), hence the question with which we start off this section: *Do we already know enough?* It's questionable whether we can infer effects of a basic income-type policy, or whether experiments or pilots for that matter can be considered legitimate means to provide those answers. We will address these two questions at the end of the discussion on existing evidence of the impacts of our case studies.

Before going into our analysis, one additional note is warranted: these results should be read in light of their specific context, considering the importance it plays in shaping the experiment, pilot, or policy before, during and after implementation, as we saw in Chapter 2. One of the important contextual variables is whether an experiment or pilot was conducted in a context with robust social assistance mechanisms. In some of our cases, like in Finland, Utrecht, or even Barcelona, an unconditional cash transfer was tested against existing or other forms of conditional transfers. Hence, we have examples where either an unconditional transfer was tested against non-existing social assistance mechanisms or conditional cash transfers with very strict measures of conditionality. In such cases, we might expect, and many times observed, positive impacts of the introduction of an unconditional cash transfer. However, an unconditional cash transfer can fare worse than a conditional one in some dimensions if conditionality is less strict or fairer (White 2017). Some data in Barcelona seems to imply that this could be the case. We will not dispute this but can certainly acknowledge that certain impacts can vary—relatively and absolutely—in relation to others, and the decision of what results should be prioritized or not is a matter of a collective debate among the interested stakeholders, and possibly also a philosophical debate of which impacts could be seen as more important, in light of communities' values or considerations of justice.

Moreover, it is also important to outline the limitations faced by social experiments, which is a relevant label for our basic income experiments, pilots, and also the ad hoc studies conducted of some policies. This means that we should perhaps keep in mind what experiments and pilots will probably not be able to tell us or will do so in a very limited way. Experiments and pilots' time frames are short—two to three years—which is an insufficient amount of time to inspire or observe structural changes in many relevant variables (e.g., well-being, education outcomes, or labor market effects). Moreover, experiments using RCTs, as many of our case studies do, are incapable of assessing community effects because they only target a particular set of the population or because their sample is small. Even when using a saturation study, we are able to observe community effects, but only in that particular context, which makes the possibility of generalizing findings very difficult. Therefore, impacts that are influenced by community effects (e.g., labor market participation, educational impacts, trust) will likely be very difficult to observe in our case studies, or when they are observed, it will be difficult or impossible to attribute them to basic income specifically.

Moving on to the discussion of existing evidence, our interviews enabled us to separate results into two sets. The first is impacts that seem to be common to all unconditional cash transfers, of which we have some degree of evidence. The second ones are more particular impacts, which may be unique to certain experiments, pilots, or policies, or have received little attention in the literature and discussion on basic income and which we will discuss more thoroughly later on in the book.

So what are the impacts that seem to be present across the board?

3.1.1 *Welfare and Health Benefits*

Almost every experiment highlighted the role of unconditional cash transfers on individuals' welfare. Most of the time, these results were related with health benefits, such as reduced mental and physical stress and reduced consumption of alcohol, drugs, and tobacco. This seems to be consistent with the evidence from the MINCOME experiment in Canada in the 1970s, where the NIT scheme seemed to reduce hospitalizations due to mental health disorders (Forget 2011).

In Finland, Ontario, and Barcelona, there was clear evidence of decreased stress, a sign of better mental health and individual well-being. This does not seem surprising considering that the people participating in these cases were either poor, marginalized, or long-term unemployed. These results suggest that receiving an unconditional cash transfer would therefore provide a more robust and also an unconditional financial safety net than the existing systems in place in each context. Ontario and the Eastern Band of Cherokee Indians' Dividend also showed reduced alcohol and drug consumption, and in both interviews, this was attributed to decreased levels of stress and better mental health of the participants. There were also significant improvements in individuals' health observed in Kenya, which was attributed to the additional income enabling people to access medical care previously unavailable to them through the country's non-existent health system.

Our case studies also provided a rich set of data for effects on individuals' welfare. The case in Finland was extensively reported in Europe, since happiness indicators seemed to have greatly improved for the participants who were granted cash transfers there. In South Korea, payments to 24-year-old citizens have increased their happiness and satisfaction with life, as well as their "dream capital" (their possibilities and future outlook on life). There was evidence of increased well-being from participants in the experiment in Utrecht as well. Although both the conditional and unconditional groups seemed to be satisfied with the additional income and support they were receiving, the unconditional group seemed to report more peace and control in their lives. These were not very significant results, but nonetheless are consistent with the evidence of other experiments, pilots, and policies.

In Barcelona, although individuals reported decreased levels of stress in the first year, this effect disappeared in the second. Our interview revealed that this result was surprising for the research team. Although the team is unaware of why this was the case, Lluís Torrens, one of the leading researchers from the experiment in Barcelona that we interviewed, believed that it may be explained by the fact that participants knew the support was coming to an end after the second year. If this is in fact what happened, it serves as a reminder of the ethical implications of basic income experiments and pilots, especially considering the effect they can have on very fragile and marginalized groups, particularly their ability to impact well-being and physical and mental health, as the evidence suggests. It also possibly indicates how implementing a policy, rather than an experiment or pilot can contribute positively to impacts on well-being and health.

Some of our case studies exhibited health impacts attributable to the unconditional cash grants, namely lower levels of malnutrition in particularly poor households. Such impacts were a result of having more disposable income, which allowed for the possibility of making different decisions, and especially to take better care of one's family. Moreover, our interviewees believed such results were attributable to the role played by women within the household. In fact, women seem to enable more favorable outcomes in health and education in children in these households. In the Namibian pilot and the GiveDirectly experiment in Kenya, there were significant improvements in the nutrition of households involved, particularly for children. This was a result of how the transfers were spent. Because they received these payments unconditionally, these households were able to buy staple products, such as food (although in Kenya, it was also used to invest in education and health, since these are not universally provided services). In Namibia, women received the unconditional transfer that was distributed to children, whereas in Maricá women were the grant holders of the *mumbucas* within the household (since it was not an individual policy). In the GiveDirectly experiment, the transfers targeted all adults aged 18 years and above, including both women and men but excluding children. However, our interviewee believed that the fact women were included as recipients had a profound impact in such results, a perspective shared by researchers of both the Maricá *Renda Básica de Cidadania* and the Namibia pilot, where transfers were indeed targeted at women within households. These results mirror what has been found in other conditional and unconditional cash transfers (World Bank Group 2020), though one can argue whether it reinforces gender roles or not (and how that could be perceived as positive or negative). Moreover, our case studies also illustrated other particular impacts related to women's autonomy and gender roles, which will be covered in Chapter 5.

3.1.2 Labor Market Participation

None of our case studies with available evidence showed any significant reduction in the intensity of work (measured in hours or days worked). However, impacts on labor markets, and particularly on labor supply, must be differentiated when considering basic income experiments and pilots in different contexts, namely with different prosperity levels. In some of our case studies, such as in Namibia, Madhya Pradesh, and Kenya, scientific literature and official reports do not reveal any significant reductions in labor supply. Rather, some signal a positive trend. For example, the unconditional cash transfers in Madhya Pradesh incentivized job creation in the agrarian sector, positions which were filled by former part-time workers. More importantly, a decrease in bonded labor was detected, while participants dubbed their likelihood of seeking out and finding a job higher. In addition, entrepreneurial economic activity performed by women also increased (Davala et al. 2015). In Kenya (Haushofer and Shapiro 2016) and Namibia (Haarmann et al. 2009; Osterkamp 2013), beyond a drastic reduction in rates of extreme poverty, similar impacts on work activation were also observed while the local economy and entrepreneurial activity were also reinforced. In Iran, apart from the reducing various urban-rural inequalities, no labor supply reduction was detected, though there was a slightly increase in self-employment (Salehi-Isfahani and H. Mostafavi-Dehzooei 2018).

Impacts in our case studies from wealthier countries are less conclusive and differ when compared with the former cases. In Ontario, the report conducted surveys of some participants after the cancelation of the experiment, which showed small increases in workplace satisfaction, labor participation, and entrepreneurial activity (BICN. Basic Income Canada Network 2019). Utrecht also reported a slight increase in labor participation and a major likelihood of finding a permanent contract. (Verlaat et al. 2020). It also detected a sort of "plateau effect" in the people receiving the conditional cash transfer; it seems they were quicker to find a job (hence the group fared better in labor activation), but then the effect would "plateau", with a percentage of the people in those groups not being successful in labor activation. Moreover, Timo Verlaat from the Utrecht experiment who was involved as one of the researchers told us that initially the unconditional cash transfer with additional earnings options made some people chose less stable jobs (part-time, for example) since working next to benefits would now provide extra income. According to the interviewee, an open question still to be answered was if these part-time jobs would eventually serve as a steppingstone to full-time employment. In Finland, the overall household economic situation improved, becoming more stable and secure, despite the detection of a slight increase in the number of hours worked by participants (particularly migrants and single mothers). This effect was not statistically significant nor even conclusive, since it cannot be attributed to the treatment per se because the government unilaterally decided on the introduction of the "activation model" during the second year of the experiment. In Barcelona, a slight reduction in the likelihood of being employed or seeking a job was observed at the end of the project, in contrast with the more positive results in this variable observed during the first year. However, it is important to highlight that this reduction on year 2 was somewhat expected by those engaged in the experiment, given that many participants either suffered from poor health, or have been excluded from the job market (and in many cases from mainstream society) for several years. Finally, in South Korea, no reduction of labor supply was detected. In sum, although there is a fair degree of evidence on the impact of basic income experiments and pilots on labor market and labor supply, it's difficult to say how a full-scale policy, particularly in more affluent contexts, would affect the labor market.

At least one of our case studies showed changes in power dynamics in the labor market. In Ontario, the payments seemed to have impacted labor market choices, with some quitting their jobs—our interview from the Ontario experiment called them "bullshit jobs", echoing the words of David Graeber (2018). Considering the limitations of Ontario's experiment, these results should not be extensively taken into account, although they suggest that some individuals were enabled to move to higher paying jobs, or to quit their jobs and take up different occupations, namely caring for relatives. As mentioned above, most experiments find that people either kept their jobs when granted an unconditional cash transfer, as in the case of the Eastern Band of Cherokee Indians' Dividend, or little evidence was found in terms of an influence on behavior when it comes to labor activation (in the cases of Finland and Utrecht). This means that compared to unemployed people subject to conditional measures, people with unconditional cash transfers did not prove better or worse at finding a job.

Two of our cases provide evidence in terms of a specific advantage unconditional transfers might offer individuals. Participants in Utrecht with lower levels of education were observed finding jobs more quickly when granted an unconditional cash transfer instead of a conditional one. The experiment did not gather more information on this, although both of our interviewees from the Utrecht experiment suggested that some of these people might be less demanding when it comes to job hunting but may also have their own tools and contacts they can utilize to find a job. Meanwhile, the conditional group had to comply with training demands and bureaucracy, thus losing time they could have spent job hunting. Back in Finland, immigrants and single mothers worked more when granted an unconditional cash transfer, as mentioned above. In these cases, the grant might simply be more money they could use or save, and hence in no way discourages labor market participation.

Finally, it should be added how labor market participation is crucial for discussing social inclusion, but not the exclusive way to achieve it. The three case studies examining how unconditional cash transfers are better or worse than conditional ones (Finland, Utrecht, and Barcelona) found positive results in terms of satisfaction with benefits and greater social inclusion in groups with some form of conditionality or activation policy. In Utrecht's case, this could be because some people were able to find a job more quickly when granted a conditional cash transfer (which improved their social inclusion) or as in Barcelona's case, it could simply be the result of the networks and encounters provided by some of the conditionality mechanisms (e.g., training, volunteering). Our interviewee from the research team in Barcelona deemed this a consequence of the fact that many beneficiaries of social assistance are also part of marginalized groups. Thus, their only connection to the social world might be through the social assistance bureaucracy and mechanisms, especially when they have been out of the labor market for quite a while. Hence, even when conditional cash grants were not more effective in promoting labor market activation, they could have more positive impacts in the social inclusion of some of their beneficiaries.

Finally, it is important to consider that all our case studies are examples of unconditional cash grants that are near (in the case of Utrecht or Ontario) or below the subsistence level (all of our other case studies). Hence, they illustrate cash transfers whose impact on incentives to work will not be considerably high (since someone will likely not be able to live off most of the grants attributed in our case studies).

These results seem to show that in certain contexts an unconditional transfer, namely at the subsistence level in many of our case studies, might be better in promoting labor market activation. However, we are not endorsing a productivist defense of basic income, and some of the reasons why in some of our case studies unconditional cash transfers increased labor market activation might be seen as normatively just or unjust. In the case of Utrecht, Timo Verlaat speculated that the reason lower educated people found a job quicker when granted an unconditional transfer was because they possibly were not locked up in training and activation programs any longer. Another explanation might be that they were no longer referred to (low-quality) jobs that they did not want to accept, but able to hunt for jobs that would match their preferences. In the Finnish case, it seems an unconditional grant led to more positive impacts in labor market activation in some of the less affluent members of society (e.g., immigrants or single mothers) either because they could earn more income (by saving their unconditional transfer) or because they had disposable income to pay for childcare services (e.g., single mothers), and hence could have more time to work.

This evidence is not compelling enough to provide a decisive answer to whether UBI leads to labor withdraw or not, considering the inherent limitations of social experiments. Their limited time frame does not offer participants the capacity to alter their labor situation in a structural way, which therefore makes experiments incapable of capturing the long-term effects on the supply-side of labor. Moreover, as mentioned, experiments usually are incapable of assessing community effects, or when they do (e.g., using saturation studies in a particular city or region), we cannot generalize findings. Hence, estimating the effect of a basic income in the nation-wide supply of labor would be very difficult under both circumstances.

The fact that our case studies are also quite different from what a basic income would be according to our definition, also generates strong limitations to our understanding of the impact of UBI on the labor market. As we discussed, our case studies are modest cash grants. A higher basic income would possibly have more significant impacts on the incentives to work (e.g., people will be more discouraged to work if they don't need it to survive or live a comfortable life). Moreover, the cases usually target marginalized populations, with lower educational levels, at times with limited safety nets, and some of them in a situation of social exclusion. Their perceptions toward employment, the possibilities they are offered, and their decisions about engaging in the labor market or not will likely be very different from other segments of the population. The case of Utrecht illustrated how people with more qualifications took longer to find a job. Timo Verlaat speculated that this was because they would be more ambitious with their employment choice, but many other variables might account for these different results. Hence, having only a certain type of participant in most experiments, pilots, or even policies is most likely biasing our perspective on the changes a basic income can have in labor supply. Finally, we should keep in mind that experiments do not (and cannot) consider how socio-institutional norms and settings actually affect (and build up) labor markets (Van Parjis and Vanderborght 2017; Tena 2018). These include the availability of public schools, care work services, gender patterns affecting women's behavior, the presence of more or less generous unemployment benefits or of a particular legal framework potentiating or penalizing part-time jobs. Moreover, experiments and pilots cannot estimate the demand-side response of labor markets, which means people might not be working not because of their choices, but because of the unavailability of jobs matching their competencies or qualifications. They are therefore only capturing a very partial effect of labor market participation.

Hence, despite existing evidence, our knowledge on the impact of basic income in labor markets is still quite incomplete, partly because of the nature of our case studies, and their differences among themselves, but also how they do not resemble a basic income according to our definition. Additionally, social experiments are also naturally limited, which in turn restricts our ability to understand and estimate impacts in the labor market.

3.1.3 Autonomy

The possible impact UBI can have on individual's autonomy is also one of the key claims for implementing a basic income (Widerquist 2018) and is part of Van Parijs' defense of the proposal (Van Parijs and Vanderborght 2017). Despite that, we found little reference to it in our interviews, and when we did, it was as a proxy for impacts gathered in the experiments, and due to their very particular contexts.

In the Eastern Band of Cherokee Indians' Dividend, we can see the impact basic income has on an individual's autonomy, due to it granting parents more time for themselves and their households. In the Madhya Pradesh and Kenyan cases, two somewhat opposite situations seemed to have happened. In Madhya Pradesh, the poorer members of the community were able to increase their self-sufficiency (by promoting farming on their own plots of land) and decrease the amount of time spent in waged labor. Therefore, they increased their autonomy by becoming less dependent on wealthy property holders (whose land they tenant farmed) and exploitative money lenders (since they could now use the additional income from the unconditional cash grant to help finance their own farming activities), thus significantly reducing the exploitation they suffered due to high-interest loans. Alternatively, in Kenya, people were able to become autonomous by freeing themselves from daily subsistence farming and instead began to think more long-term and take more economic risks. Since self-sufficient farming was the main economic activity in rural Kenya, the autonomy granted by the unconditional cash grant made it possible for participants to increase time they spend in alternatives to supplement subsistence farming. As Caroline Teti project Director at GiveDirectly told us, there were people who could not even till their land because of poverty and rented it out so that they could get income for their families. These people are no longer renting their land: they now till that land to get their own food because UBI is providing the little income floor they lacked at the beginning.

In other case studies, namely the ones in Europe, very little data was collected on the role unconditional cash grants could play in autonomy.

Only in Utrecht did some evidence seem to suggest that the unconditional group felt more in control of their lives and also had more time and space to use their networks to find a job, compared to those granted a conditional income. However, the three case studies of Utrecht, Barcelona, and Finland also highlighted the role played by activation policies and social assistance mechanisms in providing a safety net and a means for more successful social inclusion for the most vulnerable members of society. Our interviewees even claimed many of these mechanisms—group gatherings, assistance in preparing for job interviews, or periodic assessments to monitor how job hunting was proceeding—provided one of the most meaningful opportunities for social interaction for many of the recipients. If this is the case, the value of autonomy might be considered less relevant, in exchange for promoting social inclusion, begging the question of what activation and inclusion policies are the best and least stigmatizing for beneficiaries.

3.1.4 Economic Activity

Another interesting topic in the literature is the possibility of basic income influencing economic activity. As mostly a demand-side policy, basic income can stimulate consumption, hence contributing to a positive dynamism of economic activity. This is one of current arguments for implementing a basic income in the context of economic downturns. However, some also argue that a basic income without any other control mechanisms would be inflationary, therefore reducing its value and eroding its benefits for those most in need (Minsky 2013; Thomas 2020).

However, we found very little evidence in our interviews of any particular attention to the impact of basic income on economic activity or inflation (except the already mentioned discussions on the impact of labor market participation). Two of our case studies implemented local currencies—Maricá and South Korea—as ways to finance the policy and promote positive impacts at both individual and community level, while also boosting local economies. Not surprisingly, both cases have been looking for potential impacts that such policies had in stimulating local commerce, since that's one of the main goals of local currencies. In both South Korea and Maricá, though with less evidence in the latter case, the transfers in local currency naturally seemed to have boosted sales at local businesses.

In other case studies, the analysis of the impact of unconditional transfers on the economy is scattered at best. One of our interviewees who on the research team of the Namibian pilot told us that the unconditional transfer increased monetary circulation and economic activity in the community where the pilot was implemented (e.g., people were buying more products and also selling commodities). We can infer from this evidence that in the Namibian pilot the additional income per household was not mostly saved, but rather used in transactions within the community (e.g., shopping in local businesses, in new businesses that might have been created, or even in lending activities between villagers). In Kenya, one of the Directors from GiveDirectly told us that the unconditional cash grant seems to be improving entrepreneurial activity, since the amount seems at times to be considered as a capital grant (e.g., seed grant), allowing people to start their own small businesses. The results from the long-term pilot (12 years) are not published, hence we have no particular evidence on this impact. However, from the interview with Caroline Teti, one of the Directors from GiveDirectly, we gathered this had been because some of the villagers could start their own local small businesses, selling the excess they produced farming or trying out some business models (e.g., the case of an old lady living in the village who used the extra money to go and buy extra groceries outside the village, then sold them to nearby neighbors).

Besides these references to the influence of unconditional cash transfers on the economy, our interviews did not discuss any more relevant evidence. Even about inflation, no systematic analysis of its possible role has been undertaken. Maricá's *Renda Básica de Cidadania* research team wishes to include it in their analysis and are engaging with a research center connected with Maricá's municipality to study the impact of the *mumbuca* local currency on the economy, particularly on inflation. The lack of evidence for such a concern in our case studies probably reflects some of the limitations inherent to social experiments, but particularly to our case studies. On the one hand, the fact that most of these unconditional transfers are not universal makes it difficult to understand whether they have impacted local sales or lead to inflation. Moreover, considering the significant global interdependence of current economies, testing inflation might be very difficult, especially if experiments, pilots, and policies are targeting certain segments of populations within certain communities. For this reason, experiments or policies paid in local currencies might be better equipped to assess such an impact, rather than those paid in national or supra-national currencies (e.g., the euro), or targeted toward particular segments of particular communities.

3.1.5 *Investments in Education*

Finally, it is worth considering the impacts on education: contrary to the other impacts presented, we found very little reference to it in our interviews. There is a rich discussion on how basic income could promote investments in education, hence ensuring a better outlook for individuals by potentially increasing productivity, but also generally impacting the community positively. This could be achieved by enabling parents to invest more in their children's education, as opposed to pushing them to work for extra income to help support the household. It could also be a side effect of parents having more time to participate in their children's lives. Another possibility would be that basic income promotes life-long learning, or the option to engage more in learning experiences throughout their lives, especially if they are not forced to work for survival. Despite such debates, only three of our case studies mentioned education. Two case studies illustrate the role basic income plays in promoting education for the children of the community. As Caroline Teti one of the Directors from GiveDirectly in Kenya told us, parents can invest more in education. Also, the Eastern Band of Cherokee Indians' Dividend seems to have allowed parents to be more present and improve children's mental health, which in turn improves their educational outcomes (Costello et al. 2016). Only Ontario, with its small sample of interviews, had some evidence of adults choosing to quit their jobs or reduce the number of hours worked to return to school.

It is important to mention that the educational claim is a difficult one to test: we can observe whether children stay more years in school, or whether adults invest in their education by enrolling in universities or in training throughout the experiment. However, whether such investments would lead to higher productivity will probably be very difficult to test in an experimental context, given their limitations as social experiments, namely their time frame and the difficulty in capturing community effects, as Widerquist points out (Widerquist 2018, 111–112).

The survey of these impacts seems to show us that we have a fair amount of data which reinforces the idea, discussed theoretically, that unconditional transfers, such as an unconditional basic income, can have significant positive impacts on well-being and health. There is also limited evidence that cash transfers can positively impact economic activity, and that unconditional ones might also positively impact an individual's autonomy.

However, we might not be able to fully answer to our initial question: Do we already know too much on basic income? Firstly, we lack evidence on important outcomes, such as labor market participation. As discussed, this is not only because of lack of testing, but perhaps mostly because of the inherent difficulties in testing labor market participation (as influenced by community effects) in the context of a social experiment. Nonetheless, we have evidence that shows important patterns in how individuals behave when granted unconditional cash transfers, which indicate that people do not withdraw the labor market when receiving unconditional cash transfers. We also lack qualitative evidence on some of the impacts of basic income, namely in issues on community empowerment or women's emancipation, an issue which will return to after discussing other findings in Chapter 5. We also are missing evidence on a variety of commonly debated questions on basic income, such as inflation, productivity, and entrepreneurial activity. Once again, there are surely important knowledge gaps which might be very difficult to test in the context of an experiment, either because of their time frame, methodological constrains, or the difficulty in capturing community effects. Given that many of these questions—namely the labor withdrawal objection, or the economic-boost and inflation questions—are part of widespread normative debates on basic income, the difficulty in testing them might be a strong argument for those opposing a basic income—'if we cannot know how it will play out, we should not dare to implement it!'—or for those who favor implementation instead of experimentation.

We therefore conclude with two final notes. One is that we do have evidence that can be used to predict a basic income policy's effect in well-being, health, and maybe autonomy. However, these tend to be the outcomes everyone "expects to see", hence they are rather redundant, rather than impacts that could "tilt the scale" in favor of basic income (Laín 2021). In other impacts, our knowledge is more limited. This seems to be both the result of the limitation of UBI experiments, but also of the difficult interplay between empirical evidence and the ethical debate surrounding basic income as a proposal (Merrill and Neves 2021a). Moreover, these results might be expected in most experiments that offer cash transfers (perhaps even unconditional ones), hence more testing might tell us little. A second is on the role played by our case studies as illustrative of basic income experiments, pilots, or policies. On the one hand, our case studies bear little resemblance to the definition of a basic income we used in the introduction. Hence, it might be difficult to extrapolate evidence from our case studies as impacts specific to basic income. On the other hand, experiments and pilots are rigged with limitations, offer little contribution to some of the important normative debates surrounding basic income, and will most likely observe similar results from previous experiments. Therefore, how can we justify them as research, advocacy, or political tools? This is a question we will now briefly turn to before concluding the chapter.

3.2 Experiments Play Several Roles

This section aims to provide some answers to the question of what the purpose of conducting a basic income experiment is. In fact, UBI experiments can be justified by an empirical or scientifical claim—the evidence they can collect—by a deliberative claim—the role the evidence collected can have in shaping the normative debate—an evidence-based claim—how evidence can lead to policy implementations—and finally by an advocacy claim—how they can attract media attention, and spark debates and movements pro-UBI (Merril and Neves 2021b). Using some of the insights collected in the interviews, it is possible to offer some answers which are related to existing theoretical debates.

When the question came up in our interviews, we had three main clusters of opinions:

1. The first one considers basic income experiments to be important because of the role evidence can play in the media and political discussion on basic income. One of the leading researchers from the Madhya Pradesh experiment that we interviewed expressed his belief that how the evidence collected "gives weight to the discussion". From this perspective, empirical evidence is essential to portray the policy as more realistic and less abstract. This is particularly relevant for those who wish the experiment to encourage political implementation of a basic income policy in a particular context. Although similar debates of evidence-based policymaking, this perspective is somewhat different: more than providing evidence to inform the political debate, evidence is used to provide realism, regardless of the content proving to be in line with current majority political forces or

not. Empirical evidence is simply a way to give meaning and realism to what is usually seen as a farfetched, utopian policy. This is also consistent with a view expressed by some, on how existing evidence from prior basic income experiments could become relevant when the political "window" for basic income opens in a given country (e.g., as is the case in Scotland, where several large political parties, including the government in power, are endorsing either implementing a basic income, or a basic income experiment or pilot). This was the main opinion of our interview from Finland, who was one of the leading researchers involved in the analysis of the results of that experiment. In the aftermath of the experiment, evidence was not treated as relevant by the media (which our interviewee believes was a proxy of how the public opinion was not interested in the experiment). However, our interviewee also considered that the experiment could become relevant when a nation-wide discussion on the welfare state and its challenges took place. In essence, this argument shows how the experiment took place at a time when the "political window" for implementing a basic income as policy was closed. However, the experiment could still be seen as relevant, since the results will be able to be used in the future, when such a window is open.

2. A second perspective is related to the first, but the experiment or pilot is seen as even more instrumental. In this view, the evidence and data collected are less important than the role experiments or pilots can play in promoting advocacy. The "noise" made by them is the best impact they can have, and one that should be harnessed by advocacy movements wishing to see basic income implemented. If this is the case, many of the limitations on experiments or pilots are less relevant since the goal is simply to raise awareness. A somewhat related perspective is the one argued by our interviewee, Caroline Teti, one of the Directors of the GiveDirectly experiment in Kenya, who felt that one of the roles that a basic income experiment can play is increasing the number of voices of advocates for universal basic income. If basic income experiments are implemented, a large number of people will understand the impacts the policy can have firsthand, recognize its importance and relevance, and thus become advocates. This view is consistent with what seems to happen when basic income is implemented as a policy, especially a long-term and monthly one, instead of the possibly more fragile dividend and

annual policies. Maricá's ***Renda Básica de Cidadania***, after being implemented, has become so popular that it now enjoys widespread social and political support, which is highly unusual in Brazil's turbulent political context, especially considering it has been implemented by the main party[1] opposing the current party in power in the central government. It enjoys this widespread popularity, despite targeting a particular segment of the population, which might lead those not targeted to feel indifferent or even antagonistic toward it. Nonetheless, if such a perspective is right, the main role of basic income experiments is their potential to raise awareness by turning recipients into advocates. This might also be related with another important impact of basic income policies, which is their potential lock-in effect: once implemented, dismantling a basic income policy might be political suicide, partly because people are more aware of its positive impacts, particularly at the individual level. This effect will likely be more significant in policies, rather than experiments or pilots, otherwise we might have already seen a basic income implemented in places such as India or Namibia. However, and despite already counting on all of this empirical evidence, the debate is mostly moved by normative considerations, for which more additional evidence might be useless.

3. The third and final perspective mentioned is how basic income experiments are perhaps detrimental to implementation efforts. Some of our interviewees, namely the Jamie Cooke, one of the main advocates from Scotland felt that choosing to support or conduct a basic income experiment or pilot might be more of a stalling strategy than a concern for the need of evidence to move toward implementation. One might wonder if this is not the case, considering the number of experiments conducted without leading to policy implementation. In fact, when an unconditional cash transfer resembling a basic income is implemented as policy, like in Maricá, Macau, the Eastern Band of Cherokee Indians' Dividend, or even the Iranian scheme, it seems that the decision was not necessarily connected to a previous experiment. This seems to imply that no piece of

[1] The policy was implemented by a former mayor from PT—*Partido dos Trabalhadores* and has been continued with the current mayor from the same party. PT is also the party of former President Lula da Silva, the strongest political opponent to Brazil's current president, Jair Bolsonaro.

> positive evidence on basic income was the prime motivation for moving toward a dividend, policy, or unconditional cash transfer. On this account, the leading advocate from Scotland that we interviewed highlighted the need to take this option seriously: if there is political commitment, and social support for basic income, advocates and politicians should drop claims for experimentation, and argue in favor of rolling out a basic income either in each community or nation-wide. Not doing so might compromise the "political window" for basic income and squander the opportunity for implementation, which should be the end goal of basic income advocates, rather than conducting another experiment.

These are not determining views, nor our own take on the question, but rather the results of some of the discussions we had in our interviews. In the final part of the book, we will come back to this discussion and hopefully provide an answer to the question of what the purpose of implementing basic income experiments can be. Before tackling this issue in part three of the book, we will now turn to the new questions and insights we gathered from our interviews in part two.

References

BICN. Basic Income Canada Network. *Signposts to Success: Report of a BICN Survey of Ontario Basic Income Recipients*. Ontario: Basic Income Canada Network, 2019.

Birnbaum, Simon, and Jurgen De Wispelaere. "Basic Income in the Capitalist Economy: The Mirage of 'Exit' from Employment." *Basic Income Studies* 11, no. 1 (2016): 61–74.

Costello, E. Jane, William Copeland, and Adrian Angold. "The Great Smoky Mountains Study: Developmental Epidemiology in the Southeastern United States." *Soc Psychiatry Psychiatr Epidemiol*, 2016: 639–646.

Davala, Sarath, Renana Jhabvala, Guy Standing, and Soumya Kapoor Mehta. *Basic Income: A Transformative Policy for India*. London/New York: Bloomsbury, 2015.

Forget, Evelyn. "The Town with No Poverty: The Health Effects of a Canadian Guaranteed Annual Income Field Experiment." *Canadian Public Policy* 37, no. 3 (2011): 283–305.

Graeber, David. *Bullshit Jobs: A Theory*. New York: Simon and Schuster, 2018.

Haarmann, Claudia, BIG Coalition (Namibia), Evangelical Lutheran Church in the Republic of Namibia, Desk for Social Development, Labour Resource and

Research Institute (Namibia) and Namibia Non-Governmental Organisation Forum. *Making the Difference: The Big in Namibia: Basic Income Grant Pilot Project Assessment Report*. Namibia: Basic Income Grand Coalition, 2009.

Haushofer, Johannes, and Jeremy Shapiro. "The Short-Term Impact of Unconditional Cash Transfer to the Poor: Experimental Evidence from Kenya." *The Quarterly Journal of Economics* 131, no. 4 (2016): 1973–2042.

Laín, Bru. "Basic Income Experiments: Limits, Constraints and Opportunities." *Ethical Perspectives* 28, no. 1 (2021): 89–101.

Merrill, Roberto, and Catarina Neves. "Introduction: The Challenges of Basic Income Experiments." *Ethical Perspectives* (2021a): 1–5.

Merrill, Roberto, and Catarina Neves. "Editor's Introduction." *Basic Income Studies* 16, no. 1 (2021b): 1–10.

Minsky, Hyman. "Ending Poverty: Jobs Not Welfare." *Levy Economic Institute*, 2013.

Osterkamp, Rigmar. "The Basic Income Grant Pilot Project in Namibia: A Critical Assessment." *Basic Income Studies* 8, no. 1 (2013): 71–91.

Salehi-Isfahani, Djavad, and Mohammad H. Mostafavi-Dehzooei. "Cash Transfers and Labor Supply: Evidence from a Large-Scale Program in Iran." *Journal of Development Economics* 135 (2018): 349–367.

Tena Camporesi, Alberto. "La Renta Básica Universal basada en la evidencia." *Política y Sociedad* 55, no. 3 (2018): 851–871.

Thomas, Alan. "Full Employment, Unconditional Basic and the Keynesian Critique of Rentier Capitalism." *Basic Income Studies*, 2020: 1–38.

Van Parijs, Philippe, and Yannick Vanderborght. *Basic Income: A Radical Proposal for a Free and a Sane Economy*. Cambridge, MA: Harvard university press, 2017.

Verlaat, Timo, Marcel de Kruijk, Stephanie Rosenkranz, Loek Groot, and Mark Sanders. S. *Study What Works. Summary of the Final Report*. Utrecht: Utrecht University, 2020.

White, Stuart. "Should a Minimum Income Be Unconditional?" In *Social Rights in Europe in an Age of Austerity*, Stafano Civitarese and Simon Halliday (eds.), 16. London: Routledge, 2017.

Widerquist, Karl. *A Critical Analysis of Basic Income Experiments for Researchers, Policymakers and Citizens*. Cham, Switzerland: Palgrave Macmillan, 2018.

World Bank Group. *Exploring Universal Basic Income. A Guide to Navigating Concepts, Evidence and Practices*. Washington: International Bank for Reconstruction and Development/The World Bank, 2020.

PART II

New Questions the Interviews Have Raised

This second part of the book develops and critically discusses the new insights introduced in the first part of the book, based on the interviews of our case studies, which can contribute in an innovative way to the ongoing discussion on UBI experiments. Its goal is to gather, based on our interviews, the many questions, data, evidence, and debates raised by existing UBI experiments and anticipate those which will likely be raised by planned ones. The methodology of this part of the book will be the same as the one used in the previous part: we will analyze and synthesize the interviews we conducted and existing data from UBI experiments, alongside with the largely theoretical scientific literature.

Policy analysis and social sciences in general usually operate using a dual approach. According to the first approach, social scientists pose questions they would like to see answered (how a country can reduce its poverty rates, to what extent social inequality reproduces itself over successive generations, etc.). The second approach might be associated with a more "bottom-up" strategy by which, having collected and observed some small pieces of empirical information and evidence already available, social scientists try to construct comprehensive causal explanations on different social phenomena (e.g., under which conditions policymakers should design cash transfer schemas, and of which amount, to reduce poverty in a particular area). Andrew Gelman (2014) holds that most of the actual social science is performed according to this second approach among which randomized control trials (RCT) appear as the "gold standard", despite the contributions of history, philosophy, and other qualitative disciplines are also essential.

In line with the growing importance of this "bottom-up" or somehow inductive approach in the social sciences and policymaking in general, Steven Levitt and John List (2007) explained in a seminal paper that publications of peer-reviewed papers using methodologies of experimental economics have expanded exponentially over the previous five decades. Experimental methods, particularly randomized techniques, have been given an unprecedented preponderance in social analysis (Leigh 2018). As they both point out, the fact that human beings are the object of study of these experiments raises fundamental ethical questions to the attention of scholars and the academic community, particularly philosophers, social theorists, and epistemologists of the social sciences. Such ethical concerns were also raised in some of our interviews, namely in the Namibia case, where we discussed whether the downfalls of having a group of the population who is not entitled to benefits but is surveyed extensively (a control group) might be outweighed by the gains we have scientifically. Or in the case of Iran, where a lot of the people who benefited from the cash grant, refused to be surveyed about it. Nonetheless, we also had discussions where RCTs were indeed seen as superior when experimenting with a basic income, as it happened in the cases of the Finnish and the B-MINCOME experiment.

To address the most relevant questions our interviews have raised, part two is organized as follows. Chapter 4 discusses different aspects related to the decision to conduct UBI experiments. We start by asking to what extent moral and instrumental arguments are used to justify implementing these kinds of experiments and basic income-related policies. Although these two arguments mostly work together when experimenting, the second section of this chapter argues that scientists and politicians in charge of rolling out these experiments or implementing these kinds of policies differ in their respective logic and procedures, and these differences inevitably affect the design, implementation, and evaluation of basic income experiments and related programs. However, the decision to implement a basic income experiment is not solely explained by these different scientific and political decisions. The third section of Chapter 4 addresses the role of the political scenario and the actual political debate in explaining when, how, and in what manner an experiment or a policy is about to be implemented, or on the contrary, why it is rejected. Moreover, the structure, logic, and functioning of the welfare regime and of existing social policies also frame the discussion around the (in)convenience of implementing a basic income experiment or rolling out a similar in-cash policy. Finally, our last section explores the hypothesis that UBI experiments' features are more due to political reasons than scientific ones.

After exploring the framing process of decision-formation of implementing UBI experiments, Chapter 5 focuses on how their results are interpreted. As these experiments and policies are quite sensitive in social, political, and economic terms, their results are easily affected by various social, political, and economic interests. Therefore, beyond statistics and objective data, the interpretation of basic income experiments usually differs depending on the observer's point of view. Hence, the first section of Chapter 5 discusses how results have been analyzed and interpreted in light of different national and regional contexts and of the various experiments and policies' objectives. The second section considers the influence of both national and international media coverage and how it has influenced the discussion on the results of these experiments and basic income-related programs. The third section discusses some impacts which our interviews revealed have largely been ignored or have received insufficient attention from the media, scientists, and commentators in general. In this section, we consider how these UBI experiments affect individual and collective identities power patterns within and among communities, the alteration of women's and gender roles, and the empowerment experienced by some groups and individuals. Finally, we also discuss a few shortcomings observed in some of our case studies that might seem to contradict or refute the pivotal features of basic income, namely, its unconditional and universal properties.

After several years of implementing UBI experiments, a growing number of analysts and commentators are exploring the possibility of how to move from experimenting to implementing basic income as a real nation-wide policy. For this reason, in the first section of Chapter 6, we explore the pros and cons of considering basic income as an object of study to be tested through different social experiments—such as randomized control trials—or of considering it a real policy option, in which case, political and scientific implications seem far more profound. In the second section of Chapter 6, we assess to what extent and in which manners these experiments, and policies can be altered by political intervention or manipulation, and then if the so-called evidence-based policies (such as the tested basic income models) will always be condemned as a utopian project rather than a serious scientific program to inform public policies empirically and honestly. Consequently, and considering the most recent concerns of the basic income community, we thirdly and lastly explore the question whether it is preferable to continue experimenting or if these efforts should be discarded in favor of direct lobbying from different social, political, and academic pulpits to definitely implement a real basic income policy.

References

Gelman, Andrew. "Experimental Reasoning in Social Science." In *Field Experiments and Their Critics: Essays on the Uses and Abuses of Experimentation in the Social Sciences*, Dawn Langan Teele (ed.), 185–195. New Haven: Yale University Press, 2014.

Leigh, Andrew. *Randomistas: How Radical Researchers Changed Our World*. New Haven: Yale University Press, 2018.

Levitt, Steven D., and John List. 2007. What Do Laboratory Experiments Measuring Social Preferences Reveal About the Real World? *Journal of Economic Perspectives* 21 (2): 153–174.

CHAPTER 4

The Decision to Implement UBI Experiments

The aim of this chapter is to contribute to the discussion about the decision of implementing a basic income experiment. Sometimes, these experiments are evaluated endogenously—and sentenced as a success or a failure—basically in accordance with their immediate results. Nevertheless, other influential, exogenous factors are also necessary to properly understand them. We are referring to questions such as who decided to implement such an experiment and under which scientific criteria and with which political aims, when it was decided, or in which circumstances or context the decisions were made.

To deal with the above questions, this chapter's first section explores what the main formal arguments supporting the decision of testing a basic income or a similar scheme. Since poverty is morally condemnable, are UBI experiments mainly implemented to fulfill a "moral" claim, such as reducing unjust economic inequalities or putting an end to poverty? Is basic income effective in coping with these moral ends? Or should it be implemented because it might be instrumentally adequate to foster, for example, youth employability? The second section of this chapter recalls that although social scientists and politicians usually work together when designing or implementing a basic income experiment, they notably differ in their respective logic and procedures; differences which inevitably affect

R. Merrill et al., *Basic Income Experiments*, Exploring the Basic Income Guarantee,
https://doi.org/10.1007/978-3-030-89120-6_4

the design, implementation and particularly the evaluation of these experiments. However, the decision to implement a UBI experiment is not only explained by the relationship between scientists and politicians. The third section of this chapter explores how a particular political scenario and the background of the political debate also play a central role in setting up the conditions of the decision to implement an experiment or a policy or, on the contrary, of rejecting its implementation. Likewise, this section also explores the role of the welfare state model and its functioning, and the constellation of social policies it offers, in framing the discussion on rolling out a basic income experiment. As we will argue, a particular welfare regime might likely facilitate the decision, whereas a different one might restrict the range of plausible political decisions—including the one of testing a basic income scheme. We conclude, in our last section with the possibility that UBI experiments' features are more due to political reasons than scientific ones.

4.1 Moral and Instrumental Arguments to Implement UBI Experiments

When announcing or presenting an experiment with basic income or a similar schema, the policymakers and politicians responsible for the program, and sometimes the social scientists behind it as well, are asked to frame their proposal's aim. Of course, social experiments are primarily designed to "instrumentally" tackle some specific, practical issue which are assumed to require some adjustments or political intervention. For example, reducing primary school drop-out rates, increasing labor participation among a specific social group, reinforcing the welfare model's economic efficiency, increasing developmental dynamics in poor countries, or meliorating labor markets all might be targets of study. However, some experiments seem to be driven by more general moral principles which are usually put forward by their promotors to defend the program, such as reinforcing redistribution to "compensate" the worst-off, to promote social justice or personal freedom, or to reinforce social rights or gender equality, among other ends (Perkiö et al. 2019, 243). This view tends to consider that all "social policies should be judged by ethical principles" (Davala et al. 2015, 11). We are not defending that basic income experiments can or must be driven by a singular purpose, either an instrumental goal or a moral principle. However, our interviews highlight that each experiment seemed to be framed by taking this dichotomy between instrumental and moral values into account, even if in some cases both approaches were acknowledged as being relevant when designing and implementing the experiment. When the stakeholders involved in an experiment or a policy defend their vision of the program, their arguments can be situated in different points within that continuum. In the cases of Finland and the Netherlands, the disclosed, explicit purpose of rolling out these experiments was associated with an instrumental value rather than a moral principle. As Minna Ylikännö from the Finnish experiment told us, the experiment was implemented primarily to assess labor activation. The explicit goal was therefore quite instrumental: to understand whether an unconditional cash transfer could be better or worse in promoting labor market activation. Hence, the considerable amount of effort put into designing a scientifically robust experiment to assess this very specific outcome. The same happened in the experiment in Utrecht. The city council as well as the research team also pursued the aim of assessing labor market activation. Hence, the experiment's objective was also quite instrumental. In the Province of Ontario, the declared aim of the experimental project was somewhat less specific since it ranged from supporting vulnerable workers, to improving health status and education for low-income people, all while ensuring that nobody was excluded from Ontario's economic growth.

The case of Barcelona was defended as a measure to improve participants' lives and increase their autonomy in the mid and long-term, while it also declared to be designed to alleviate the "historical poverty and social exclusion" faced by some of the poorest areas of the city (Laín and Torrens 2019; Riutort et al. 2021).Therefore, it was framed as a solution to an instrumental problem—solve the poverty problem in the city—but also at the same time, it was also framed as an experiment who wished to test a solution to advance the moral aims of increased autonomy for Barcelona citizens.

In the experiments in Namibia, India, Maricá, and Macau, and to some extent the experiment in Ontario too, moral arguments related to social justice seem to be even more salient than in the case of Barcelona. For example, and as we will explore in Sect. 4.3 in more detail, proponents of the experiment in Namibia and supporters of basic income in general wished to extract lessons for an eventual nation-wide policy. The aim of their pilot seemed to be more driven by the possibility of advancing a national program rather than testing or experimenting any specific tool instrumentally. Behind this aim of scaling the program, the project was supported by wider moral principles, such as fostering social cohesion, reducing poverty, and generally boosting the situation of the worst-off. As a consequence of colonization and apartheid, among other factors, Namibia being one of the most economically unequal countries in the world, the people involved in the experiment expected that it would be portrayed by media and defended by national and international politicians in light of these moral ends, and such a context (Haarmann and Haarmann 2007). In India, the experiments conducted in New Delhi and Madhya Pradesh were primarily defended to redress the existing inefficient welfare model and the food price-subsidizing policy, though the underlying motto was to guarantee the "right to food" as a moral claim forged by a long campaign and, more importantly, considered a fundamental right under the Constitution (Mehta 2019). Similarly, in Maricá, the most prominent argument when defending the experiment was to lift several thousand people out of poverty. However, our Fábio Walternberg, the lead researcher from Universidade Federal Fluminense hired to assess some of the results of the Maricá local currency basic income policy revealed that the baseline argument was also fueled by the ambition to provide families and households with a "sense of security and dignity" which was the argument participants used to defend the program. In Macau, something similar can be observed: the official message is that the program is a matter of "justice", serving as a mechanism to redistribute the profits of the casinos, making everybody a shareholder of the wealth created by this economic activity. This case is also similar to the Eastern Band of Cherokee Indians' Dividend, which was created as a mechanism to reduce Native American poverty in the shadow of generations of displacement from their traditional lands and to mitigate their situation of being disadvantaged in terms of economic and social opportunities. We can also consider the Stockton SEED case as a representative example. Ex-Mayor Tubbs' primary motivation in pushing for a basic income experiment was to alleviate poverty and exclusion while enhancing dignity in poor people's lives by eliminating the stigma they carry due to other social programs in the United States, such as the food stamps policies and similar measures. Even researchers acknowledged that such an experiment, and the push for basic income in Stockton, could not be dissociated from the impacts of the 2008 financial crisis, and the impoverishment and destitution that many communities there have been feeling with globalization and ongoing unequal economic growth in the country.

There is a third group of more heterogeneous cases. The Kenyan experiment driven by GiveDirectly seems more agnostic in terms of "social justice" values since it focuses on the "instrumental" improvement of recipients' economic and living conditions through a more "efficient" platform to perform charity and provide solidarity donations across the globe. After Alaska, the largest quasi-basic income program in the world took place in Iran (De Wispelaere 2016), where its implementation was justified as a monetary policy to offset the impact of ceasing to subsidize certain commodities, justified by the necessity of macroeconomic reforms, rather than as a basic income experiment specifically. Similarly, and although the South Korean Youth Dividend introduced in South Korea was explicitly portrayed as a program to promote the local economy and small business owners, it has also the wider aim of forging political alliances to advance a basic income on a national scale.

There would seem to be a correlation, on the one hand, between rich countries with robust welfare regimes and the instrumental justification of conducting basic income experiments and, on the other hand, between poor or developing countries and moral or philosophical justifications. Nevertheless, the three groups of countries previously analyzed reveal that the background justification of rolling out experiments always melts down into both moral and instrumental principles. Indeed, moral claims, such as condemning poverty because it degrades the human condition, are inextricable from the instrumental tools we use to tackle such claims. As Widerquist (2006) suggests, the central question with basic income experiments is whether the tested scheme is about to produce the greatest increase in welfare for poor per unit of cost. However, although "instrumentally" speaking basic income is usually perceived as an efficient mechanism to eliminate poverty, that does not divest it from its moral implication, i.e., that it contradicts the traditional reciprocity principle (White 2003; Neves 2021), for example. Undoubtedly, this inescapable combination between instrumental gains and moral principles is what makes basic income experiments so appealing (and controversial) in public opinion, a discussion we return to in part three of the book.

4.2 Social Scientists and Politicians

In some of our case studies, the research-led experiments in the global South seemed to be driven primarily by moral ends, while the ones implemented in more developed contexts with significant influence from politicians—the B-MINCOME program and the Finnish and Utrecht experiments—seem to be more instrumentally driven and significantly more concerned with scientific outputs and with the experiments' robustness. Although in some of our case studies our interviewees from the B-MINCOME, Utrecht, or Madhya Pradesh experiments frame them through instrumental or moral reasons, this distinction is sometimes difficult to disentangle. Moreover, any correlation between this dichotomy and the place where an experiment is being conducted—a western country, with a well-developed welfare state, versus a country in the global South, for example—seems to be too hasty or even misguided. Take the work from developmental agencies: in 2014, the World Bank alone was evaluating in a clear and explicit "scientific" and "instrumental" way more than 67 randomized control trials (out of 89 ongoing different program evaluations), and paradoxically they were all being conducted in Africa and regions with high levels of poverty regions (Banerjee and Duflo 2014, 79). So, is the distinction between poor and rich countries a valid division to classify and study basic income experiments and policies, or is the role played by scientists or politicians within them more informative?

First, let's not forget that UBI experiments usually involve social scientists and politicians alike and that, as Evelyn Forget and her colleagues warn us, "science and politics do not mix well" (Forget et al. 2016, 7). On the one hand, scientists are expected to perform their work in a disinterested manner, regardless of whether they prefer a bottom-up, inductive technique or a deductive, top-down approach. Therefore, they should research mostly in accordance with their own inquiries and the hypothesis they establish, which must then be checked in light of observed causal relations or correlation dynamics among variables. On the other hand, politicians do not necessarily follow this logic, and indeed they do not in most cases. Sometimes, a politician involved in a UBI experiment might be smeared as "vile" when trying to accommodate science to their non-scientific interest.[1] Although the evidence-based policy narrative has been established as a paradigm of efficient policymaking procedure, politicians also operate according to other factors. For example, they ultimately rely

[1] "When a man seeks to ***accommodate*** science to a viewpoint which is derived not from science itself (however erroneous it may be) but from ***outside***, ***from alien***, ***external interests***, then I call him 'base'" [vile]. (Marx, *Capital*, Vol. 4. Chap. 9. §4, §2. emphasis original, quoted by Raventós 2007, 203).

on their electorate and operate within a particular ideological framework which altogether determines the range of available moral ends they might pursue as well as the instrumental tools to do so. Moreover, a particular institutional, legal and budgetary framework generally restricts the possibilities of policymaking. Finally, in democratic-representative regimes, politicians' options are usually restricted by parties' competition and power-equilibriums which are always present both within their own party and among the whole political spectrum. Thus, due to these and other factors they must deal with, politicians are not scientists and vice versa, an issue which more or less explicitly emerges when deciding to implement—and of course when designing and evaluating—an experiment.

The Finnish experiment was perceived to be "scientific", though this did not stop the government from altering the experiment as it was being designed, and to introduce an "activation model" once the experiment had already started, which altogether reveals the "political" nature of the experiment itself (Halmetoja et al. 2018). For its part, the newly elected conservative government in Ontario abruptly canceled the experiment just twelve months after it started. In this case, neither scientific rigor, nor moral concerns about those participating were taken into consideration. In Utrecht, as in other cities in the Netherlands, the decision to test a basic income was advanced by various NGOs, grassroots organizations and particularly by municipal politicians and policymakers, who to a certain extent defied the central government. However, once the *participatiewet* law was passed early in 2015, which authorized municipalities to experiment with their social assistance policy portfolio, the national government also tried to alter some local pilot projects by toughening some experimental conditions and participants' requirements (Groot et al. 2018) or by even conducting their own analysis mainly focusing on labor activation.

The B-MINCOME experiment resulted from an explicit political decision of the city council (Laín 2019). Although it was designed, assessed, and evaluated by researchers, the decision to test innovative cash transfer policies was mostly a political goal rather than a purely scientific one. Similarly, the decision of rolling out a basic income pilot in Namibia was highly politicized. It was the Namibian Tax Commission (created by the government in 2001) that recommended the adoption of a universal monthly income grant to all adults in the country (Haarmann et al. 2019). Just a few years after, in 2005, the BIG Coalition was created as a large conglomerate of the Council of Churches led by the

Evangelical Lutheran church, the National Union of Namibian Workers, different NGOs and AIDS organizations, and the Labour Resource and Research Institute, among other organizations, which took the political lead fueling the debate on basic income and the necessity of implementing it nationally. Although the experiment was not directly driven by the government, political agreement was necessary to implement it. However, political and economic pressure from both inside and outside the government prevented the experiment from extending beyond its end and using the results as encouragement for a nation-wide policy. In Madhya Pradesh, SEWA was pushing the government to implement an unconditional cash transfer program as a test for a viable alternative to existent malfunctioning welfare programs and benefits. The program was entirely funded by UNICEF India, was innovative in its design, and fully in accordance with the developmental strategy recommendations of the international community. Although there was a continuous dialogue from the beginning, between public and private institutions and the different levels of government—both the states' and the central one—the Indian experiments might be considered "less politicized", particularly when considering the discussion of its implementation and of its methodological design. Along with this case, the ongoing experiment in Kenya is also an example of a pilot with minor political "interference", considering its implementation was decided by the NGO GiveDirectly.

The Iranian and the South Korean cases, although very different in their political contexts, represent two examples of a clear political decision. The former is a program implemented nation-wide (with notable internal opposition both from the right and from the left political forces) by former president Ahmadinejad's decision and supported by the International Monetary Fund and World Bank. The latter case is a product of Governor Lee Jae-Myung in his effort to advance the idea of basic income nation-wide. It is important to highlight that while the unconditional cash grant in Iran stemmed from a political decision, it was not based on the idea to implement an explicit, universal basic income sort-of scheme (Tabatabai 2011, 2012; Salehi-Isfahani and Mostafavi-Dehzooei 2018). It was the result of the perceived need to compensate for the subsidies that were being withdrawn. The Stockton experience might be also placed alongside these two cases. The decision to test an unconditional cash transfer was fueled by the Economic Security Project, the Reinvent Stockton Foundation, several grassroots organizations, and citizens of the city. However, as our interviewees Stacia West and Amy Castro told us, it was then-Mayor Tubbs leading the proposal under the auspices of the campaign "Mayors for a Guaranteed Income" (MGI)[2] which joins municipal initiatives together with a similar political-discourse framework supporting the necessity of testing basic income at the local level. Similarly, the policies implemented in Macau, Maricá, the Eastern Band of Cherokee Indians' Dividend, and also the UBI experiment under development in Scotland should all be understood as programs mostly or entirely decided and promoted by regional governments or other political institutions.

Even though some of our interviewees framed a given experiment as a scientific endeavor as Minna Ylikännö from the Finnish experiment, or Lluís Torrens from the B-MINCOME experiment, our case studies are all in some way or another judged mostly politically, rather than scientifically. Of course, the academic community would be eager to assess any new program or social policy precisely because they have the tools to properly evaluate its design, effectiveness, and adequacy as a pure scientific endeavor. However, they represent only a fraction of a population, and they are not those deciding the next election. Moreover, an explicit political decision is in some way or another present in most of the experiments. It cannot be forgotten that, despite its history and the rich public debate, basic income is still relatively unfamiliar for most people, including most politicians. It is a rather disruptive policy for countries with highly developed welfare states and entrenched norms of contribution and work-ethics, but also for countries in the global South, where international institutions, such as the International Monetary Fund or the World Bank have been endorsing strong conditional policies for decades, and charity-based and means-tested frameworks are still the norm (Lo Vuolo 2015). Therefore, all these national contexts and particularities undoubtedly affect the experimental design of basic income pilots and the features or basic income-related policies, as well as the mere possibility of conducting them.

[2] The webpage of the campaign might be accessed at: https://www.mayorsforagi.org/

4.3 How the Debate, Political Scenario, and the Welfare Model Frame the Decision to Implement UBI Experiments

The basic income movement has experienced three historical waves. The first ranged from 1910 until 1940. The second spanned the 1960s and 1970s coinciding with a period of frustration with the conditional cash transfer programs in the USA and Canada, though it vanished from public debate because it did not gain enough political and popular support. The difference with the third wave, which began around 2010, is that the "grassroots support and international media attention are more extensive than ever, and the third wave represents the first truly global Basic Income movement" (Widerquist 2019, 40). There are various reasons explaining this new popularity, particularly in western countries, and two are especially relevant. First, the growing popular perception of the failure of the actual welfare model to respond to new phenomena such as the working poor, the threat of robotization, the long-term unemployment, and the insecure labor markets for youth, migrants, single mothers, and the "precarious class" (Standing 2011). The second reason is the increasing popular disagreement with actual social policies, conditional welfare programs, and the general intensification of the workfare and activation features of social assistance.

Guy Standing (2017, 57) warns that any new social policy is usually attacked as being futile, perverse by triggering negative consequences, and of endangering other political and social goals. This third wave challenges these critics by placing basic income experiments in the center of the debate precisely because they empirically and normatively face these very same issues. Of course, these experiments do so differently according to each national context since, as we already pointed out, experiments do not occur in vacuum. Thus, arguments justifying rolling out an experiment must also differ as an idiosyncratic framing process. Beyond what we did in Chapter 2, where we analyzed the context of the experiments more broadly, this framing must also be understood as a process in policy change, attitude formation, and popular persuasion which are necessary to properly understand the political economy of basic income experiments and related policies (Perkiö et al. 2019). This process is in turn influenced by two major factors: the political debate and scenario on the one hand, and the structure and functioning of the welfare model on the other. We are hence talking about a full policy option. Therefore, when framing an experiment within a particular policy paradigm, we are defining problems within a certain political scope, whose causes we diagnose from a specific perspective and upon which we formulate moral judgements. Our interviews reveal how this process was undertaken in each case.

This framing process was central in Finland hence the reason why the experiment attracted so much attention worldwide. Finland's welfare model is historically grounded on a strong universalistic principle and features extensive social policies, though its social protection system reflects an individualistic logic rather than a household based one. By the end of the past century, some political parties brought the idea of UBI into the political discussion. However, the recession of the early 1990s turned the Finnish welfare model toward the new "activation paradigm" and the debate on basic income partially vanished from the political debate and policy agenda. However, it never disappeared completely, and the Finnish experiment was built on a large period of public and policy discussions on basic income and related policies. From the Nordic model to the activation logic, the way basic income is now framed reflects a historical debate preceding the decision of launching a basic income experiment. Therefore, it is not surprising that the new scenario of growing precariousness and the reinforcing of the workfare paradigm of the early 2000s again brought about the debate, culminating in the experiment being implemented. As Minna Ylikännö explained in our interview, such a framing meant that the government was willing to test out what is perceived as a radical or quite transformational policy such as basic income by framing it as a mechanism that can help promote the activation logic of the remaining social assistance mechanisms in the country.

In Utrecht, the already-mentioned activation paradigm of the late 1990s also altered the former universal character of the Dutch welfare model, which stirred up both popular and political discontent. In the early 2000s, the existing minimum income guarantee was toughened by limiting its duration and imposing stricter conditions and sanctions. The process of framing the debate on testing a basic income was also influenced by the decentralization of the Dutch social protection system. Since 2001 and funded by a national allowance resulting from a specific calculus (according to the number of inhabitants, the labor market trends, etc.), municipalities are responsible for providing social assistance by themselves and, precisely because of that, they have strong incentives of rationalizing social expenditure in terms of overall cost and number of beneficiaries. The new law (*participatiewet*) passed in 2015 imposed severe new sanctions, controls and conditions to the existing minimum income guarantee and then threatened municipalities with additional administrative and bureaucratic burdens which in turn boosted their disaffection (Groot et al. 2018; Muffels and Gielens 2019). Nevertheless, the law also allowed experimenting with the minimum income schema. Our interviewees, particularly Roger van Loon from the Utrecht Municipality pointed out that only this legal change allowed the testing of basic income within the municipality, but also in other cities in The Netherlands. So, although the experiment was in fact never identified nor considered a basic income, the changes of the legal framework, the transformative logic of the welfare model, and the decentralized governance system, have favored the conditions to experiment with forms of unconditional cash transfers.

Similarly, both the Spanish multi-layer governance and the particularities of its legal framework were also fundamental in the decision to test an innovative cash transfer experiment in Barcelona. The framing process was shaped by a complex and highly fragmented social protection system where municipalities became the last resort of the welfare protection system. Until May 2020, there was no national comprehensive minimum income schema in Spain, while the Catalan *renda garantida de ciutadania* was insufficient to meet people's basic needs. To fill that gap, the city of Barcelona decided to launch the B-MINCOME project to test an innovative cash transfer schema. The legal Spanish framework also restricted the range of policy options which in turn affected the possibilities of implementing such an experiment. Spanish law does not permit municipalities to offer minimum income benefits. This might have obstructed the possibility of testing a "true" basic income model, but paradoxically it permitted the justification of the pilot on strictly experimental grounds. Such framing—"experimental" rather than "policy-oriented"—was crucial to attract the necessary support of all political parties in the city council. Hence, the Spanish multi-layer governance, along with its complex legal framework, did not facilitate the decision of implementing the experiment as was the case in Utrecht, but rather forced Barcelona to test its own pilot. Though the destination was the same in both cases, different roads were taken to arrive to a similar situation.

Despite being a municipal initiative, the framing process in Stockton was quite different. In the USA, the idea of basic income dates back to Thomas Paine's *Agrarian Justice*. In the 1970's, different models of negative income tax were tested, and a few bills were passed though they were finally abandoned because of a lack of political support. Since then, the basic income idea has been collecting heterogeneous support from academics, politicians, and activists. For its part, the plan to launch the SEED was initiated in 2017 when then-Mayor Tubbs decided to address the city's poverty rates, which were especially high among African Americans. He partnered with the Economic Security Project—a basic income advocacy group created by Facebook co-founder Chris Hughes—which was seeking a city to test a cash transfer pilot. The framing process in this case was fueled by three major factors. First, a historical tradition in the USA of experimenting with similar basic income schemas, followed by a debate that inspired positive momentum and led to experimenting. Second, an enthusiastic mayor and municipal team exploring solutions to complicated, chronic challenges. Third, an external group funding the experiment which diminished risk for the municipality since they did not have to take on most of the financial burden of what could still be perceived as a bold idea.

Canada was one of the first countries to test a negative income tax, a relative of basic income, as we saw in our introduction to the book, through its MINCOME experiments between 1974 and 1978 (Forget 2011). However, like the European experience, during the 1980s and 1990s, the social security model, particularly social security programs, experienced a retrenchment across all the country. During the 1980s, the Economic Union and Development Prospects for Canada recommended rolling out a basic income for the whole country, but most part of the labor movement and progressive organizations forcefully opposed the proposal. During the more pronounced neoliberal period, the basic income proposal faded away, until recently when the Liberal party officially adopted several resolutions supporting a nation-wide basic income policy. In 2016, the formerly opposed (or at least highly skeptical) Canada's New Democratic Party adopted a new resolution in favor of the policy. This also paved the way for multiple progressive, non-governmental and grassroots organizations to endorse the proposal. Finally, in April 2017, the leader of Liberal Party and Premier of Ontario, Kathleen Wynne, announced a basic income experiment in Ontario, which illustrated a definitive shift in how public and political debate of testing this proposal is politically framed (Hamilton and Mulvale 2019).

The decision in Namibia was also a result of the malfunctioning of the welfare model, its mismatch with the labor market and how the political debate shifted in recent years. Though the government subsidizes the labor market, public and private wages are still extremely low. Different job-creating programs have been rolled out, but the government's capacity to create new jobs has never substantially reduced unemployment. As a result, self-employment and deregulated work appear as the only alternative for most workers in Namibia (Haarmann and Haarmann 2007). This situation creates two problems. First, fiscal policies are incapable of redistributing wealth and hence have difficulty breaking down the cycle of poverty. Second, the lack of money-in-cash in local economies prevents investment and hampers economic growth, particularly in rural areas where loan sharks have multiplied. Thus, the basic income debate is framed mostly by the desire to boost labor markets, and by the need of securing a minimum level of economic activity, especially for those in rural areas where subsistence farming is at times the only way to survive. Beyond these factors, the political and social debate framing the discussion expanded during the 2000s. Widespread poverty, rising inequalities, and high unemployment rates, combined with optimistic macroeconomic prospects, made Namibia an ideal place to test a cash transfer scheme. Though conditional cash policies were recommended by the IMF and other international institutions in places like Namibia in the early 2000s, the BIG Coalition pushed for an unconditional model, thus becoming a focus of international attention. It is also important to note that such a debate was also fueled by the work of BIEN, which organized a conference on basic income in South Africa at the time. In our interview, Dirk Haarmann pointed out how BIEN International congress taking place in Africa, and its international audience, had a profound impact in boosting the BIG Coalition in Namibia.

The case of Kenya was quite different from Namibia. There was no pre-existing debate on basic income there, nor a grassroots movement endorsing the idea of a policy or experiment. So, it seems no framing process developed in the country, hence endogenous factors seemed to have played no role, or minor roles in inspiring the experiment. Nevertheless, as Louise Haagh (2019, 266) sustains, it cannot be a "surprise that unconditional cash grant experiments in Sub-Saharan African countries, with lower levels of public finance, such as Kenya, are dominated by an aid logic". Aid and development agencies have long been working in these countries, and the lack of government money to undertake such policy experiments would likely pave the way for international NGOs to become the main actors in such contexts. Moreover, many of these NGOs are operating in countries where the debate on basic income has increased (as in the USA).

Despite also being externally funded, the Indian case differs from Kenya since an internal framing process was behind the decision of implementing the two Indian experiments. One of the most influential factors was the malfunctioning of the existing welfare model. Despite persistent economic growth, India has been criticized because of the state's asymmetric distribution of resources (Davala et al. 2015; Mehta 2019). The poorest captured fewer public resources and social benefits than the richest, an imbalance which fuels social tensions. Thus, the Indian welfare model failed to properly and symmetrically allocate and apply most social benefits and policies, such as schooling grants or providing grain, energy, and fertilizer at subsidized rates. These factors contributed to the debate on basic income, framing it as a policy that could help secure fair and equal development across the country, especially through its potential to solve the challenge of extremely high rates of poverty (Haagh 2019, 281). Hence, the debate on basic income started in the early 2000s and intensified in 2008 when many of the existing social protection schemes were reformed. The discussion moved from the idea of subsidizing prices and social services, as had been the norm, to implementing cash grant benefits with no strings attached. In 2008, the government introduced a system of "direct cash transfer" benefits, directly granting cash so people could buy gas and other basic commodities. While the debate on this new cash transfer model was heating up, a trade union (SEWA) managed to launch the experiments in New Delhi with the funding support of the United Nations Development Program (UNDP) and then the experiment in rural Madhya Pradesh with the funding support of United Nations Children's Fund (UNICEF).

Maricá's experience is similar, as there were also strong factors framing the debate, regarding both welfare models and the political and social situation in the country. During the 1990s, the welfare model in Brazil was running between a contributory and non-contributory rationale. It was not until 2003, after unifying four existing federal social assistance programs that *Bolsa Família* was created to complement private income. It now reaches 5,570 municipalities and has become one of the most fundamental pillars of the country's social protection system. Driven by IMF and World Bank directives, almost all cash transfer programs for poor people in Brazil require households to meet some conditions, such as attending hospital and medical appointments and assuring school attendance. Thus, it is usually seen somehow as a "natural" precursor of a full basic income designed for developing countries. However, the structural shortcomings of *Bolsa Família* are consistent with other neoliberal dynamics such as deconstructing much of the welfare system, deactivation of social programs, and the reduction of such programs' funding (da Silva et al. 2019). These factors framed the debate on basic income until 2004 when former president Lula passed a law implementing the so-called Citizenship Basic Income. However, this law was never enforced because of budgetary restrictions and strong political opposition in the country.

The welfare model and political scenario also inspired and framed the cash transfer policy in Iran. In this case, basic commodities, utilities such as gas, water, electricity, and bread were subsidized by oil revenues. "The result was overconsumption, inefficient production, waste, pollution, smuggling to neighboring countries, and [...] a lopsided distribution of benefits, as the bulk of subsidies went to the better-off sections of the population who consumed more" (Karshenas and Tabatabai 2019, 340). The annual cost of this system was around 100–120 billion US dollars, of which 70% was captured by one third of the population, living mostly in urban areas (Tabatabai 2012). This maintained the discussion until 2008, when President Ahmadinejad proposed replacing it with 45 US dollars monthly, direct, unconditional, individual grant to Iranian citizens. This triggered intense disagreements, though almost everybody was concerned about the inefficiency of the existing system of subsidies. The debate on the new reform was then framed by the assumed necessity of compensating lower income households. The reform took about seven months to be presented by the government, thus paving the way for furthering the discussion, which focused first on targeting only the poorest, and secondly on whether it might not be better to prioritize investing in public infrastructure. The policy discussion and social unrest grew rapidly, and the government was forced to declare all household heads eligible for the new cash grant. Although the government did not renounce targeting, protests and social upheaval, along with bureaucratic and administrative difficulties in managing the new scheme, allowed "the resulting universal coverage by default heralded the uniformity of the transfer amount for all" (Karshenas and Tabatabai 2019, 341). Hence, in this case, the political framing was key in moving for an unconditional cash grant, although such a debate had very little to do with basic income as a policy goal.

In Germany, the debate has been well-established for a long time. In 2003, however, the Hartz IV reforms revived the idea of basic income due to the strengthening of the conditionality and sanctioning logic of most social assistance programs, unemployment benefits, and the entire welfare model generally. Moreover, from 2005 onwards, people receiving unemployment benefits were obligated to seek a job. This "incentivized" unemployed people and then reduced unemployment rates by creating a large class of "working poor" in the process, thus revealing that even having a full-time job could no longer protect people from poverty (Perkiö 2013). The German welfare model, though historically quite universally oriented, has shifted toward the activation model in accordance with the developments in other European and OECD countries. In particular, the beginning of the debate around the basic income proposal might be situated in the mid-1970s, but rapidly disappeared from public and policy debate after German reunification (Van Parijs and Vanderborght 2017, 207). However, the aforementioned Hartz IV reforms triggered the "Freedom, not full employment" campaign and consequently boosted the popularity of the proposal. Therefore, and despite the deeply established "workfarist" character of the German welfare model, the idea of basic income is present in everyday politics, policy debates, in the press and social media platforms, and in the work of different NGOs, such as the *Mein Grundeinkommen*.[3]

The same occurred in Scotland, where the idea attracted much attention from political parties and also from civil society, especially around the independence referendum in 2014, where the redesigning of Scottish welfare model and its social policies was at stake. Nevertheless, the Scottish debate on basic income seems to be mostly framed in political-institutional terms. The underlying concern is how to reform the existing social security model and so, in 2015, a cross-party group in the Scottish Parliament was established to examine the basic income proposal. This group integrated members from the Scottish National Party, the Scottish Labour Party, and the Scottish Greens. Soon after, the government agreed to explore testing a basic income at the municipal level. In order to be feasible in political, legal, and budgetary terms, however, the

[3] The NGO *Mein Grundeinkommen* has developed several crowdfunding campaigns that were used to raffle off basic income for one year for several German citizens, and it can be accessed at: https://www.mein-grundeinkommen.de/.

proposal was required to be in accordance with the institutional framework set by the UK Government and British political institutions (William Danson 2019, 96). Regarding the experiment, the Scottish Social Security Committee debated the idea from mid-2016 until 2017, when the Glasgow City Council and the Royal Society for Arts Scotland launched a study on the viability of implementing its own experiment. The initiative was quite well-received by the North Ayrshire and the Edinburgh Councils, who expressed their aim to conduct their own experiments as well. In this way, the Scottish case clearly illustrates how popular political discussion, political parties' relationships and multilateralism, and the institutional framework all contribute to establishing the manner in which basic income is discussed.

The South Korean Youth Dividend also reveals how a particular political scenario frames the discussion, which was in turn conditioned by the weakness of the welfare model. Basic income has been discussed for years because of rising inequalities and unemployment. While there seems to be a widespread consensus that a new system of income support is required, there is a clear debate between those advocating for a traditional employment insurance system, and those associations and minority parties supporting a basic income. Within this debate in 2016, the then-mayor Lee Jae-Myung introduced a youth dividend reaching 3,500 youth inhabitants in Seongnam. After becoming governor of the Gyeonggi Province in 2018, he extended the program granting 175,000 youth aged 24 across the entire Province with about 727 euros in local currency per year to use in local businesses. During the 2017 presidential election, the term "basic income" came to the forefront of the debate, though it was confused by most of the parties with traditional subsidies, probably because the national government was then embarked on an income-led growth strategy and the name was strategically used to support the new governmental policy. However, the COVID-19 pandemic invigorated and clarified the debate and forced the Democratic Party in the government to propose a Universal Disaster Relief grant to the entire population. On March 30, 2020, the National Assembly agreed to fund an Emergency Relief Payment of 9.1 trillion won (almost 8 billion US dollars) to support 70% of all South Korean households. Just one month after that, on April 30, the Assembly passed a second emergency relief program of 12.2 trillion won (almost 11 billion US dollars) to grant each household 1 million won ($US 876) paid to the household of four or more family members. In households of one people, it pays 400,000 won, households of two people are paid 600,000, and households of three people are given 800,000 in the form of local currency to encourage consumption. These direct relief packages contributed to building widespread popularity for basic income. In this line, a survey published in December 2020 reported that 48.6% of the population supported a "universal basic income at a minimal level of livelihood" (Gyeonggi Research Institute 2020; Young Seong et al. 2019). At the institutional level, however, the proposal lacks this large support since it is only endorsed by a small party in the National Assembly—the Basic Income Party under the alliance of the Democratic Party, the South Korea Basic Income Network, some small trade unions, and several social movements and grassroots platforms.

4.4 Experiments' Features Are More Due to Political Reasons Than Scientific Ones

As we have seen, we do not need to have an extremist view, namely the one that contends that there is no border separating a laboratory from the external real-world (Latour 1983). Rather, we argue that scientific knowledge is always an output or a mix of both internal scientific and external non-scientific factors. Basic income experiments are a clear example. In other words, and as we discussed in Chapter 2, scientific research does not occur in vacuum and a particular societal context will affect, alter, or simply facilitate all scientific endeavors or production in a specific way. In this case, and to understand how basic income experiments have come to be decided upon and implemented it is important to both understand whose actors are behind the decision to roll-out the UBI experiment, but also the motivation and goals that guide such a decision, namely whether is it a way to obtain empirical evidence to further or advance an already existing social policy? Or is it rather a government aim to promote a particular political goal?

Some of our case studies do not appear to be a simple "experiment" to obtain evidence to be used scientifically in order to inform further policies, but more properly, a policy or public program which is being tested for a particular policy or political purpose. As Banerjee and Duflo (2014, 85–87) point out, most pilots "are being designed and evaluated not only to show the average treatment effect for a particular policy or program", but also "to understand the way institution's function". In this line, one might say that a basic income experiment is moving away from "really being" a basic income experiment inasmuch its aims differ from evaluating, for example, the effects of the cash transfer on the autonomy of the beneficiary. Nevertheless, the aim of evaluating an experiment on its reduction of the administrative or bureaucratic burden experienced by the responsible institution does not make this experiment different nor less a basic income experiment than in the former case. In other words, a basic income experiment is not defined by the variable it attempts to evaluate—whether an impact on individual behavior or on institutional functioning, but on how it is designed, the methodology it uses and the way in which it is implemented and evaluated. This would lead us to differentiate between those considered "pure" experiments from those seen as policies, a topic we discussed at length in Chapter 2. In some cases, this differentiation influences the way the experiment is designed, others in the "political" motivation behind them.

Cases like Finland, Utrecht, India, Germany, and Kenya might be properly considered experiments rather than policies, as they are driven by and designed according to an explicit scientific motivation. In Finland, the primarily goal was to increase labor activation by eliminating conditionality, as in Utrecht replacing the traditional sanction model by incentivizing job seekers. In India, the goal was poverty reduction by reforming the weakness of the subsidies system for poor and farming families, whereas in Germany the aim was rather to test a new cash transfer mechanism reducing sanctions of assistance and unemployment programs. Finally, the pilot in Kenya is apparently a "pure experiment" following scientific and pre-established experimental parameters reducing the possibility of being politically biased.

Some of our case studies might be a bit far from this former "pure scientific" pattern and aim, as they might be seen closer to simply testing a new policy, implementing a particular social program or be instrumental of a pure political aim. Among these, one might place the Namibian experiment, which was designed with no control group and with the goal of being a precursor to a national policy to alleviate poverty and inequality in an upper-middle income country with high inequality rates. The SEED project in Stockton, although designed on quite robust scientific parameters, was likely more of a way to generate momentum for change promoting the basic income idea, as opposed to a scientific experiment driven by "disinterested inquiries". Iran is an illustrative example where the experiment was a pure policy—in this case, replacing the price-subsidizing system for political and macroeconomic purposes. The

Eastern Band of Cherokee Indians' Dividend, though a clear communitarian policy implemented for political purposes (to boost members' well-being and reduce their historically high poverty rates), was used as a natural experiment, by the Great Smoky Mountain Study of Youth (Costello et al. 1996). In this case, the non-randomized control group was made up of the children that did not benefit from the treatment (the extra income provided) due to their age, but also non-Indians who were not eligible for the dividend. In the case of South Korea, there is no control group, nor are the parameters of the policy exclusively scientifically oriented, since it is a provincial program first and foremost designed to reduce growing inequality and boost local commerce. This would be much the same as what occurred in Maricá where the program was politically established to fight poverty and not so much to gather empirical evidence scientifically.

The cases of Ontario, Barcelona, and Scotland might be more controversial. The Ontario case was clearly an experiment, designed, and implemented as such, but was interfered with politically, since the government repudiated its own electoral commitment and disregarded any scientific and ethical standard regarding the participants by abruptly canceling the experiment. In the case of Barcelona's experiment, although being designed with robust experimental design standards, the political implications of its implementation sometimes blurred its former scientific character. The Scottish case is not easy to classify since, while the designing phase is quite robust in scientific and methodological terms, its multiple political implications, and the underlying independence issue behind threats to exercise overtly political influence.

As seen across all cases, each national political scenario, as well as the welfare model, including its design and functioning, are two fundamental factors in framing how basic income experiments are seen and discussed in each setting. In some cases, the debate is more mature, in the sense that it is fueled by a historical record of public and social discussion, which is fundamental in determining how political and economic forces endorse the idea, as we discussed in our interview with Amy Castro and Stacia West from the SEED project in USA, or with Lluís Torrens from the B-MINCOME experiment in Barcelona. In contrast, namely in some of the cases where the debate is more recent, the discussion is much more framed by elites and political parties according to their interests, power-balances, and the political-institutional settings in which they operate, as Sarath Davala from the Madhya Pradesh experiments explained us in our interview. As Karl Widerquist (2018, 33) sustains, although basic income experiments are commonly seen as "pure" scientific endeavors they, as well as basic income-related policies, are simultaneously an outcome and input of the political process. Therefore, if one wants to understand them, the scenario, and the political debate, and how each particular welfare model frames the "political" decision of implementing them, all have to be carefully considered.

References

Banerjee, Abhijit V., and Esther Duflo. "The Experimental Approach to Development Economics." In *Field Experiments and Their Critics: Essays on the Uses and Abuses of Experimentation in the Social Sciences*, Dawn Langan Teele (ed.), 78–114. New Haven: Yale University Press, 2014.

Costello, E.J, et al. "The Great Smoky Mountains Study of Youth." *Goals, Design, Methods, and the Prevalence of DSM-III-R Disorders*. 1996. https://doi.org/10.1001/archpsyc.1996.01830120067012

da Silva, Ozanira, Maria Sila, and Valéria Ferreira Santos de Almada Lima. "Citizen's Basic Income in Brazil: From Bolsa Família to Pilot Experiment." In *The Palgrave International Handbook of Basic Income*, Malcom Torry (ed.), 319–338. Cham, Switzerland: Palgrave Macmillan, 2019.

Davala, Sarath, Renana Jhabvala, Guy Standing, and Soumya Kapoor Mehta. *Basic Income: A Transformative Policy for India*. London/New York: Bloomsbury, 2015.

De Wispelaere, Jurgen. "Basic Income in Our Time: Improving Political Prospects Through Policy Learning?" *Journal of Social Policy* 45, no. 4 (2016): 617–634.

Forget, Evelyn. "The Town with No Poverty: The Health Effects of a Canadian Guaranteed Annual Income Field Experiment." *Canadian Public Policy* 37, no. 3 (2011): 283–305.

Forget, Evelyn, Dylan Marando, Tonya Surman, and Michael Crawford. "Lessons Affecting a UBI Pilot. Pilot Lessons: How to Design a Basic Income Pilot for Ontario." Mowat Research n. 126, 2016.

Groot, Loek, Ruud Muffels, and Timo Verlaat. "Welfare States' Social Investment Strategies and the Emergence of Dutch Experiments on a Minimum Income Guarantee." *Social Policy and Society* 18, no. 2 (2018): 277–287.

Gyeonggi Research Institute. 2020. *Gyeonggi Youth Basic Income Program Satisfaction Survey. Q4/2019*. Available at: www.gri.kr. Accessed 5 May 2021.

Haagh, Louise. "The Philosophy and Political Economy of Basic Income Revisited." In *The Palgrave International Handbook of Basic Income*, by Malcom Torry (ed.), 253–299. Cham, Switzerland: Palgrave Macmillan, 2019.

Haarmann, Claudia, and Dirk Haarmann. "From Survival to Decent Employment: Basic Income Security in Namibia." *Basic Income Studies* 2, no. 1 (2007): 1–7.

Haarmann, Claudia, Dirk Haarmann, and Nicoli Nattras. "The Namibian Basic Income Grant Pilot." In The *Palgrave International Handbook of Basic Income*, Malcom Torry (ed.), 357–372. Cham, Switzerland: Palgrave Macmillan, 2019.

Halmetoja, Antti, Jurgen De Wispelaere, and Johanna Perkiö. "A Policy Comet in Moominland? Basic Income in the Finnish Welfare State." *Social Policy & Society* 18, no. 2 (2018): 319–330.

Hamilton, Leah, and James Mulvale. "'Human Again': The (Unrealized) Promise of Basic Income in Ontario." *Journal of Poverty* 23, no. 7 (2019): 576–599.

Karshenas, Massoud, and Hamid Tabatabai. "Basic Income by Default: Lessons from Iran's 'Cash Subsidy' Programme." In *The Palgrave International Handbook of Basic Income*, Malcom Torry (ed.), 339–356. Cham, Switzerland: Palgrave Macmillan, 2019.

Laín, Bru. "Desigualdad, redistribución y gobernanza. Las políticas redistributivas municipales en la ciudad de Barcelona." In *Politicas Publicas para la Equidad Social*, P.R. Vargas, J.M. Saavedra, R.M. Olivares, and S.B. Hijerra (eds.), 319–331. Barcelona: Universidad de Santiago de Chile and Universitat de Barcelona, 2019.

Laín, Bru, and Lluís Torrens. "The Minimum Living Wage Initiative of Barcelona." *Transfer. European Review of Labour and Research* 25, no. 3 (2019): 386–391.

Latour, Bruno. "Give Me a Laboratory and I Will Raise the World." In *Science Observed: Perspectives on the Social Study of Science*, Karin Knorr-Cetina and Michael Mulkay (eds.), 141–170. London: Sage, 1983.

Lo Vuolo, Ruben. "The Limits of Autonomy in Latin American Social Policies: Promoting Human Capital or Social Control?" *European Journal of Social Theory* 19, no. 2 (2015): 228–244.

Mehta, Vanya. *The Great Indian Basic Income Debate*. Karkhana, India: India Network for Basic Income & INBI Foundation, 2019.

Muffels, Rudd, and Erwin Gielens. "Job Search, Employment Capabilities and Well-being of People on Welfare in the Dutch 'Participation Income' Experiments." In *Empirical Research on an Unconditional Basic Income in Europe*, Lei Delsen (ed.), 109–138. Cham, Switzerland: Springer Nature, 2019.

Neves, Catarina. "Basic Income Experiments: Expanding the Debate on UBI and Reciprocity." *Basic Income Studies* 16, no. 1 (2021): 55–74.

Perkiö, Johanna. "Basic Income Proposals in Finland, Germany and Spain." Transform Discussion Paper No. 2, 2013.

Perkiö, Johanna, Leire Rincón, and Jenna van Draanen. "Framing Basic Income: Comparing Media Framing of Basic Income Canada, Finland, and Spain." In *The Palgrave International Handbook of Basic Income*, Malcom Torry (ed.), 233–251. Cham, Switzerland: Palgrave Macmillan, 2019.

Raventós, Daniel. *Basic Income. The Material Conditions of Freedom*. London: Pluto Press, 2007.

Riutort, Sebastià, Albert Julià, Bru Laín, and Lluís Torrens. *Resultados finales del proyecto piloto B-MINCOME (2017–2019). Informe ejecutivo*. Barcelona: Ajuntament de Barcelona, 2021.

Salehi-Isfahani, Djavad, and Mohammad H. Mostafavi-Dehzooei. "Cash Transfers and Labor Supply: Evidence from a Large-Scale Program in Iran." *Journal of Development Economics* (2018): 349–367.

Standing, Guy. *The Precariat: The New Dangerous Class*. New York: Bloomsbury Academic, 2011.

Standing, Guy. *Basic Income: And How We Can Make It Happen*. London: Penguin Random House, 2017.

Tabatabai, Hamid. "The Basic Income Road to Reforming Iran's Price Subsidies." *Basic Income Studies* 6, no. 4 (2011): 1–24.

Tabatabai, Hamid. "From Price Subsidies to Basic Income: The Iran Model and Its Lessons." In *Exporting the Alaska Model: Adapting the Permanent Fund Dividend for Reform Around the World*, Karl Widerquist and Michael Howard (eds.), New York: Palgrave Macmillan, 2012.

Van Parijs, Philippe, and Yannick Vanderborght. *Basic Income: A Radical Proposal for a Free and a Sane Economy*. Cambridge, MA: Harvard University Press, 2017.

White, Stuart. *The Civic Minimum: On the Rights and Obligations of Economic Citizenship*. Oxford: Oxford University Press, 2003.

Widerquist, Karl. "The Bottom Line in a Basic Income Experiment." *Basic Income Studies* 2 (2006): 1–5.

Widerquist, Karl. *A Critical Analysis of Basic Income Experiments for Researchers, Policymakers and Citizens*. Cham, Switzerland: Palgrave Macmillan, 2018.

Widerquist, Karl. "Three Waves of Basic Income Support." In *The Palgrave International Handbook of Basic Income*, Malcom Torry (ed.), 31–46. Cham, Switzerland: Palgrave Macmillan, 2019.

William Danson, Michael. "Exploring Benefits and Costs: Challenges of Implementing Citizen's Basic Income in Scotland." In *Empirical Research on an Unconditional Basic Income in Europe*, Lei Delsen (ed.), 81–108. Cham, Switzerland: Springer Nature, 2019.

Young Seong, Yoo, et al. "Analysis of the Effects of the Youth Basic Income Policy in Gyeonggi Province: Comparison of the Ex-Ante and Ex-Post Survey." *Gyeonggi Research Institute Policy Study*. 2019. Available at: https://www.google.com/url?sa=t&rct=j&q=&esrc=s&source=web&cd=&ved=2ahUKEwjC7qXhz_zzAhXoyYUKHcb8BNsQFnoECAMQAQ&url=https%3A%2F%2Fbasicincomefair.gg.go.kr%2Fdownload.php%3Fdownloadfilename%3D605daEaABiERofWUzd5Ho

CHAPTER 5

How Results Are Interpreted

After exploring the decision of rolling out experiments and basic income-related policies, the debate and political process behind them, and the influence of the welfare model in each case, this chapter builds on the discussion from Chapter 3 and looks at the impacts or effects of basic income experiments and similar policies. Particularly, it discusses how these impacts have been analyzed, and how some outcomes have received much less attention, partly because of how UBI experiments' results have been interpreted and discussed. Basic income experiments are highly sensitive in social, political, and economic terms, and so the interpretation of their results is likely to be affected by multiple social, political, and economic interests and, of course, by press and social media coverage. In a nutshell: although data and statistics remain unaltered, the interpretation of an experiment's results might (and usually does) differ depending on the way in which a given observer sees and communicates them. Therefore, beyond the "objective" experimental results, the first section of this chapter discusses how results have been analyzed and interpreted. The second section considers the influence of both national and international media coverage, and how it has influenced the discussion on results and impact of experiments. The third and final section discusses some observations from our interviews which have received little attention to date

R. Merrill et al., *Basic Income Experiments*, Exploring the Basic Income Guarantee, https://doi.org/10.1007/978-3-030-89120-6_5

and are worthy of mention, such as how experiments have affected individual and collective identity roles, power dynamics, women, and gender roles and the status and empowerment of certain communities. This final section identifies some shortcomings associated with these experiments and policies which might be seen contrary to the unconditionality and universality features of basic income and which requires further debate.

5.1 How Results Are Interpreted and Analyzed: The Context and the Objective of Experiments

As pointed out in the introduction of this book and in more detail in Chapter 3, it seems we already know much about the results of unconditionally granting people cash through experiments. A general overview of all the case studies indicates positive results across different indicators, ranging from welfare, happiness and subjective well-being, economic activity, and different psychological aspects. Additionally, effects on labor market participation, though not conclusive in many cases, are not as negative as some would expect and in some cases, they have been very positive, as both Sarath Davala from the Madhya Pradesh experiments and Dirk Haarmann from the Namibia pilot pointed out, and which we already explained in Chapter 3. However, as Karl Widerquist points out, basic income "has many complex economic, political, social, and cultural effects that cannot be observed in any small-scale, controlled experiment" (Widerquist 2018, 3). By definition, any experiment is methodologically incapable of advancing all possible effects of a hypothetical basic income, both at individual-behavioral and collective-structural levels. This is precisely one of the most convincing arguments employed by those opposing conducting more experiments, that is, since basic income's general effects are untestable and unpredictable, further experiments do not make sense. Right or wrong, the discussion is appealing from a scientific and methodological point of view, and has triggered interesting debates on epistemology, philosophy of science, and scientific methodology (Heckman 2020; Langan Teele 2014; Luetge et al. 2014).

In general, there are high expectations put upon these and other social experiments. However, social experimenting (particularly the use of RCTs) poses several challenges that the public does not consider when discussing the potential outcomes and findings from experiments. For example, RCTs necessarily rely on assumptions which are hard to verify in real-world settings, such as the observable rationality of people's behavior.

An RCT is a deductive method, and hence one can never be sure if an assumption is right. In a deductive affirmation, the conclusion is already inserted in the premises. Thus, controlling a particular dependent variable by several independent ones does not assure the latter are true; the only thing it assures is that the model (and the conclusion) is consistent in *presupposing* the assumptions are right. In dealing with this, rolling out an RCT to assess basic income's effects must imply facing several methodological obstacles.

First, there is always an environmental dependency or "external validity" which makes empirical evidence dependent on its contextual setting. How can we be sure these effects would be maintained in a different scenario? Second, there are always problems caused by various biases when selecting participants. Obviously, when participation is mandatory, biases associated with voluntary participation vanish rapidly, as it was in Finland. However, when it is voluntary, several variables alter the sample (educative level, country of origin, being single or married, having a job or being unemployed, income level, etc.), as it is in all social experiments (Betkó et al. 2019, 139). Third, and related with the first shortcoming, there is always an "equilibrium effect" (Banerjee and Duflo 2014, 102), meaning that evidence gathered by a small study is hardly scalable when it is performed in larger areas or even nationwide. Fourth is the "heterogeneity effect", which is observed when a RCT focuses exclusively on the mean impact. An RCT "might reveal an average positive effect although nearly all of the population is hurt, with a few receiving very large benefits, a situation that cannot be revealed by the RCT, although it might be disastrous if implemented" (Deaton 2014, 164). For example, granting cash to male breadwinners resulted in positive mean effects, such as boosting the aggregate household income, as Djavad Salehi-Isfahani, our interviewee pointed out. However, it might impact women within the household, which might become more dependent and tied-in to the household, because of the increase in monthly income.

These methodological obstacles might not be fully considered or understood by the public when experiments are being conducted and results are disseminated. Rather, the non-expert public usually expects scientists to be able to solve the "entire puzzle" (Virjo 2006) by answering all the fundamental "bottom-line questions" (Widerquist 2006). However, due to the mentioned methodological obstacles, UBI experiments cannot address in a definite way whether basic income works at all or whether should we implement it, for example. Considering these inherent methodological and policy limitations, and despite the heterogeneity of our case studies, most of them have collected positive and, to some extent, quite similar results, as we saw in Chapter 3. This is true particularly at the individual and household level, where increases in happiness and decreases in stress and anxiety were observed across the board, in contexts such as Finland, Barcelona or even Kenya. Moreover, it is also important to point out how some of our case studies observed improvements in child nutrition and school attendance, namely in Namibia, Kenya, or Madhya Pradesh. However, a more systematic analysis of all these results shows how difficult it is to compare all of them and devise a general conclusion when contextual factors are considered. Such a general and even simplistic overview is what the public usually perceives and media outlets report: did it work at all?", "are these results good or bad?" However, as we suggest in Chapter 3, the evaluation of the experimental results cannot be understood out of their social, political, and economic context.

For example, considering an experiment as a success or failure just because recipients worked a few hours more or less than the control group is a simplification of a more profound and complex causal explanation. However, these kinds of reductionist conclusions are the ones scientists, policymakers, and those in charge of experiments should deal with when evaluation reports and news are published and disseminated among the public and press. This danger of reaching reductionist conclusions is one important reason why inherent contextual differences and their effects on results should not be ignored when assessing the effects of basic income experiments and similar cash transfer policies.

Usually, there is a clear difference between the effects observed from experiments and policies conducted in rich countries and those in poorer ones, with less robust and institutionalized welfare mechanisms, labor markets, and tax and transfer systems (Torry 2019, 9; 531). Hence, more relevant and conclusive empirical evidence on issues such as severe poverty, education, malnutrition, and health status can be found in countries such as Kenya, Namibia, Iran, and in the case of the Eastern Band of Cherokee Indians' Dividend. Increased food security and quality of food consumed were also detected in places such as Ontario and Barcelona. Despite being rich countries, participant populations were those in need in both places and therefore improvements in these kinds of basic indicators were expected.

Regarding physical and mental health effects, the "rich-poor" cleavage persists. In both contexts, once a minimum economic threshold is guaranteed, general health status tends to improve substantially, though there seems to be a slight qualitative difference: while improvements in mental health are firstly and mostly observed in richer contexts, more salient, positive effects on physical health are firstly reported from less affluent places. Therefore, in places such as Kenya or Namibia, enjoying a more stable and secure economic situation has potentiated health treatments and hospital attendance, thus improving overall physical health, as Caroline Teti from GiveDirectly told us. In contrast, in richer places like Finland, Ontario, and Barcelona, positive effects on mental health were prominent. Participants in these last cases experienced a significant stress-relief due to having a more secure and stable economic situation. As our interviewee Lluís Torrens, director of social innovation at Barcelona city council, pointed out, the decrease anxiety and stress were quite salient in the first year of the B-MINCOME experiment, and it was consistent with the results observed in the Finnish experiment. Overall, these improvements in mental health have ended up improving the quality of the sleep and subjective well-being and happiness in almost all of these places. This is the case of Finland, for example, where participants reported feeling more satisfied with their lives and secure with their future. In Ontario, although results are limited because the pilot was canceled, participants also reported being more confident and satisfied with their lives. It should be noted, however, at least in Barcelona, that improvements in mental health and stress-relief were less statistically significant by the end of experiment, according to the survey conducted two months before it finished. Lluís Torrens mentioned this could be because participants pessimistically anticipated the end of the cash grant and the return to their previous vulnerable situation.

The Barcelona case points out that interpretation of the results is not only affected by the differences in social, political, and economic contexts, but also by the experimental design and the manner in which results are collected. As discussed in Chapter 3, and despite some methodological and scientific limitations, most of these results might be extrapolated favorably onto a hypothetical basic income schema, even if we have limited comparability in our case studies. However, and even though these positive results have already been published and broadly disseminated, basic income continues to suffer the same objections from its opponents.

These objections have resulted from a genuine concern over the potential for generalization of these findings and their overall importance given the inherent limitations of basic income experiments, and from a deliberate attempt to minimize these positive findings in favor of other, more traditional social policies or other normative welfare principles.

The first objection is based on skepticism about basic income experiments and policies and portrays their outcomes as expected, in the sense that it would be odd to have results which are null or quantitatively insignificant. Indeed, "in large-scale, expensive trials, a zero or very small result is unlikely to be welcomed, and there is likely to be considerable pressure to search for some subpopulation or some outcome that shows a more palatable result, if only to help justify the cost of the trial" (Deaton 2014, 165). Although these results might be considered "redundant effects" (Widerquist 2018; Laín 2021), it is always important and even strategically necessary to count on empirical evidence supporting an idea such as basic income. Depending on the context, some results might be more expected or redundant than others. As we have seen, results such as reduction of severe poverty and malnutrition, or improvements in physical health and child education, are expected in poor countries precisely because of the problems these communities are facing, as well as the aims of experiments and policies implemented there. Caroline Teti from GiveDirectly explained how many of the preliminary findings on consumption patterns, improvements in nutrition, and investments in education were to be expected, even if their magnitude was nonetheless surprising. In contrast, in richer places results on mental health and stress-relief, happiness and subjective well-being along with the effects on labor participation in institutionalized labor markets are the most salient ones, once again, precisely because they are considered important issues in these places: it is important to remember how our interviewees from the Utrecht experiment—Roger van Loon and Timo Verlaat and Minna Ylikännö from the Finnish experiment both insisted on the fact that both experiments were aiming to understand how unconditional transfers could improve labor market activation. As redundant as they might be, most of these effects are highly relevant in their own contexts, since they are dealing with issues which are considered of importance in each case to achieve this societal goal. So, the point is not only if these results are expectable or redundant, but rather which is the moral value we, as a society, assign to them.

The second objection is about how this positive trend in the effects of UBI experiments have been side-lined by opponents and the mainstream media at times. If we disregard the position of the "scientific skeptics"—a position we share to a certain extent given the inherent limitations of experiments, but which are not exclusive to basic income experiments per se—we are left with a second group. This group, composed of social scientists, commentators, politicians, and the general public, tends to prioritize the narrative and the results on labor activity, to the detriment of the positive results discussed previously. This narrative giving priority to labor activity is based on a certain perspective of reciprocity, as Stuart White (2003) and Gijs Van Donselaar (2008) have pointed out, grounded both in normative concerns and also in instrumental ones, namely in macroeconomic effects of basic income. This position, paired with a normative position on the value of work, is also often echoed by politicians and NGOs. The discussion on the basic income experiments' outputs, and on their actual effects, ends up being dominated almost exclusively by labor market effects and possible labor withdrawal, hence overshadowing other impacts that have been present in almost all the case studies and which might entail more social value, as we have already seen. This has happened in the cases where labor market activation was indeed the prime variable being assessed, as Minna Ylikännö from the Finnish experiment pointed out, but also in how the media sometimes portrays experiments taking place, as discussed with both Stacia West and Amy Castro from the SEED project.

Beyond labor activation and its impact on how results are interpreted, there are usually two different goals when basic income experiments and policies' results are interpreted. The first goal, which is typically promoted by researchers is to seek empirical evidence to promote scientific investigation on for example the reduction in poverty rates. The second goal comes from the basic income movement, is boosted by national and international NGOs, grassroots movements, and activists alike, which aims to understand how UBI experiments' results can contribute to advance and promote this proposal both at national and international levels. These two different goals when interpreting and disseminating the results of UBI experiments most often do not coincide, leading to multiple interpretations that, on first sight, could be considered straightforward, but whose discussion is always the subject of different perspectives. Beyond the differences regarding the national contexts and the different goals promoted by scientists and politicians and by basic income movement, the national and international media is another agent whose goals may differ from the previous stakeholders, and whose actions can amplify a given set of goals different from or directly opposed to the formers' agents (including, scientists, politicians, and policymakers, the basic income advocates, etc.). We will now turn to the discussion of how the media's and the press' coverage frame the ways in which UBI experiments' results are interpreted.

5.2 National and International Media Coverage

The idea of basic income has never been so frequently mentioned or debated throughout history as during the last five or ten years. In 2013, a European campaign promoted a European Citizens Initiative (ECI) which needed to collect a minimum of one million signatures from at least seven-member states over the course of a year to force the discussion of the proposal by the European Commission. Though the ECI campaign did not collect the necessary number of signatures, it did succeed in bringing the idea of basic income to the center of media and political debate, reaching sectors and places where it had never been heard before (Van Parijs 2016). New platforms and grassroots movements popped up across Europe informing their fellow citizens and petitioning their governments for a basic income. In Europe, and to a great extent in the rest of the world, the debate around basic income was bolstered in 2013 with the announcement of a referendum in Switzerland asking citizens whether they wanted to be granted a monthly basic income equivalent to 2,500 Swiss francs (2,800 US dollars). Less than 50% of the electorate participated in the 2016 referendum, among which almost 77% rejected the proposal, whereas just 23% voted in favor.[1] Despite failing, the Swiss referendum substantially contributed to fostering an unprecedented debate on basic income in Europe and beyond.

In 2015 amid this context, a new organization called Unconditional Basic Income Europe (UBIE) was created, with a goal to organize a new ECI to be submitted in two years. This renewed activism captured media attention as never before. Therefore, it might be said that the basic income community at large has attracted "media attention via new

[1] The referendum outputs which were reported by Swissinfo are accesible at: https://www.swissinfo.ch/eng/directdemocracy/vote-june-6_basic-income-plan-awaits-voters-verdict/42200378.

forms of cooperation outside the realm of traditional politics" (Van Parijs and Vanderborght 2017, 207). Meanwhile, the implementation of several UBI experiments since 2008 attracted additional media attention, as it was the case of all of case studies and most recently in the previously mentioned platform of Mayors for Guaranteed Income in the USA.

In these cases, and in the coverage of the results of the experiments in USA and Canada during the 1960s and 1970s, the media played a significant role. However, one can see differences in the perspectives and assessments made by media outlets. On the one hand, in the aftermath of these experiments in USA and Canada, a complete misalignment in their coverage seemed to exist since, as Widerquist notes, "neither the results nor the disagreements about how to interpret the results were understood by politicians or the media" (Widerquist 2005, 50). In contrast, the more recent experiments in Namibia (2008–2009) or India (2012–2013) led to an outburst of media coverage, which favored the presentation and dissemination of their results, and inspired ongoing discussion on the possibilities of basic income. However, these two last experiments were reported when the basic income debate was not as popular as it is today, while their results were widely covered across the globe. Soon after, the Finnish experiment (2017–2018) came at a moment when the basic income movement was much more solid and widespread across many countries, and there was therefore a significant interest from the press. This experiment and its media coverage fueled the debate and the movement even more, particularly in Europe, and contributed to the ongoing discussion.

These historical events lead us to ask ourselves what the role of media and press coverage is in understanding basic income experiments and similar cash transfer policies in general and their impacts in particular. From our case studies, we were able to define two key roles for media coverage which usually do not receive much attention when analyzing the impact of the national and international media and press coverage of basic income experiments and related policies.

The first role is the attention an experiment receives when it finishes, namely when results are published and broadcasted by different media outlets. For example, Dirk Haarmann from the Namibia experiment told us how the experiment was declared to be a success by national and international press, up to the point that it is now considered a textbook example of a "basic income experiment" and a benchmark of the whole basic income movement in general. Several documentaries and news pieces have been disseminated across the globe depicting it as a success. Within Namibia, press coverage contributed to the creation of the idea that it left a relevant corpus of evidence, which in turn made the basic income concept appear more plausible and less utopian for the public. The importance of the experience and its positive results led to widespread international and national coverage, a coverage which likely contributed to the United Nations referencing it as "good-practice" (UNDP 2017; UN 2018). Hence, in this case, media coverage and institutional promotion was key to fueling the international debate and raising awareness on basic income experiments in general. Even today, it serves as a prime example of a basic income pilot, and it contributed to inspire the contemporary surge in the basic income movement, including the implementation of the experiment in India, as Sarath Davala mentioned.

Finland was another case where national and international media coverage was significant, mostly after the experiment published its results. The expectations from other European countries and basic income advocacy groups were substantial. However, the extensive media coverage of this case was subject to criticism by many from the basic income debate, as well as from the research team involved in the experiment. The results, which showed that labor activation was not stimulated by granting unemployed Finns an unconditional income as compared with conditional measures, pointed out that unconditional cash grants did not appear effective in addressing this specific challenge the government wished to tackle the most. Again, these were quite narrow objectives, since they pertained to labor activation of unemployed jobseekers in Finland. But the media coverage focused on how these results showed "basic income" was not successful. In accordance, the experiment was characterized as "useless" and "unsuccessful" by mainstream media[2] even if it simply focused on answering whether unconditional transfers could be better or worse than conditional ones in labor market activation, a goal which is strongly linked to the framing of the experiment, and it is not necessarily a widespread or theoretical objective of basic income as policy. As Minna Ylikännö from the Finnish experiment pointed out, in this regard, the experiment was quite successful since it provided an answer to its initial framing question.

[2] An illustrative example of such a discourse, see The Independent's report accusing the Finnish experiment as "useless", accessible at: https://www.independent.co.uk/news/business/news/universal-basic-income-finland-useless-says-trade-union-a7571966.html.

The Utrecht experiment was another case where results were scrutinized by the media, though somewhat more modestly when compared to Finland. Here the results on labor activation were well covered, especially in Europe. After the results were published, they spurred a lot of debate about whether basic income led to a reduction in working hours or not. Roger van Loon and Timo Verlaat repeatedly highlighted in our interview how the experiment was not a testing a basic income. However, when one politician publicly labeled them "basic income experiments", it led to a surge in international media coverage, which interpreted the results through the lens of the ongoing basic income debates.

The second role is media coverage received before or just after the experiment is implemented. Here it seems that recent events, which take place against a background of a strengthened basic income movement, have led to an increase in the media coverage of basic income experiments.

The increasing interest of politicians and the general public in basic income in Spain over the last five years, as well as the growing coverage in the media are giving to the topic, contributed to the Barcelona City Council's decision to implement its own UBI experiment in 2017, as Lluís Torrens pointed out. Similarly, in Germany, the debate gained momentum in 2005, and since then not a day passes without a public event or discussion on basic income (Perkiö 2013). This ongoing and growing debate is backing the actual plans for experimenting in Berlin. The project, we were told by Maheba Goedeke Tort who is coordinating the experiment in Germany, is every day covered by German newspapers as well as by some TV channels and by international social media platforms. The coverage is not only extensive, but quite positive, indicating a general curiosity to find out what would be the results of the experiment in a country as Germany. Similarly, basic income was broadly discussed across the USA, becoming a topic of media interest. This may have influenced the decision to launch an experiment (or a so-called demonstration) in Stockton, although both Stacia West and Amy Castro from the SEED project where not sure whether the ex-mayor's decision resulted more from increased interest in the USA for basic income, or from an idiosyncratic municipal necessity to cope with rising poverty and trending inequality. The Stockton experience is even more notable since it harnessed the power of media and recognized its role from the onset. From the beginning, the experiment included families who agreed to engage with the press and provide their take on the process and its results. We don't know if any individual or participant household did not agree in responding to the media' requests but the press acknowledged the general participants' active role and incorporated at least some of them as key players when covering the implementation and the results of the experiment. This led to more positive, accurate coverage of the experiment's results by the media and has also reinforced the media as a key agent in framing the debate on the results and the general perception of their success or failure. The Canadian and USA cases happened in the aftermath of the experiment in Finland, which alongside the Swiss referendum and to a certain extent the pilot in Namibia, are cornerstone moments for the basic income movement, as described above. However, these are countries where the movement, and specifically its grassroots element, is well-established and has been influential for several years. This way, if a UBI experiment is implemented in a country or region where the idea has long been discussed, one can predict that a significant amount of press will cover the implementation of the experiment and its first steps, and not only its results.

A final note on the case of Barcelona: despite being a renowned European experiment, mostly because it was part of the first round of the European Urban Innovative Action program, and despite having taken place in a country where the basic income movement is quite significant, no major national or international media outlet gave much coverage to the experiment. Lluís Torrens seemed to believe this lack of media coverage resulted from the fact that the experiment was never a political issue, either within the city council or among the political opposition. This uncontroversial character and its positive results in several dimensions of impact assessment did not lead to significant interest from the press, nor the possibility of labeling it as a failure as a basic income experiment, even if results showed that some treatment groups slightly reduced their labor market participation.[3]

A related aspect resulting from our interviews was how much the international media coverage was not necessarily representative of intense national coverage, or the other way around. Considering the international media attention, it received, we expected our interview on the Finnish case to discuss media coverage extensively. We were surprised to learn

[3] See the piece "El 'pinchazo' del experimento de la renta mínima de Barcelona: redujo el empleo en 10 puntos", published by the Spanish journal El Confidencial, accesible at: https://www.elconfidencial.com/economia/2021-05-07/renta-minima-barcelona-bmincome-desincentivo-empleo_3070400/.

there was hardly any national media interest in the experiment. Minna Ylikännö formulated the hypothesis this happened because the experiment was dealing with unemployed people, a group which is usually not subject to media attention in the country.

Maricá is also notable in this respect. The policy and its assessment have received international media coverage, partly because of the involvement of international researchers. However, national media coverage is scarce. The research team decided to monitor the traditional and social media right from the beginning according to the same program description.[4] The local media have been publishing positive reports of the policy, and are enthusiastic, as opposed to national media, which gives no significant coverage. This is striking, given not only the international coverage, but also the fact that Brazil has been in the spotlight of the basic income movement for some time. However, it is also a result of the current political environment in the country. The lack of media coverage at the regional and national levels may be related to pro-Bolsonaro and conservative movements across the whole country. This indicates that when assessing the role of media, one should not be tempted to believe that international coverage implies national coverage nor a widespread national interest either.

Beyond some of these cases, in general, the implementation of UBI experiments and the press coverage they have received may have boosted some positive insights on the concept of basic income, particularly on the debate about poverty traps and the conditionality associated with traditional cash transfer mechanisms. In the face of the actual current economic insecurities exacerbated by the crisis caused by the COVID-19 pandemic, the existing administrative and psychological costs assumed by a growing number of beneficiaries of means-tested benefits, with the increasing bureaucratic burdens they entail, are turning media attention toward UBI as a potentially more efficient policy. These shortcomings associated with the traditional means-tested and conditional benefits seem to back the idea of the "desirability" and the "inevitability" of basic income. Social media and traditional press coverage are playing an important role in framing the discussion as such. In this sense, it must be noted that due to mainstream media structures, usually controlled by elites, it is also indicative of the arguments or parts of the debate that have

[4] The description and the agencies involved in media monitoring can be accessed at: https://www.maricabasicincome.com/s/Marica-Basic-Income-Fact-Sheet.pdf.

been picked up by those who hold power in society (Perkiö et al. 2019, 242). As such, it is not surprising that some important press pulpits still accuse basic income of being a "thoroughly wrongheaded idea",[5] not only because of its supposedly disastrous economic consequences, but also because it wrongly rejects that laziness and selfishness are the two major attributes monopolizing human anthropology.

Our case studies revealed that the two moments with most intense media coverage—the beginning and aftermath of the experiment and policies—are precisely those critical to understanding how they will be framed and discussed in later months or even years. This should come as no surprise, given what was seen in the years after the USA and Canadian experiments in the '70s. To this day, social scientists discuss their labor market effects, and why such negative perception was prevalent, given the positive results the experiments showed in other dimension. If an experiment or a particular social program is labeled as "basic income", its implementation and results will be framed within existing national and international debates on "basic income". Therefore, media coverage and press framing are two fundamental factors in this equation, either to promote and disseminate the idea, or to deter and refrain its real implementation.

5.3 Additional Related Effects That Received Less Attention

This section aims to present and discuss some additional related outputs of basic income experiments and related policies that are not always considered when assessing their impacts. These were particularly salient in our interviews, and though they were considered secondary results at times (versus labor market activity, for example), at others they were highlighted by our interviewers as some of the most staggering and long-lasting results. Though these are important results, there still is a lack of attention in the existing literature around them, although some of them have been discussed as possible impacts in theory. This way, we will explore topics related to identity and power relations within communities and how social engagement might have benefited from these experiments

[5] See the piece "Universal Basic Income: A Thoroughly Wrongheaded Idea" published by Forbes, accessible at: https://www.forbes.com/sites/miltonezrati/2019/01/15/universal-basic-income-a-thoroughly-wrongheaded-idea/#6c2e89b045e1.

and cash transfer policies. Another salient topic we discuss is how gender and women's roles within communities and households are affected in some of our case studies. Likewise, as women's roles are sometimes altered by these programs, granting people cash also alters power dynamics and power relationships within communities and households, as well as the perception society might have upon some particular groups or communities. This section also analyzes how trust among citizens and toward public institutions is affected.

Moreover, many of our case studies used RCTs, and qualitative methods were often not as extensive, nor as deeply researched when they were used, leaving many questions unanswered. Therefore, we will also discuss some of the most salient shortcomings when these UBI experiments provide cash transfers on an unconditional basis in comparison with some which feature more conditional schemes.

5.3.1 *Identity, Power Relations, and Community Engagement*

One of the clusters of impacts collected in our interviews is about issues of identity and class and power relations in a given community. They were highlighted in many of our interviews, namely the cases of Ontario, Kenya, South Korea, or Namibia. Though they are not usually discussed extensively in the reports on basic income experiments or similar policies, since their goal usually prioritizes other impacts. Almost all of our case studies reported improvements in community engagement and belonging this was the case with the small sample from Ontario, where people felt more part of the community during the year, they received the unconditional grant. This was detected by the non-official report (BICN. Basic Income Canada Network 2019) and mentioned in our interview. The same results were observed in Namibia, where relationships between neighbors, and even with some of the beggars in the villages, were better and more accepting and engaging. Even in South Korea, the basic income for 24-year-old people yielded a "positive impact on the perception and attitude of youths in Gyeonggi Province" (Yoo et al. 2019, 7), as Hyosang Ahn also pointed out. In the case of the Eastern Band of Cherokee Indians' Dividend, the unconditional grant seems to have even contributed to reducing crime committed by children of the reservation, which our interviewee also highlighted. Another case was in Utrecht where it was observed that participants felt their position had changed, as we were told during out interview, "from victims being exploited to participating members of the community". Increased feelings of personal autonomy were also mentioned as important impacts, as well as an increase in having more time and care available to participants and their relatives as briefly discussed in Chapter 2.

This community engagement and sense of belonging seem to be a result of the underlying consequences of having an obligation-free grant, hence reducing the burden to receive it, but also potentially reducing the stigmatization involved with being a beneficiary. This seems to be the case in Barcelona, where our interviewee believed this was a combination of the impacts of the cash transfer schema and the framing of the experiment: participants were able to contribute to the results by taking part in active policies, instead of being merely "the poor" ones eligible to receive "charity payments". Participants were in quite vulnerable situations, mostly excluded from the community, so their positive reaction was quite significant. In this sense, they reported not feeling stigmatized and rather "proud of being part of a European project", in which and through the active policies put in place, "they had a voice and an active role in the very same experiment and in designing their own life plans" (Riutort et al. 2021; Laín 2019). Similarly, the case of Maricá, where the policy covers a large percentage of the population including many well above the poverty line, also illustrates a possible underlying impact of basic income responsible for better community engagement and belonging.

In the Namibian, Kenyan, and the two Indian cases, where the cash transfers were granted almost universally in the villages where it was implemented, all three interviews highlighted the important impacts in power relations generated by the unconditional grant, namely how it made people feel they were on more equal footing with one another. Dirk Haarmann highlighted that in Namibia poor neighbors felt more comfortable helping beggars, but also demanding accountability from them, since now they were also receiving grant money. In Kenya, Caroline Teti told us people were able to start borrowing from people they trusted, and less often, instead of appealing to their own families or other members of the community out of pity for their situation, often burdening their relatives and creating resentment through their personal socioeconomic situation. Lastly, in Madhya Pradesh, Sarath Davala told us the cash transfers implemented by the two experiments had the striking impact of allowing people to stop borrowing from loan sharks, enabling them instead to become more self-sufficient by borrowing from a community created bank or from people they trusted more. Recipients of the payments were then able to stand on equal footing with other members in the community and escape the sometimes-exploitative lending practices of money lenders in the region, creating a shift in the power balance (Davala 2019, 377).

5.3.2 *Empowering Women*

In Chapter 2, some of our interviews namely the ones focused on the Maricá policy or B-MINCOME experiment revealed the impact such experiments had in reinforcing or shaping women's positions and roles, but also how they contributed improve the lives of their son's and daughter's. This was particularly true in less affluent contexts, where giving women money led to a reduction of children malnutrition and improvements in school attendance, giving more time to women. These results confirm findings of other experiments with other kinds of cash transfers schemas in poor regions (World Bank Group 2020). The "gender-reinforcement claim" (Widerquist 2018, 110) postulates that a UBI can lead to women's emancipation from abusive or submissive contexts within household and community alike. Contrary to our findings, however, there are also fears that basic income could reinforce some traditional gender roles and be detrimental to women's emancipation, for example, keeping them away from participating in the labor markets as having their material existence guaranteed (Baker 2008; Miller et al. 2019). Despite little evidence from UBI experiments regarding this claim, and the difficulty in testing it, our case studies highlighted some possible insights on how basic income can promote women's emancipation.

In India, the cash transfer schemas, particularly the one tested in Madhya Pradesh, helped emancipate women, regardless of their economic position. Everyone participating in the pilot project received cash transfers and their own bank account. In the beginning, some of richer families in the village initially refused to participate out of fear of losing their property or wealth, or to avoid being monitored. However, Sarath Davala, our interviewee, was surprised to see that after a while, women from these households started growing curious about some of the initiatives that were being implemented—namely workshops on financial literacy—and persuaded their husbands to participate. This allowed these women access to these activities, and to receive their own basic income and bank account, ensuring them greater independence and autonomy. As our interviewee told us: "basic income has a way of helping every marginalized member of society".

Besides the Indian cases, very little evidence has been collected on the possibilities of women's empowerment through basic income (Miller et al. 2019). Nonetheless, this case highlights how basic income can contribute to mitigating women's subalternity and generally meliorating the situation of other marginalized groups.

5.3.3 *Community Empowerment and Trust*

Besides the role played by unconditional cash grants in reinforcing community belonging and engagement as explained previously, some of our interviews also highlighted the potential impact of receiving unconditional cash payments in empowering some vulnerable or deprived communities. Likewise, receiving cash grants has been reported to improve some individuals' positions and their roles within their communities, as well as some underrepresented or excluded social groups within the communities they belong to or in front of the entire society. In this line, recent scientific literature and reports from basic income experiments and unconditional cash transfer policies (Kosec and Mo 2019) do also reveal that, on average, recipients tend to increase their trust in their fellow citizens and in the political institutions.

In India, Namibia, and Kenya, the cash transfers implemented through the experiments led people to create their own dynamics and modes of organization for self-governance. In Namibia, the experiment contributed "to a process of mobilization, consciousness-raising and self-empowerment; an entirely organic process initiated and developed by the community without outside interference". As a result, Dirk Haarmann told us the community elected a "BIG Committee" of 18 members comprised of local teachers, the nurse, the police, some business, and bars owners and other community members, who "mobilise the community and advised residents on how to spend the BIG money wisely". This suggests that the introduction of a BIG [basic income grant] can effectively assist with community mobilisation and empowerment (Haarmann et al. 2009, 37). Finally, the community demanded more accountability from their local politicians to the point that our interviewee considered local politicians fearful of some of these communities, who are now more demanding and mobilized. In Kenya, although much less information has been reported in this respect, Caroline Teti, our interviewee, reported that participants in the experiment are organizing themselves and creating their own community banks to improve their own lives and their community members. Being unconditionally granted cash for several years, as we were told by Caroline Teti, also promotes participants' empowerment by enabling them to demand better or different material conditions for the whole community.

In Madhya Pradesh, after the experiment ended, people did not want to revert to being exploited by money lenders and persuaded SEWA to establish a revolving fund to provide low-interest loans to farmers to buy seeds at the time of the sowing season. This further lead to farmers themselves establishing a communitarian seed-bank (SEWA—Self Employed Women's Association 2014). In Iran, as explained in Chapter 4, and although the effect appeared prior to rolling out the cash grant policy precisely as a reaction of its announcement, the growing political controversy, social unrest, and popular mobilization forced the government to implement the cash grant on universal grounds instead of targeting the most in need as the government originally planned.

Community empowerment could be interpreted as a side effect of the reinforcement of community links and trust between people granted a basic income. In the interviews from both Kenya and India, we discussed the impact basic income had in promoting trust between individuals. Caroline Teti from GiveDirectly in Kenya told us that the experiment showed people coming together to pool savings in anticipation of larger sums of money for bigger projects, or that parents have come together to contribute money to pay community teachers for primary schools in their villages. Such results seem to show there is more trust among villager as they see basic income as an equalizer, giving all of them a basic starting point each month. In Madhya Pradesh, Sarath Davala told us the end of exploitation by money lenders resulted partly from people feeling it was better to borrow from their friends or fellow villagers, starting a chain reaction of trust and reciprocity and thus reinforcing the existing community ties. The Finnish and Stockton cases, although quite different from these previous ones, also highlighted increases in trust in a significant way. In Finland, the unconditional monthly grant seemed to slightly increase trust between individuals, though primarily built trust in institutions. Minna Ylikännö from the Finnish experiment suggested this could be a result of having to deal with less bureaucracy and conditional "activation policies", which could have a positive impact on how individuals perceive and trust public institutions. Simply put, it's possible that when institutions place more trust in people, people return this trust to institutions. Results from the Stockton experiment also seem to indicate similar impacts in institutional trust (Baker et al. 2020). As Stacia West and Amy Castro revealed, poor people in the USA, particularly in deprived locations, "do not trust public institutions but in cash". That was clear when observing the participants' spending patterns and their relationship with the cash grant. We were told that, when the monthly payment was deposited on the beneficiaries' cards, "an overwhelming majority of people converted the money into cash, to save it on their own, or to save it in banks they trust and are familiar with". Though it might seem paradoxical, the experiment had a positive impact in increasing trust in local administration, since it was granting people a monthly transfer which beneficiaries might convert to cash whenever they pleased with no-strings or requirement attached.

Unfortunately, beyond these examples, it seems there is a lack of scientific literature and official reports looking into these issues of community empowerment and trust when considering UBI experiments. Despite this lack of consideration and of empirical evidence, at least two final considerations should be summarized and highlighted. First, in poor and strongly unequal societies, such as India, Namibia, or Kenya, community empowerment seems a salient and primary effect of basic income experiments. This might be because the cash transfers implemented during the experiments represented a substantive difference from the beneficiaries' poor material conditions in which they used to live. This resulted in very significant economic improvements in their immediate situation, which in turn ended up benefiting their households and their communities' well-being. As confirmed in our case studies, in less affluent contexts both individual and communitarian economic empowerment is likely to be translated into enhancing individuals' and communities' possibilities to participate politically and socially. However, positive impacts on community empowerment in richer contexts were also reported from places such as Finland, Utrecht, and Barcelona, for example. The experiments in these places were usually less-universally implemented and as already explained, tended to target poor individuals, social services users, or long-term unemployed people. In doing so, they reached out the most marginalized members of affluent societies. These three cases represent highly individualized, urban, rich societies, where poor people tend to be highly excluded and marginalized from social, cultural, political, and economic spheres. This way they are usually suffering from a lack of effective social, community, and even familial support. In the experiments implemented in these countries, participants interacted with social assistance institutions, were heard by social workers, took part in activities related with the experiments, or got involved with other participants' concerns and daily lives. Hence in most cases, these experiments might have possibly been a significant opportunity for social interaction for these groups and individuals, which in turn might be easily transformed into an improvement of their subjective well-being, their self-confidence, their empowerment, and their trust in their fellow citizens and political and social institutions.

5.3.4 *Shortcomings of Unconditional Cash Grants*

Another salient issue from some of our interviews was the discussion on social inclusion and community empowerment when considered in accordance with the debate on conditional and unconditional policies. Despite the overwhelmingly positive results of unconditional cash transfers schemas on community empowerment in developing countries, such as India, Kenya, or Namibia, other cases like Barcelona, Finland, or Utrecht also revealed significant impacts concerning individual and collective empowerment and increase of trust though, as seen, in a qualitatively different way. By taking part in the inclusion policies incorporated into the design of the B-MINCOME pilot, conditional participants (more than those unconditionally granted) were able to create new friends, form new groups, and strengthening their socio-communitarian ties. This led to increases in their social networks and their knowledge of public and community resources available in their neighborhoods (Hill-Dixon et al. 2020). As Lluís Torrens told us, the conditional policies allowed many of the participants to create new friends and gave them an opportunity to social inclusion, which in many cases was not available before.

In Finland, some participants did not opt out of the public employment services, but apparently wished to be activated, that is given services to enhance employability. According to our interviews, they were able to experience a form of social interaction with their case workers through the conditional measures they were required to perform. Minna Ylikännö, our interviewee, mentioned how for many people this "could be their only connection to the society", explaining why they would favor conditional measures over an unconditional schema.

Utrecht and Barcelona experienced a similar phenomenon. In the Dutch case, for example, policymakers and researchers were convinced that they were right in having designed different treatment groups (conditional and unconditional) since this would have fit different people's characteristics. For example, some beneficiaries may be better off receiving some sort of tailor-made support to potentiate their labor activation (particularly the long-term unemployed), and so they would perform better in the conditional group. In contrast, other profiles might perform better in the unconditional group. So, different profiles might have benefited from the program in different ways according to their different abilities, education level, labor experience, or status. For Timo Verlaat and Roger van Loon this might help explain the different results the experiment in Utrecht had in terms of labor market activation, given different people's educational level. In the case of Barcelona, the most socially excluded, less-educated participants, mostly women from other countries with low levels of literacy in Catalan and Spanish, had better results in terms of well-being, happiness and social inclusion and were better off as compared with other categories of participants, including those in the unconditional treatment groups (Bonilla and Sekulova 2019). However, the explanatory variable here is not the "obligation" requirement, but rather the fact of having been involved in the inclusion policies designed by the B-MINCOME pilot project. In fact, the most salient difference regarding subjective well-being and happiness was not found between the "conditional" and the "unconditional" treatment groups, but rather between those that took part in the inclusion policies and those who did not do so at all. So, regardless of being obligated or not, those who participated in these policies were given the opportunity to connect with other people, and so to enrich their social interactions with other participants, and with the researchers and social workers involved in the pilot.

Social interaction, involvement in collective projects, and group cohesion undoubtedly increased participants' subjective well-being, happiness, and self-confidence (Sianesi 2008). This is not to say that unconditional cash grants do not work, nor that conditioned programs always perform better. It just demonstrates the importance of socially inclusive policies or social activities and involvement, especially for those who are worst-off, regardless of whether they are implemented through a social experiment or performed "naturally" without anybody being coerced. This might be particularly true in marginalized urban contexts, where social networks can be fragile or non-existent. Here, activation or social-inclusion policies, even if not mandatory, can play a significant role in ensuring marginalized populations can secure a place in the community.

The impacts reported in this section, particularly those on identity, power relations, community empowerment, and trust, were highlighted in most of our interviews, albeit in different ways due to specific contexts. As we already signaled on multiple occasions, experiments in urban, developed contexts can exhibit different results from rural, less affluent ones. However, our interviews also made clear that many of the impacts lack either additional evidence or information on the narratives behind them. In the latter case, our understanding of basic income and community engagement or empowerment is incomplete. In many experiments, the methodological design did not allow for further or complete understanding of some results. This might be the case in Finland, where the increase in trust in institutions would require further explanations. Likewise, the fact that some people preferred activation or inclusion policies because of engagement in social interaction, as in Barcelona and in Finland, also requires a better theoretical and empirical explanation.

This circles back to one of our final conclusions from Chapter 2, namely the significance scientific and political goals, the sociocultural and economic context, and the methodological features play in determining the basic income experiments' (and similar policies') outcomes. It also shows that despite already having some relevant evidence that can be extrapolated to basic income, there is still certainly a lack of understanding of the impact can have on communities, including its ability to promote inclusion, autonomy, empowerment, and belonging. The way results are interpreted and the reason why some are considered more relevant by key players, the public in general, as well as by the media (as we will see in the next chapter), reinforce a narrative and side-line many of these "other", less-considered impacts. In turn, this also reinforces a general trend not to look for these kinds of impacts within basic income experiments, and thus not assess what they might mean for the basic income debate in general. Hence, while we can claim that *we already know much* on the potential impact of basic income, as we saw in Chapter 2, we can still find important gaps in our common understanding of the possibilities and downsides of implementing a basic income in specific contexts.

References

Baker, John. "All Things Considered, Should Feminists Embrace Basic Income?" *Basic Income Studies*. 2008. https://doi.org/10.2202/1932-0183.1129

Baker, Amy, Stacia West, Sukhi Samra, and Meagan Cusack. "Mitigating Loss of Health Insurance and Means Tested Benefits in an Unconditional Cash

Transfer Experiment: Implementation Lessons from Stockton's Guaranteed Income Pilot." *Population* 11 (2020): 100578.

Banerjee, Abhijit V., and Esther Duflo. "The Experimental Approach to Development Economics." In *Field Experiments and Their Critics: Essays on the Uses and Abuses of Experimentation in the Social Sciences*, Dawn Langan Teele (ed.), 78–114. New Haven: Yale University Press, 2014.

Betkó, János, Niels Spierings, Maurice Gesthuizen, and Peer Scheepers. "The Who and the Why? Selection Bias in an Unconditional Basic Income Inspired Social Assistance Experiment." In *Empirical Research on an Unconditional Basic Income in Europe*, Lei Delsen (ed.), 139–170. Cham, Switzerland: Springer Nature, 2019.

BICN. Basic Income Canada Network. *Signposts to Success: Report of a BICN Survey of Ontario Basic Income Recipients*. Ontario: Basic Income Canada Network, 2019.

Bonilla, Fabricio, and Filka Sekulova. "B-Mincome's Impact on Life Satisfaction Bellaterra." Universitat Autònoma de Barcelona—Institute of Environmental Science and Technology (ICTA), 2019.

Davala, Sarath. "Pilots, Evidence and Politics: The Basic Income Debate in India." In *The Palgrave International Handbook of Basic Income*, Malcom Torry (ed.), 373–387. Cham, Switzerland: Palgrave Macmillan, 2019.

Deaton, Angus. "Instruments, Randomization, and Learning About Development." In *Field Experiments and Their Critics: Essays on the Uses and Abuses of Experimentation in the Social Sciences*, Dawn Langan Teele (ed.). New Haven & London: Yale University, 2014.

Donselaar, Gijs van. *The Right to Exploit. Parasitism, Scarcity, Basic Income*. Oxford: Oxford University Press, 2008.

Haarmann, Claudia, BIG Coalition (Namibia), Evangelical Lutheran Church in the Republic of Namibia, Desk for Social Development, Labour Resource and Research Institute (Namibia) and Namibia Non-Governmental Organisation Forum. Making the Difference: The Big in Namibia: Basic Income Grant Pilot Project Assessment Report. Basic Income Grand Coalition, 2009.

Heckman, James J. "Randomization and Social Policy Evaluation Revisited." National Bureau of Economic Research Technical, 2020: Working Paper n. 107.

Hill-Dixon, Amanda, Hannah Davis, Gitanjaliand Patel, and Victoria Boelman. *The Voices of Basic Minimum Income. Report Evaluating Experiences of a B-MINCOME trial in Barcelona*. London: The Young Foundation, 2020.

Kosec, Katrina, and Cecilia Hyunjung Mo. "Does Relative Deprivation Condition the Effects of Social Protection Programs on Political Attitudes?" International Food Policy Research Institute—Discussion Paper, 2019.

Laín, Bru. "Report on the Preliminary Results of the B-MINCOME Project (2017–2018)." Barcelona: Ajuntament de Barcelona, 2019.

Laín, Bru. "Basic Income Experiments: Limits, Constraints and Opportunities." *Ethical Perspectives* 28, no. 1 (2021): 89–101.

Langan Teele, Dawn (ed.). *Field Experiments and Their Critics: Essays on the Uses and Abuses of Experimentation in the Social Sciences*. New Haven: Yale University Press, 2014.

Luetge, Christoph, Hannes Rusch, and Matthias Uhl (eds.). *Experimental Ethics. Toward an Empirical Moral Philosophy*. New York: Palgrave Macmillan, 2014.

Miller, Annie, Toru Yamamori, and Almaz Zelleke. "The Gender Effects of a Basic Income." In *The Palgrave International Handbook of Basic Income*, Malcom Torry, 133–153. Cham, Switzerland: Palgrave Macmillan, 2019.

Perkiö, Johanna. "Basic Income Proposals in Finland, Germany and Spain." Transform Discussion Paper No. 2, 2013.

Perkiö, Johanna, Leire Rincón, and Jenna van Draanen. "Framing Basic Income: Comparing Media Framing of Basic Income Canada, Finland, and Spain." In *The Palgrave International Handbook of Basic Income*, Malcom Torry (ed.), 233–251. Cham, Switzerland: Palgrave Macmillan, 2019.

Riutort, Sebastià, Albert Julià, Bru Laín, and Lluís Torrens. *Resultados finales del proyecto piloto B-MINCOME (2017–2019). Informe ejecutivo*, Barcelona: Ajuntament de Barcelona, 2021.

SEWA. Self Employed Women's Association. *A Little More, How Much It Is... Piloting Basic Income Transfers in Madhya Pradesh*. India, New Delhi: SEWA Bharat and UNICEF, 2014.

Sianesi, Barbara. "Differential Effects of Active Labour Market Programs for the Unemployed." *Labour Economics* 15, no. 3 (2008): 370–399.

Torry, Malcom (ed.). *The Palgrave International Handbook of Basic Income*. Cham, Switzerland: Palgrave Macmillan, 2019.

UN—United Nations. *Some Lessons from Microfinance and Basic Income*. United Nations Conference on Trade and Development, Geneva: United Nations, 2018.

UNDP Programme—United Nations Development. Universal Basic Income. A Policy Option for China beyond 2020? Working Paper, UNDP, 2017.

Van Parijs, Philippe. "The Worldwide March to Basic Income: Thank You Switzerland!," *Social Europe*, 2016.

Van Parijs, Philippe, and Yannick Vanderborght. *Basic Income: A Radical Proposal for a Free and a Sane Economy*. Cambridge, MA: Harvard University Press, 2017.

Verlaat, Timo, Marcel de Kruijk, Stephanie Rosenkranz, Loek Groot, and Mark Sanders. *Study What Works. Summary of the Final Report*. Utrecht: Utrecht University, 2020.

Virjo, Ilkka. "A Piece of the Puzzle: A Comment on the Basic Income Experiment Debate." *Basic Income Studies* 1, no. 2 (2006): 1–5.

White, Stuart. *The Civic Minimum: On the Rights and Obligations of Economic Citizenship*. Oxford: Oxford University Press, 2003.

Widerquist, Karl. "A Failure to Communicate: What (If Anything) Can We Learn from the Negative Income Tax Experiments?" *Journal of Socio-Economics* 2005: 1–51.

Widerquist, Karl. "The Bottom Line in a Basic Income Experiment." *Basic Income Studies* 2 (2006): 1–5.

Widerquist, Karl. *A Critical Analysis of Basic Income Experiments for Researchers, Policymakers and Citizens*. Cham, Switzerland: Palgrave Macmillan, 2018.

World Bank Group. *Exploring Universal Basic Income. A Guide to Navigating Concepts, Evidence and Practices*. Washington: International Bank for Reconstruction and Development/The World Bank, 2020.

Yoo, Young Seong, Jeong Wonho, Rhie Kwanhyung, Yun Sungjin, and Ma Jooyoung. *Analysis of the Effects of the Youth Basic Income Policy in Gyeonggi Province: Comparison of the Ex-Ante and Ex-post Survey*. Gyeonggi: Gyeonggi Research Institute—Policy Study, 2019.

CHAPTER 6

From Experiment to Policy Implementation?

After having witnessed several experiments over the last decade, more and more researchers, politicians, analysts, and members of the basic income community in general are wondering how to move from experimenting to implementing a real basic income scheme. This was also a key discussion present in most of our interviews, not only from experiments which have finished and have not seen a basic income implemented, but also from ongoing and planned experiments, which could potentially contribute to a nation-wide implementation of the policy. This chapter will examine our interviews to understand the existing gap between conducting basic income experiments and having this measure in place. The first section explores the pros and cons of considering basic income as an object of study to be evaluated through social experiments or, on the contrary, as an actual policy to be implemented as part of a welfare services' portfolio. We will draw from our case studies to discuss some of these arguments. Looking at experiments from this perspective reveals a more complex setting which determines the need to look at both the scientific and political process. The second section will discuss whether experiments are affected by political manipulation or tampering and, if so, in which manner. Keeping this in mind, the third and final section of this chapter

R. Merrill et al., *Basic Income Experiments*, Exploring the Basic Income Guarantee, https://doi.org/10.1007/978-3-030-89120-6_6

explore the duality between experimenting and lobbying, when considering moving from experimenting to really implementing a basic income scheme.

6.1 Basic Income Experiments: Their Role as Political and Research Tools

Experimenting in the social sciences has a long intellectual history, but has only recently expanded into the realm of social policies. In recent decades, experimentation has rapidly grown to gather scientific evidence to help inform the design and implementation of various political programs or social policies. As James Heckman stated, we have moved from the "first great awakening" of experimentation evaluating manpower, education, and health programs, to the "second great awakening" which "came in developmental economics in the wake of a variety of micro programs targeting to [sic] less-developed countries funded by influential NGOs, billionaires, and various world institutions" (Heckman 2020). However, it was not until recently that experimentation reached its zenith of social relevance with the 2019 Nobel prize in economics being awarded to Abhijit Banerjee, Esther Duflo, and Michael Kremer for their research on experimental methodologies in the fight to reduce global poverty. When considering all experimental methodologies, randomization has achieved prominence, particularly within the new evidence-based policy paradigm (Cartwright and Hardie 2012). Indeed, the RCT has become the most prominent mechanism to determine whether a particular policy or program is properly functioning (Leigh 2018). For at least 60, scientists have been using RCTs to test and compare medicines and new drugs and they are now becoming fundamental in the behavioral economics research agenda, as well as in some developing economic programs implemented in poor regions to reduce inequality or to boost school attendance, for example. No doubt, "RCTs are increasingly used in international development to compare the cost effectiveness of different interventions for tackling poverty", although "they are not yet common practice in most areas of public policy" (Haynes et al. 2012, 6) as seen in Fig. 6.1.

Despite this disproportionate difference in the use of RCTs between health sciences and social policies, the basic income debate is not alien to these new trends in experimentation. As our research clearly illustrates, many of the concluded basic income experiments and pilots have included

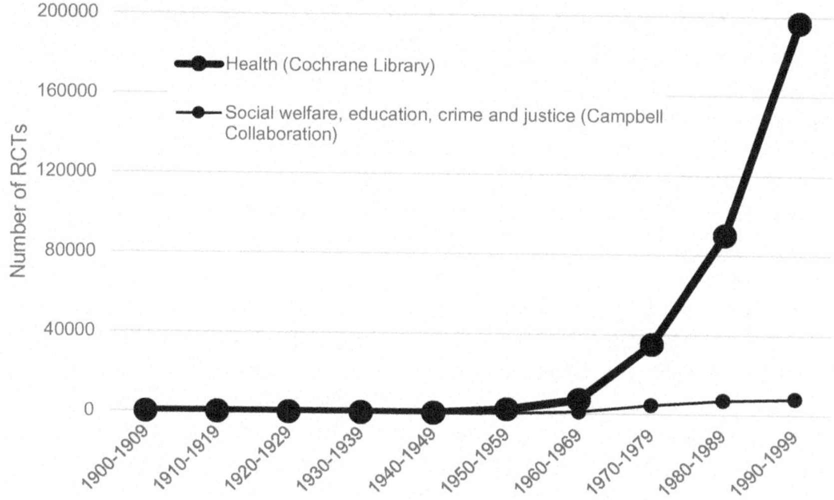

Fig. 6.1 Use of RCTs across the twentieth century in health and social welfare, education, crime, and justice related policies and programs (*Source* Haynes et al. 2012, 6)

randomization in their methodology, and many of those currently being designed plan to as well. Indeed, almost all our case studies identified as experiments have in some way or another featured an RCT in their methodology. Our aim here is not to scrutinize these experiments' methodologies, nor to discuss whether they obey all required scientific parameters. Rather, we wish to suggest that this fact might reflect Karl Widerquist's concern that "the demand for the current round of experiments [on basic income] seems to be driven more by the desire to have a UBI experiment than by the desire to learn anything specific about UBI from an experiment" (Widerquist 2018a, 3). No doubt, the actual debate about experimenting with basic income highlights a fundamental obstacle, namely that all these experiments deal with a sensitive political topic, which is not only researched in scientific terms, but in most cases, also supported in ideological and political terms. One might be tempted to perform both activities—researching and advocating—through the same strategy: experimenting. In facing such a dilemma, "one must separate basic income as a *research object* from basic income as a *political goal*" (Virjo 2006). Thus, we should differentiate when a UBI experiment is understood as a "research object", used to collect and evaluate evidence to determine which elements of a particular design might be featured in a basic income policy (or a related-social policy), from a UBI experiment used as an ideological device or a strategy to promote a particular political aim or interest. Both uses might be legitimate, and in some cases both aspects are likely to be involved in the decision to implement such an experiment, but if we want to understand them properly, these two uses—both scientific and political—need to be clarified from the very beginning.

On the one hand, if basic income experiments are conducted and designed as scientific endeavors, they are expected to collect robust evidence capable of informing the full implementation of a basic income scheme, or other related policies. In this sense, an experiment is useful in predicting some of the basic income's potential impacts, such as mental and physical health, subjective well-being and happiness, social participation, poverty, or social exclusion reduction, for example. However, as we have already seen, there are a lot of things an experiment cannot estimate, such as the long-term, macroeconomic effects, the economic feasibility of a nation-wide basic income scheme, the reaction of the high-income earners, or the impact on labor markets, to mention just a few limitations (Deaton 2014; Groot 2006; Laín 2021; Standing 2012; Tena 2018).

Our interviews indicated how UBI experiments are useful for informing how political actors and their decisions affect, constrain, and distort the design and implementation of social policies. For example, the Ontario experiment has shown how UBI experiments can be sensitive to political decisions, and that scientific reasons might be seen as secondary. Similarly, even in the Finnish case, where the scientific nature of the experiment was a key goal, politicians were able to unilaterally alter the design by imposing the "activation model" on the original design. In Namibia, although important political figures supported the idea, pressure, and lobbying from civil society was necessary to finally implement the experiment. We have also learned from Iran and South Korea that basic income is best anchored in political coalitions, as opposed to being framed as a one-party proposal, or one-person agenda. Although in some way, the Maricá and Stockton cases might weaken this conclusion, popular mobilizations were also fundamental there, but not a specific political-party coalition.

Our interviews also gathered useful insights on the limits, constraints, and opportunities of policymaking and the potentialities of a particular institutional policy context. In this sense, Finnish researchers are now more aware of the dynamic effects of unconditional cash transfers and better able to predict how a hypothetical basic income scheme in Finland might accommodate itself and perform among the other social policies within the Finnish welfare model. In Ontario, the recent cash benefits implemented due to the COVID-19 pandemic were very much informed by its canceled experiment, namely in the decisions behind the amount being granted, as Wayne Lewchuk, researcher involved in the Ontario experiment pointed out. The B-MINCOME experiment in Barcelona showed that active inclusion policies might be of help to regularize migrants' legal status, as well as that unconditionality likely empowers women inside and outside their homes. In the case of Namibia's experiment, it was expected that in a context of high poverty and inequality rates, an unconditional cash benefit would lead to positive individual and communitarian impacts, as Dirk Haarmann pointed out. The case of the Eastern Band of Cherokee Indians' Dividend indicates some possible ways of how historically excluded communities might use actual legislation (the federal law on casino revenues) to establish their own unconditional cash transfer program to improve their own situation. In a nutshell, UBI experiments are valuable, and worth being conducted in scientific terms since, as seen, they might provide a baseline against which other social policies' results may be compared (Groot 2006). These examples do not pretend to be an exhaustive list of all the lessons gathered by UBI experiments when accommodating themselves within existing social policies and welfare models. However, these few examples do illustrate that a lot can be learned from a UBI experiment in terms of policy making (Virjo 2006), even in a context where a rapid implementation of a full basic income scheme is hardly conceivable in the short-term.

On the other hand, sometimes politicians in charge of launching and implementing an experiment are more concerned about the political debate it might trigger rather than about the empirical evidence it might or should gather. In opposition to laboratory experiments with pre-established and well-controlled environmental variables, in social experiments using an RCT model, for example, optimal methodological and experimental factors are hardly to be expected, and then results need to be carefully analyzed. Being aware of these methodological boundaries, those in charge of the experiments (most often politicians) might feel discouraged in letting researchers and social scientists assess the results independently, and therefore charge non-academic institutions or technicians with evaluating the experiment's impacts. The resultant discussion is thus "built upon policy reports, white papers, discussion papers [...] but not on scientific evidence" (Füllbrunn et al. 2019, 172). In the most extreme cases, a UBI experiment might divert itself from its intended-formal aim and become a mere political-ideological device to further a particular political goal, which might include—though not necessarily—implementing a full basic income scheme. This might be an acceptable option, but only as long as those in charge announce this aim explicitly and publicly from the very beginning, something that admittedly does not occur frequently. In these cases, however, those in charge should know that "there is a danger in focusing too much on the strategic value of the experiments to supporters and opponents" since in fact, when conducting an experiment "there is more to scientific inquiry than political advantage" (Widerquist 2005, 69). Experimental results will always be contested from one side or another, as our interviewee from the Finnish experiment pointed out, and advocates and detractors of basic income alike might be tempted to affirm or reject those results as inevitable anyway.

In sum, and as explained before, UBI experiments and unconditional cash transfer policies are an output of political processes where there are political interests (against or in favor) in testing unconditional cash transfers. This does not necessarily imply that the experimental results might be used to advance a particular political-ideological goal—defending or criticizing the very idea of basic income, for example. However, given the inherent political nature of social experiments as well as the fact that basic income is highly sensitive in political and ideological terms, there is always the risk of political manipulation in the use of UBI experiments as political, electoral, or populist devices.

6.2 Experiments: Political Opportunity Costs, Manipulation, and Populism

As we already pointed out before, basic income is a controversial issue because any kind of welfare reform tends to be a sensitive issue in political and ideological terms. Consequently, most of the experimental evidence gathered by our case studies is usually discussed according to a political context in which different positions tend to be already polarized. José Noguera and Jurgen De Wispelaere noted UBI experiments will then be "assessed in a highly politicized environment, one that is hostile to universal welfare schemes; and this in turn might render the science hostage to outright political manipulation" (Noguera and De Wispelaere 2006, 3).

When conducting a basic income experiment (or another similar, large social program or policy) there has always been a certain "political opportunity cost" that any government (or institution in charge) must face. The case of Ontario reveals how important the political landscape is particularly the opinion polls in convincing a government to keep an electoral promise. However, once the electoral period has passed and the government takes office, the political opportunity cost tends to decrease rapidly, as the Ontario experiment's cancellation also demonstrated. In a very different context, the political landscape also affects the experiments and policies' possibilities and prospects. Similar to Finland and Ontario, Maricá's UBI experiment was also an outcome of a topic long discussed before it was implemented. In this case, however, it was rolled out during a period of high sociopolitical unrest and tension. This situation may lead to fear of rolling back the policy once the political climate changes, as Fabio Waltenberg from the Maricá policy pointed out. In South Korea, debate on basic income is attracting greater attention since the introduction of the Youth Basic Income program. As we were told during by Hyosang Ahn, national government and other relevant political actors at the national level used the popularity of the term "basic income" and co-opted it to attract more electoral attention, despite defending traditional, means-tested benefits rather than an unconditional cash transfer scheme. The case in Namibia is also relevant when discussing the political opportunity cost. As Dirk Haarmann told us, despite positive results, international media attention, and the fact that one of the main stakeholders involved, Bishop emeritus Dr. Zephania Kameeta of the Evangelical Lutheran Church was appointed by the President as the First Minister for Poverty Erradication of the Government, basic income was never implemented.

Despite their differences, these cases highlight important ways in which the political process influences the experiment—before, during, and after its implementation—and most importantly in the aftermath of publishing results: namely in the decision to roll-out basic income as a policy or not. As discussed, our case studies illustrate how UBI experiments and similar cash transfer policies are a result of political processes, subject to political pressures and motivation, even before being implemented.

Therefore, a first important observation is that no politician or policy-maker who wants to remain in office is willing to carry out an experiment or introduce a new policy whose results are so negative that they might lead to questions regarding the relevance of the experiment or the policy, or even implementing them in the first place. Indeed, "the smaller scale of this research design requires less funding, less political or bureaucratic support, and (in part for that reason) is less likely to attract political attention" (Noguera and De Wispelaere 2006). In these small experiments, the political opportunity cost would tend to be low, and then neutral or even negative results might be more readily tolerated in political terms. This might be the case in Barcelona, where the small scale of the experiment and the fact that it was partially funded by an external body—the European Union—reduced the risk of conducting it. This might help explain the lack of political opposition and of adverse media coverage and thus the low political opportunity cost this experiment dealt with.

In contrast, "in large-scale, expensive, trials, [sic] a zero or very small result is unlikely to be welcomed, and there is likely to be considerable pressure to search for some subpopulation or some outcome that shows a more palatable result, if only to help justify the cost of the trial" (Deaton 2014, 165). The size and the cost of an experiment represent two key factors directly linked with its political opportunity cost and this, in turn, with the possibility that the interpretation and dissemination of results or the experimental design might even be politically altered, as in Finland with the introduction of the "activation model" during the experiment. This seems to have occurred in many of our case studies, for example, where the choice of only targeting more vulnerable groups with lower levels of income was a result of given political agendas, which in some cases might fear or respond to a general public aversion of giving money to people who "do not really need it". Among others, this might be the case of South Korea only targeting young people, Iran where only the poor households were included in the original plan, or Barcelona where only social services beneficiaries from a very particular, poor area were eligible.

Even more, a government may be opposed to a basic income for political or ideological reasons and thus try to alter or manipulate the results of the experiment to justify its inappropriateness. An additional point to stress is that "those who sponsor trials, those who analyze them sometimes, and those who set evidence-based guidelines using them sometimes have financial stakes in the outcome, which can cast doubts on the results"

(Deaton 2014, 175). Certainly, there is always a risk of political manipulation. However, we do not want to highlight this risk per se, but the fact that politicians are usually seeking good press. Therefore, they always tend to justify and extol the achievement of their own political actions. Indeed, most of the time, "scientific curiosity is not why trials are happening. They are an outcome of the political process" (Widerquist 2018a, 71). Consequently, an experiment's results might not be particularly positive, but what responsible politicians—regardless of being advocates or detractors of basic income—will not allow is for the experiment to be perceived as a failure in itself and, since experiments are the "outcome of the political process", it might take a toll on them in the next elections.

A second related discussion is the possible use of experiments as political instruments, which might happen in a trio of ways. First, experiments might be used to advance the basic income debate by a supportive party, or one who has committed itself to basic income. This seems to be the ongoing situation in Scotland, where even the First Minister, Nicola Sturgeon, has supported the idea. This was also clear in Ontario, where the Liberal party was sympathetic to the idea of a basic income and had committed to it, hence the experiment was implemented. The timing of its implementation, near the end of the government's term shortly before elections, could call into question the government's motives. In some of our interviews, we discussed this as a strategic move, whether the parties in charge of experiments knew they were behind in the polls and thus implemented a widely popular program to build support for themselves, or as a way to force the experiment onto an eventual new government. This was an hypothesis we discussed in the case of Namibia, by Dirk Haarmann, but also in the case of Ontario, as Wayne Lewchuk told us. Either way, it shows how experiments might be a way for a given party to push their pro-basic income agenda, or in contrast, a strategic move aimed at reaping electoral benefits.

UBI experiments might also be used to stall debate surrounding a basic income's actual implementation (Widerquist 2018a, 43–59, 77–85, 145–49). This might be a plausible explanation for what happened in Namibia, in India, or perhaps even in Finland: experiments allowed the debate on basic income to be focused on the experiments' design and results for at least three years, if not more. This can be a long period of time in the democratic political process, which in turn would allow the government to try to justify why its full implementation is not adequate for the country.

Finally, UBI experiments might be also used as political banners—and hence susceptible to the influence of populistic actors. This might also be the case in Maricá where the basic income program is a flagship policy of a mayor from the Workers' Party, one of the main opponents of the current President, Jair Bolsonaro, as Fabio Waltenberg pointed out. There is concern that a mayoral change in Maricá might threaten the policy, although this seems less likely as time passes, and it becomes more deeply ingrained in the city's sociopolitical landscape. Widespread local support for Maricá's *renda básica*, driven by its obvious positive impacts on the local economy and poverty alleviation, may make it too politically costly to be dismantled. But the Maricá experiment also cautions that basic income might become the tool for populistic parties or politicians to gain influence, due to its positive results on individual and community levels. In our interview with Sarath Davala on the Madhya Pradesh's experiment, such concerns were clear. Illustratively, a recent program of an unconditional cash transfer to farmers received widespread support, leading to a victory in local elections for the party who implemented it. Potential electoral benefits could increase support for basic income, as opposed to it being included as part of policy reform to promote a particular ideological project, or to solve some existing challenges. It can also lead to a wrongful appropriation of what the word "basic income" means, a threat that resonates with the multitude of experiments that are dubbed basic income but fall largely outside the definition of what basic income is.

In sum, and as noted previously, "there is nothing inherently wrong with using a study [...] to promote a policy, as long as the evidence is presented honestly and aimed at improved understanding" (Widerquist 2018a, 6). However, when assessing whether and how basic income experiments might be an instrument to implement a real basic income policy, various political factors must be considered. We now know that the decision to roll-out an experiment or a policy, and eventually to move toward full implementation of a basic income measure, usually relies upon a political opportunity cost. As seen before, the scale, the cost of the experiment, and media coverage can all influence this opportunity cost, and any government, the political party, or institution in charge must be willing to pay it if a basic income is to be implemented as policy. These are key factors to be critically considered when studying UBI experiments and assessing their results.

However, as we have seen across this section, the decision of launching a UBI experiment and even implementing a basic income scheme, is always the output of a political process which might easily suffer political influences, manipulation, or even to be used as a populist instrument. Political parties and politicians in charge find themselves under pressure because of press coverage and the electorate's opinion. Consequently, they would have incentives to use experiments to justify their own agenda. In this way, they might use experiments to promote their own ideological or policy aims, whatever these might be: either by using experiments' results to promote the basic income idea, or deterring its implementation by wasting time by conducting experiments. Likewise, politicians or institutions in charge of UBI experiments might also use them as political banners to differentiate themselves from a particular political rival or to appear as an advocate of a widely supported cause. In both cases, there is a danger of a populist manipulation of experiments and of the idea of basic income in general.

6.3 Experimenting or Lobbying: Which Path Forward?

In light of the issues, doubts and skepticisms raised to this point, which most of our interviews have reinforced, the question one could legitimately pose is: to what extent is it worth continue to experiment with basic income? Would it not be better or more strategic to lobby and push governments to implement a basic income? Answering such a question is not easy and hardly fits into a black or white discussion. However, if experiments continue to be implemented, tested, and evaluated, the cost of not addressing will likely increase for the whole basic income community. Our interviews reveal a lack of consensus, though this mainly reveals how ambiguous the debate might be.

On the one hand, UBI experiments—those already conducted and those still being designed—are sometimes perceived as a "distraction", keeping those involved (scientists, politicians, policymakers, or merely basic income supporters) away from the political debate and the policy-making process of implementing a real basic income policy. Moreover, in other cases, misunderstanding or failing to disseminate the experimental and policies' results might even contribute to deterring the implementation of a real basic income policy (Widerquist 2005, 2018b). On the other hand, however, these experiments are also perceived as positive and useful in advancing the implementation of a full basic income schema (Standing 2008). In these cases, experiments are justified as, first, being useful for reforming or improving other related policies, such as child benefits or guaranteed income schemas and, second, as a useful means of gathering insightful information for policymakers and the basic income community in general to use for promoting such a proposal. This is a perspective discussed in some of our interviews, namely with Lluís Torrens, in the case of B-MINCOME or Timo Verlaat and Roger van Loon from the Utrecht experiment. Within this last defense of UBI experiments and related programs, two main approaches might be differentiated among the basic income advocates. First, those who support continued experimentation as a strategy for accumulating as much evidence as possible to finally make evident *enough* the need for implementing a basic income policy. Second, those who instead would situate basic income experiments within an "incrementalist" strategy. According to this view, dreams of full, at-once implementation would be discarded as experiments would contribute to reinforcing other similar policies (such as minimum income schemas, conditional and means-tested benefits, refundable tax credits, child grants, etc.), which in the mid or long-term *would be turning* themselves into a de facto basic income. Therefore, while the first strategy would then prioritize rolling out the basic income directly through the "Royal Way", the later would defend its implementation by stealth or through "the Back Door" (Groot 2006; Groot and Van der Veen 2000).

Both strategies possess important pitfalls which must be considered. The first option—the Royal Way—could be criticized as being overly optimistic, as there is considerable "doubt that a generous unconditional basic income will ever be introduced anywhere as a result of a big triumphal revolution" (Van Parijs and Vanderborght 2017, 214). Nevertheless, the latter option—the Back Door—is also haunted by doubts of the incrementalistic strategy's efficiency. In fact, as more experiments are being conducted and empirical evidence accumulated, "there might be good reasons to worry about diminishing returns to the research resources invested in a given stream of research; that scholars will be learning more and more about less and less" (Shapiro 2014, 233). This might make each experiment less useful in fostering public debate, and could instead necessitate extremely specific discussions, in which only experts and scientists in the field could participate. Paradoxically, this might deter basic income experiments and similar cash transfer policies from step-by-step, convincing more and more people, politicians, and non-expert public in general of the merits of implementing a basic income.

The discussion between these two views seems to be framed by an inescapable logic of "reform or revolution". On more empirical grounds, however, our research shed some light on the debate, though it is hardly conclusive since the discussion remains merely speculative. In Finland, for example, the experiment attracted worldwide attention and promoted unprecedented debate on basic income in many countries around the world. However, the fact that the mass media heavily criticized its "failure" to increase labor participation, as well as the fact that the government did not wish to discuss the possibility of a different experiment, or implementation of basic income, pose some doubts as to whether the "window of opportunity" is now closed, if it was actually opened, or if it might be open again. Minna Ylikännö discussed in our interviewee how nonetheless the experiment Will potentially be quite useful in framing and advancing the debate when a broad discussion on the welfare state in Finland takes place, and where a basic income can be considered as a relevant tool for that reform. A quite different case is Namibia, where results were indisputably positive in several indicators. Therefore, the platform pushing for basic income in the country, the BIG Coalition, criticized the government for ignoring these positive results. Consequently, both the BIG Coalition, but also Dirk Haarmann in our interview, pointed out how the experiment showed that the effort should push for rolling out a basic income nation-wide, instead of calling out for expanding the pilot that took place, or pushing for a new one.

In a quite different context, the experiment in Stockton helped the basic income community and supporters in "fueling the match [of basic income debate]" as long as they know they appear as a "catalyst" of the proposal in front of the entire country, as both of our interviewees from the SEED project pointed out. In this sense, the Stockton pilot might likely be useful both to redesign and improve other related-social programs, as well as to promote the implementation of a basic income in the mid-term via the "Royal Way". The example of India reveals a similar case, since the empirical evidence collected added weight to the discussion and contributed in situating the basic income proposal in the Indian context. As long as India is usually seen internationally as an "object of study" of developing policies worldwide, it is easy to understand why Sarath Davala reported that basic income supporters in India are blaming scientific efforts to be "just one part of the game" and opting to "make noise" instead.

In Scotland, the previous reports on the design and the feasibility of their pilot projects were instrumental in triggering the debate and framing it beyond theories and abstract discussion on basic income. These reports and all previous work have contributed significantly in exploring the possibility of a UBI experiment. Thus, supporters and researchers are worried about not being able to profit from this propitious moment and "waste their time and efforts" conducting an experiment that might provide ambiguous or inconclusive results. A perspective shared in our interview by Jamie Cooke, from RSA Scotland. Lastly, in Barcelona, Catalonia, and Spain in general, basic income is attracting attention from people who have never heard about it, and more interestingly, from people who were formerly opposed but are changing their opinion because of the global financial crisis of 2008 and the crisis created by the COVID-19 pandemic coupled with the inability of the Spanish and the Catalan minimum income schemas to tackle its consequences. However, the rigidities and institutional constraints of the Spanish political system (De Wispelaere and Haagh 2019; Noguera 2019) dampen any sense of optimism of causally linking rolling out more experiments and the advancement of a basic income policy, through either the "Royal Way" or the "Back Door" strategies.

Basic income has been promised in many political parties' electoral campaigns across much of the ideological spectrum, although it usually vanishes as parties gain more political and institutional power (De Wispelaere and Noguera 2012; Laín 2021). In some places where experiments and unconditional cash transfer policies have been conducted, the basic income idea has advanced to some extent, and in others it might have contributed to slightly reducing some cash transfer schemas' conditionality (Standing 2008). Nevertheless, none of the countries where these experiments or policies have been conducted and implemented has established a basic income policy after all. Unsurprisingly, basic income is a proposal with a huge redistributive capacity, larger than unemployment benefits or retirement pensions. In doing so, it would trigger a great political and social controversy. It would be naïf then to assume that a government would implement it just because some positive results are obtained from an experiment. From an evidence-based policy perspective, it would be fully rational to roll-out a basic income if its experimental results are generally perceived as positive enough. However, political decisions often do not follow this scientific reasoning. Beyond this "naïf scientism", the fact that a government implementing such a policy does not depend on the magnitude of the experimental results, but on its political determination and, more importantly, on the political and economic resistance and support this proposal would likely raise. Considering the collected interviews and of the actual development of real-world politics, "we need to revise the recent narrative according to which the basic income experiment constitutes a genuine window of opportunity" (De Wispelaere et al. 2018, 17). Our research, including both the conducted interviews and the analyzed scientific literature, lead us to conclude that none of the experiments or cash transfer policies conducted thus far have proven themselves capable of inspiring or forcing a government) to implement a nation-wide basic income policy. However, this does not mean that a future experiment or policy might not do so, nor that it cannot contribute to its implementation.

References

Cartwright, Nancy, and Jeremy Hardie. *Evidence-Based Policy: A Practical Guide to Doing it Better*. New York: Oxford University Press, 2012.

De Wispelaere, Jurgen, Antti Halmetoja, and Ville-Veikko Pulkka. "The Rise (and Fall) of the Basic Income Experiment in Finland." CESifo Forum. ifo Institute—Leibniz Institute for Economic Research at the University of Munich 19, no. 3 (2018): 15–19.

Deaton, Angus. "Instruments, Randomization, and Learning About Development." In *Field Experiments and Their Critics: Essays on the Uses and Abuses of Experimentation in the Social Sciences*, Dawn Langan Teele (ed.). New Haven & London: Yale University, 2014.

Füllbrunn, Sascha, Lei Delsen, and Jana Vyrastekova. "Experimental Economics: A Test-Bed for the Unconditional Basic Income?" In *Empirical Research on an Unconditional Basic Income in Europe*, Lei Delsen (ed.), 171–199. Cham, Switzerland: Springer Nature, 2019.

Groot, Loek. "Reasons for Launching a Basic Income Experiment." *Basic Income Studies* 1, no. 2 (2006): 1–7.

Groot, Loek, and Robert van der Veen. "Clues and Leads in the Policy Debate on Basic Income in the Netherlands." In *Basic Income on the Agenda: Policy Objectives and Political Chances*, Robert van der Veen and Loek Groot (eds.), 197–223. Amsterdam: Amsterdam University Press, 2000.

Haynes, Laura, Owaine Service, Ben Goldacre, and David Torgerson. *Test, Learn, Adapt: Developing Public Policy with Randomised Controlled Trials*. London: Cabinet Office Behavioural Insights Team, 2012.

Heckman, James J. "Randomization and Social Policy Evaluation Revisited." National Bureau of Economic Research Technical, 2020: Working Paper n. 107.

De Wispelaere, Jurgen, and Louise Haagh. "Introduction: Basic Income in European Welfare States: Opportunities and Constraints." *Social Policy & Society* 18, no. 2 (2019): 237–242.

Laín, Bru. "Basic Income Experiments: Limits, Constraints and Opportunities." *Ethical Perspectives* 28, no. 1 (2021): 89–101.

Leigh, Andrew. *Randomistas: How Radical Researchers Changed Our World*. New Haven: Yale University Press, 2018.

Noguera, José A. "The Political Debate on Basic Income and Welfare Reform in Spain." *Social Policy & Society* 18, no. 2 (2019): 289–299.

Noguera, José A., and Jurgen De Wispelaere. "A Plea for the Use of Laboratory Experiments in Basic Income Research." *Basic Income Studies*, 2006: 1–6.

Shapiro, Ian. 2014. "Methods Are Like People: If You Focus Only on What They Can't Do, You Will Always Be Disappointed." In *Field Experiments and Their Critics: Essays on the Uses and Abuses of Experimentation in the Social Sciences*, Dawn Langan Tee (ed.), 228–239. New Haven: Yale University Press.

Standing, Guy. "How Cash Transfers Promote the Case for Basic Income." *Basic Income Studies* 3, no. 1 (2008): 1–30.

Standing, Guy. "Basic Income Pilot Schemes: Seventeen Design and Evaluation Imperatives." In *Wege zum Grundeinkommen*, D. Jacobi, and W. Strengmann-Kuhn (ed.), 133–152. Berlin: Bildungswerk, 2012.

Tena Camporesi, Alberto. "La Renta Básica Universal basada en la evidencia." *Política y Sociedad* 55, no. 3 (2018): 851–871.

Van Parijs, Philippe, and Yannick Vanderborght. *Basic Income: A Radical Proposal for a Free and a Sane Economy*. Cambridge, MA: Harvard University Press, 2017.

Virjo, Ilkka. "A Piece of the Puzzle: A Comment on the Basic Income Experiment Debate." *Basic Income Studies* 1, no. 2 (2006): 1–5.

Widerquist, Karl. "A Failure to Communicate: What (if Anything) Can We Learn from the Negative Income Tax Experiments?" *Journal of Socio-Economics*, 2005: 1–51.

Widerquist, Karl. *A Critical Analysis of Basic Income Experiments for Researchers, Policymakers and Citizens*. Cham, Switzerland: Palgrave Macmillan, 2018a.

Widerquist, Karl. "The Devil's in the Caveats: A Brief Discussion of the Difficulties of Basic Income Experiments." CESifo Forum. ifo Institute - Leibniz Institute for Economic Research at the University of Munich 19, no. 3 (2018b): 30–35.

PART III

How to Answer the New Questions About Basic Income Experiments, Pilots and Policies?

Parts one and two provided the main insights and questions from our fifteen interviews conducted with stakeholders involved in basic income experiments, pilots, and policies. Many of these questions and conclusions have been at the center of the debate on basic income and its pilots and experiments. The six chapters in parts one and two will hopefully give a comprehensive overview of the insights and questions that emerged from our fifteen interviews. These insights and questions focused on the context of the experiments, pilots, and policies, their design and implementation, their main findings, and how they have been interpreted. They should also contribute to many of the ongoing questions on what some common pitfalls in the design and implementation of experiments and pilots are, or the role different stakeholders played in the understanding and impression of each case. Both parts one and two, because of our interviews, raised important normative questions on how we discuss and perceive basic income experiments, pilots, and policies, which we will take up here in part three, the last chapter of the book, and finally in the conclusion, when summing up our main arguments and lessons.

The first normative issue is about the scope of experiments, and how goals often compete. Our interviews clearly showed how we, as basic income advocates, are at times indistinctively talking about the goals of UBI (as a movement) and the goals of a particular basic income experiment, pilot, or policy in each context. This can result in misperceptions on the success or failure of the experiment, and its intended or *de facto* significance for the basic income movement. This is true on both local and national levels. Hence, we will discuss how these different goals should be addressed and interconnected with the local or national movements. This will also lead to a discussion on whether experimentation should be more focused on local or national contexts, in the hopes of reconciling these at-times competing interests. Such lessons can be important for basic income experiments, pilots, and even policies moving forward.

The second normative issue is about the design of the experiment or pilot (or even policy, when it is being evaluated). We discussed at length the role of both researchers and politicians in the design and implementation of experiments. The quest for "unbiased" results has led some to advocate for microsimulations as a better option for testing a basic income, instead of social experiments (Noguera and De Wispelaere 2006). While we acknowledge the inherent difficulties of social experiments, and of many of existing quantitative and qualitative methodologies (such as the discussion on the limitations of RCTs), we call for the need to acknowledge the influence of political actors and the political process when conducting an experiment. In fact, even the most "scientifically driven" experiments are still mostly an outcome of a given political process. As such, one should not necessarily condemn its pitfalls, but rather acknowledge them, and work with those limitations and challenges in mind from the beginning. Opening up experiments and pilots to embrace political processes should also make the case for the need to consider other potential challenges and downfalls of experimenting, namely ethical challenges of deciding to engage in an experiment or pilot. We will therefore highlight the need to be more cautious and develop more strategies to account for these limitations in any basic income experiment, pilot, or policy that is planned or started going forward.

The final normative question will build from our analysis of the findings from our case studies. We moved from the apparent conclusion that we already know much about the impacts of cash transfers, to acknowledge that we have important knowledge gaps: on labor market participation, on investments in education or even how migration patterns can change and be affected by basic income. Others might also be worth considering, such as the impact of cash transfers on consumer patterns and the effect on environmental sustainability, or how it might reinforce competition based on positional goods. As such, this section will firstly present an evident conclusion: we have much information, which is typically scattered. Hopefully, the analysis and the opportunity granted through the fifteen interviews in this book help shed light on results from basic income experiments, pilots, and policies. This also allows us to understand which results we know less about. Secondly, we will discuss whether we need to know more or not. Do we still have questions? Can our questions be answered with social experiments? How can we use experiments to help answer our pressing questions, whether they are instrumental or normative?

Besides discussing the three normative issues presented above, we will conclude Chapter 7 by discussing what our interviewees told us about how the COVID-19 pandemic shaped the debate on basic income, and particularly on the need to have UBI experiments. Hence, the final section of the chapter will discuss the possibility for the pandemic to inspire a short-term basic income policy. We will start by discussing the role of external shocks, such as COVID-19, in the basic income movement, and then move to the debate of whether this will lead to implementation of short-term or long-term basic income at national or regional scales. If this could be the case, what might the consequences of having such a basic income be? Will it reinforce the debate for basic income caused by COVID-19? Or could it be detrimental, considering the timing and the increasing challenges that COVID-19 has brought, especially if they may potentially not all be solved through a basic income? Or can we perhaps discuss a possible "lock-in effect", as acknowledged in some of our interviews? If this is the case, once implemented, a basic income might be very difficult to dismantle, given its potential popularity.

Reference

Noguera, José A., and Jurgen De Wispelaere. "A Plea for the Use of Laboratory Experiments in Basic Income Research." *Basic Income Studies* 1, no. 2 (2006): 1–8.

CHAPTER 7

How the Findings Help Advance the Basic Income Debate and Advocacy

7.1 Do We Still Have Questions?

As discussed in Chapter 2, there is significant evidence on the impact of cash transfers. These are a result of basic income pilots, which are part of our case studies, such as the Namibia experiment, or the GiveDirectly experiments in Kenya. They are also a result of so-called basic income experiments, which actually test cash transfers but feature some important characteristics that make them relevant for a discussion on basic income. This is the case with most of our case studies. Finally, they also come from some quasi-basic income policies, namely the ones in some Native American reservations, Maricá's policy in Brazil, Iran's universal subsidy scheme, and Macau's Wealth Partaking Scheme.

Though there are significant results, there are also significant limitations in assessing them. Firstly, because of what was discussed in Chapter 2: our case studies, inasmuch as they can be considered relevant to discuss basic income, since they are all unconditional cash transfers, (hence we dubbed them basic income experiments) share very little, which reduces the possibility of confidently comparing and generalizing findings from all of them. Moreover, a second related challenge, discussed in Chapter 5, is also about how much evidence seems to be underexplored or overlooked. Our interviews have highlighted impacts on migration, power relations, and women's emancipation, though evidence on each of these results is quite scarce.

R. Merrill et al., *Basic Income Experiments*,
Exploring the Basic Income Guarantee,
https://doi.org/10.1007/978-3-030-89120-6_7

Amidst this background, and after coming back and forth between claiming that "we know much on basic income" but we also might "still need to know more", since some evidence is scarce or non-existent, it is important to present our position on the subject.

On the one hand, we know much on the specific impacts of cash transfers, particularly of unconditional cash transfers. In fact, we already know that cash transfers promote individuals' and families' well-being, which our case studies demonstrate, and we discussed in Chapters 3 and 5. They lead to increases in reported happiness and reduce feelings of stress and anxiety. Unsurprisingly, they also contribute to better health, particularly mental health, reinforcing the claims discussed when the impacts of Canada's MINCOME experiment in the '70s were analyzed (Forget 2011). Other reported benefits include how cash transfers promote economic activity, namely through increased consumption and commerce, although there is little detail on how it impacts entrepreneurial activity, consumer patterns, or wages. Two important notes on these results: the first is that they are not considerably distinct from what we could expect. It is not surprising that when granting people money, especially those with low incomes, their anxiety or stress will decrease, hence we could consider them "redundant effects" (Laín 2021). Secondly, and notwithstanding the importance of these results, one could argue they are not necessarily attributable to basic income. The example of Barcelona is particularly illustrative: the experiment compared ten treatment groups with one control group. Two out of the ten treatment groups had no "activation" policy, and only one of those two were guaranteed, and hence did not see their payment (the Municipal Inclusion Support-SMI) reduced when receiving extra income (Laín 2019, 10–11). Within the three activation policy groups, half of the recipients received an unconditional income, meaning they were not obligated to participate in the activation policy. Hence, only five out of the ten treatments groups were unconditional. Impacts on well-being were significant across the board: all ten treatment groups experienced improvements in well-being when receiving the SMI cash transfer. However, improved well-being was particularly salient in groups with compulsory activation policies, especially when they were "conditional"—which in the experiment meant compulsory activation policies. As discussed in our interviews and in the published results of the experiment, the target group of B-MINCOME (excluded and marginalized people from poorer contexts in Barcelona) might bias our findings. Hence, compulsory activation policies might have increased the sense of community, belonging, and overall inclusion of many of these people. Our interviewee, Lluís Torrens, discussed how many of the treatment groups created their own communication channels, or organized meetings and events among themselves, connections they failed to have before joining the experiment. Hence, reported increases in well-being in some of our case studies might not be attributed only to having implemented an unconditional cash transfer. They might be a result of several factors, which include the existence of a guaranteed or additional income stream, but also other policies that might be implemented. Moreover, such results on well-being may also be more pronounced in certain population groups, as the B-MINCOME experiment seems to show. Hence, although most of our case studies reported positive well-being results, and such improvements seem to be more pronounced when unconditional cash transfers are implemented, instead of conditional ones (World Bank Group 2020), these may not be exclusive to UBI experiments, pilots, or policies.

As we also discussed in Chapter 3, there are other impacts which are perhaps less "redundant" as defined above but seem to be common in our case studies. These include the acknowledgment of the role of women: money granted to women seems to lead to positive results in nutrition, education, health of the entire household. This is not only observed in our case studies, but also in other reported studies on cash transfers, even if conditional ones (Barber and Gertler 2010; de la Brière and Rawlings 2006). Impacts on individual autonomy also seem to be salient in some of our case studies, where receiving unconditional cash transfers allowed people to be more independent, and enhanced their autonomy vis-à-vis employers, lenders, or even elements of their own households, as also discussed in Chapter 2. However, and contrary to the impacts on well-being or health reported above, these results are less "redundant", either because we do not have enough evidence from our case studies, or because they were not observed in most of our case studies. Moreover, they raise questions, which are not settled: will the unconditional nature of a cash transfer amplify these results (e.g., would autonomy be enhanced in particular groups, like marginalized ones?)? Or will the results be reproduced in the context of a basic income policy or not?

An extra note on this is warranted. Despite the diversity of our case studies, we do indeed have some cases which fall much closer to the ideal definition of a basic income as presented in our introduction. In our experimental cohort, we have the Namibian pilot, the GiveDirectly scheme in Kenya (the longer one, which is still running) and the experiments in India, particularly the one in Madhya Pradesh. In the non-experimental case studies, we have three which are also closer to this definition, namely the Eastern Band of Cherokee Indians' Dividend, Macau's Wealth Partaking Scheme, and Iran's universal subsidy scheme. These three are all examples of unconditional and universal experiments and pilots (although they have some control groups) and policies. However, as mentioned in Chapter 2, they also have differences to such a definition of basic income as we introduced. Each experiment, pilot, and policy have its own relationship with our definition, fulfilling or falling short of various aspects of it in particular ways and degrees. In all of these cases, the value of the cash grants attributed is usually quite below a sufficient threshold to allow "a life with dignity". Nonetheless, these six cases—three experimental and three non-experimental—are the closest of our case studies to our definition of a basic income.

On the other hand, we still have many unanswered questions on the possible impacts of basic income, both at local and national levels. For example, we know little about the large-scale effects on labor supply (nor even less on demand side), as we discussed in Chapter 3, or the possibility of inflation (if only at a local level). We do not know how consumer patterns might change; if people will consume more, invest in positional goods, or if they will choose to buy more sustainable products. Another controversy and interesting case is the impact on migration. Only one of our case studies—Namibia—was able to clearly observe the impacts of migration into the community, which was a side effect of implementing an unconditional cash transfer and improving the socioeconomic situation in the Otjivero-Omitara region. In the second year of the pilot, the impact of migration into the village presented difficulties for observing and documenting the impacts of the experiment, since many households' numbers increased, reducing the overall value per capita of payments in the village. During the pilot a significant number of people from other regions moved to the village for economic gain. For Dirk Haarmann this was a positive outcome of basic income, since it enabled the opportunity to reunite families, instead of driving them apart out of economic necessity. However, there is basically no evidence on the relationship between basic income experiments and migration dynamics, therefore the theoretical discussion on the role basic income might play in migration cannot be conclusive either. Finally, our case studies also showed us the key role played by the context of each experiment, pilot, or policy. Hence, besides the results we have, which are scarce, scattered, or limited, we also know that such results may probably be very distinct according to the context of the case study we are analyzing.

Hence, based on our discussions in both Chapters 3 and 5, we can draw two conclusions. The first is that it seems we have substantial information on impacts, such as well-being, happiness, and health, and even trust and autonomy. But in many cases, we are not sure whether such impacts can be attributed to basic income, or whether they are common to most cash transfer programs. Moreover, for the most part, these are results which might be expected when granting money to people, particularly in the most vulnerable contexts. Hence, they are not necessary novel nor surprising in our understanding of basic income. Therefore, we do have evidence, but it might be incomplete in terms of understanding whether basic income is responsible for them, and how it could change for different segments of the population. The second is the acknowledgment of the existing gaps in our knowledge on certain potential impacts of basic income, namely issues of labor market participation, and the overall impacts on labor supply and demand. The evidence on consumer patterns is also scarce, which might limit our understanding on the role basic income can play as a policy that helps or undermines collective efforts toward sustainability (e.g., might reinforce collective bargaining for less sustainable products, by increasing demand for such products). Moreover, changes in migration patterns can have negative feedback effects, particularly if they were to be manipulated by populistic and nationalistic movements or parties. We also have little information on community-based impacts, even though some of our case studies, particularly those representatives of pilots, showed some changes in community engagement and empowerment, and shifts in power relations.

These all seem important gaps in our understanding of the potential effects of basic income. Moreover, and as discussed in both parts one and two of our book, they are the result of multiple factors. First, the difficulty in comparing and generalizing findings, given the differences between experiments, pilots, and policies and how they relate to the definition of basic income. Also, the role of methodological decisions, which for the most part focus on using RCTs and assessing certain labor market participation outcomes and collect very little qualitative evidence. Lastly, and as pointed out by Karl Widerquist, there are many claims which cannot be adequately observed or tested[1] by social experiments such as basic income experiments and pilots. This is because such experiments are limited on what they can tell us as effects which are attributed to the unconditional transfer that is granted to a treatment group. Many of such untestable or difficult-to-test claims are outcomes we included when discussing our current knowledge gaps on potential impacts of basic income. Hence, we consider them to be important to our understanding of basic income. If we side with Widerquist, basic income experiments, pilots, and even some policies which may be evaluated won't be able to shed light on such effects. If we won't be able to satisfy our knowledge gaps on the potential impacts of basic income, can we legitimize basic income experiments and pilots on the grounds of needing to gather more evidence on such impacts?

Considering the limitations of testing a basic income, should we focus on knowing more about its potential impacts? Widerquist tells us that, for the most part, disagreement on whether to implement basic income is grounded on ethical disagreements: "Little if any empirical investigation addresses the question of whether UBI can significantly raise net-beneficiaries' incomes whether they work, because there is overwhelming evidence and very little disagreement that it can; the disagreement is whether it should. Empirical investigation of the effects of UBI does little to settle that basic moral disagreement" (Widerquist 2021). Hence, the problem with the debate on basic income, and its potential implementation, is largely grounded on ethical disagreements, and not on lack of evidence of the potential impact basic income could have. If this is the case, rather than focusing on evidence, we should mostly focus on normative claims.

In this section, we discussed the role of evidence when discussing basic income experiments, pilots, and policies: can we say that we know enough, giving existing findings, and the evidence discussed in our interviews? This is closer to the positivistic point of view, where experimental

[1] Widerquist presents 24 claims which are considered untestable with existing techniques (Widerquist 2018, 110). These include the "consumerism claim", the "migration" and "the economic-stimulus claim", the 'exploitative claim' among others. He also discusses nine claims are considered testable but are so saturated with limitations so as to not allow for any conclusive argument regarding them, namely the "welfare claim" (Widerquist 2018, 109). Lastly, he offers five "claims that don't need a test", which include the "freedom claim", related to our discussion on enhanced autonomy, or the "poverty claim", namely the impact basic income could have in relative poverty (Widerquist 2018, 105).

case studies are judged based on the evidence they can gather (e.g., positive, or not, in the sense of helping to achieve the goals of the experiment). However, as we discussed, the answer is ambiguous, and it also seems that answering many of these questions is scientifically difficult or impossible. Moreover, and as discussed in Chapter 4, even when experiments were framed as "scientific" they were always and notably judged politically or ideologically. Hence, Widerquist seems to be right: we probably won't be able to settle the debate on basic income through scientific evidence, and even if we were, scientific evidence is hard to obtain for many basic income claims, which are ethically grounded. Therefore, should we or should we not drop arguments in favor of basic income experiments or pilots because of their limited scientific nature?

We do not think so. Basic income experiments and pilots might still be justified on other grounds, a topic we will return to in the conclusion of the book. For now, it is enough to consider how they might contribute to both the advocacy movement as well as promoting ethical judgments and discussions on basic income. In our interviews, when discussing evidence, normative debates were frequently raised. For example, when discussing the impacts of the experiment in Utrecht, to claim whether one considers the experiment successful or not would most likely move us away from the abstract results, into discussions about work and what to expect from people. In the experiment, when granted an unconditional transfer, people with different levels of education showed different results in labor market activation: the higher educational group seemed to take more time to find a job. Our interviewees mentioned this could be because they expected to find a job more tailored to their needs, and with better conditions. In this case, to ascertain whether one result is better than the other (e.g., better to find a job quicker, or not) implies discussing what is best when it comes to find a job: find any job, find a job that suits our needs and qualifications, among other aspects. When we discussed the role the unconditional cash transfer had on power relations in the village in Namibia, we also considered whether the impact of this scheme in leading to people demanding more responsibility and accountability from certain members of the community—namely beggars—was potentially good, or if it could have important downsides (e.g., leading people to stop helping others, on the grounds that all benefited from the unconditional grant). Also, our two interviewees who were involved in the Stockton experiment discussed how we should look to use evidence beyond its direct interpretation. For example, when discussing the impacts of the experiment in Stockton, they believed we should not only discuss how the income provided a safety net, and people continued working, but rather also take the opportunity to discuss how work should be considered beyond participation in formal employment, and beyond its benefits as means of survival (e.g., a mechanism for social inclusion as well). Hence, it seems that looking at basic income experiments, pilots, and even policies as mechanisms to gather evidence can be justified because of an "ethical claim", where experiments are considered important for promoting debates around salient ethical (dis)agreements, such as the importance of state redistribution through cash transfers or issues related to labor market participation (Laín and Merrill 2021; Merrill and Neves 2021). A second justification relates to how experiments can not only spark debates, but also contribute pieces of evidence to inform such debates. Again, these won't be helpful to settle the debate, but they can expand our knowledge on how basic income impacts labor preferences, or investments in children's education or life-long learning. Again, this was clear from our interviews: evidence not only contributed to sparking normative debates, but it also showed aspects which had not been considered as often. If we take the same example from the city of Utrecht, on the one hand we see that it challenges our view on whether taking up a job faster is morally superior. On the other hand, it also allows us to discuss how conditional policies tend to be stigmatizing (Calnistsky 2016) and can also be detrimental to people's social inclusion. In fact, the other side of the equation on labor market activation in the Utrecht experiment was that whereas the people with higher qualifications took more time to find a job, the less qualified participants found a job more quickly with an unconditional cash transfer. For our interviewees this could be attributed to the fact that they did not have to navigate bureaucracy or comply with certain requests involved in activation policies. Hence, they were "free" to use their networks and had time to pursue a job or related occupation.

As a final note, we need to focus not only on the experiments and pilots' "bottom-line" questions as Widerquist (2018) suggests, but perhaps also on how different findings from different experiments and pilots might be similar or different. This more general perspective of our fifteen case studies aims to provide just that. Discussing how findings relate to each other, or how different contexts and methodologies showcase different or similar findings, might help in using evidence beyond a mechanism to reinforce existing ethical judgments. Having a comprehensive view of different sets of results could contribute to using evidence to spark normative debates on the ethical questions surrounding basic income. It could also amplify our understanding on what key variables we might be missing when discussing certain ethical objections or arguments regarding basic income as a policy, hence enhancing our general discussions on the moral desirability of implementing a basic income.

7.2 In Between Motivations: The Interplay Between Stakeholders Involved in Designing and Implementing UBI Experiments

One of the key discussions underpinning all our case studies was the apparent dichotomy between those who based a UBI experiment on moral motivations, and others whose motivation was instrumental. As discussed in Chapter 4, however, this is partly a false dichotomy: most experiments fall in between both extremes, juggling both instrumental and moral motivations. But even if this is so, understanding the primary motivations of experiments, pilots, or policies, or how they were framed, might help identify common pitfalls in designing and implementation, and can help make sense of the results.

When we discussed how both moral and instrumental ends were involved in the motivations behind our case studies, we said little on what "instrumental" might mean. In essence, it can consider both political agendas and purposes, or scientifically driven goals. Hence, we mentioned how instrumentally driven experiments are usually designed to tackle some practical issue, which is assumed to require adjustment or political intervention. Experiments can be grounded in a motivation to understand how a different economic instrument can shape existing programs to help promote better nutrition, for example. Therefore, one could frame an experiment or pilot solely on these instrumental terms, and consider its design and implementation according to them, hoping that the subsequent results will also be judged and interpreted along those lines. However, as discussed, this has not always been the case. In both Finland and Utrecht, the experiments were presented as a mechanism to assess the role of unconditional cash transfers in labor activation. In Barcelona, despite the normative position linked with historical rates of poverty in the city, most of the framing of the experiment was quite instrumental, aiming to assess how cash transfers, with various configurations of activation policies attached, were better or worse in promoting social inclusion. But these three cases were all mostly framed as "scientific" experiments, even if the aims they wanted to tackle are related with certain moral ends (e.g., reduce poverty rates and increase social inclusion of marginalized populations). In Finland, this was because scientific rigor, and the idea of having a very robust experiment, where a causal link between the unconditional transfer and the impact on labor activation could be made, was publicized as a key goal of the experiment. In others, such as in Barcelona, framing the experiment as a scientific endeavor was a conscious decision. On the one hand, the team involved believed it would be a more neutral experiment for politicians with different ideologies and hence they would be more favorable to its implementation. On the other hand, the past example of the MINCOME experiment in Canada was used as an example, since it showed that such a framing was better because it reduced participants' stigmatization (Calnistsky 2016). In this sense, the case in Barcelona illustrates how framing served both instrumental goals—convincing and engaging politicians on practical matters from an instrumental perspective—but also moral ones, such as avoiding stigmatization. These three cases lead us to the first conflict which might contribute to some of the challenges and pitfalls of experiments, pilots, and policies. This is the conflict between a "scientifically-driven agenda" and the "political agenda".

As we mentioned in Chapter 4, it is worth highlighting that politicians' and researchers' agendas are usually not the same. A commonly held view is that scientists are primarily moved by a "quest for knowledge", whereas politicians have their own agendas and might therefore look to accommodate the experiment not only because it helps mitigate the challenges, they and their electorate care about, but also, they can interpret and misuse the results to fit into their own programs. These lead to different behaviors toward an experiment: not only in terms of how they are designed and implemented, but also how results are communicated and interpreted. The tampering with of the experiment by the Finnish government illustrated this point. Such tampering happened despite the government—who was mainly responsible for the experiment—having initially framed it as a scientific endeavor, in line with the researchers' ambitions. Our interviewee was not sure what led the government to implement these changes, given that there was not a change in office to account for them. It might simply be the case that they did not acknowledge the impacts it could have in the experiment, or rather that they were not so concerned with the robustness of the experiment in the first place. The recent experiment in Stockton is another case where there was tension between the research agenda and the political one. In this case, it was mostly an experiment whose goal was rather "open-ended" and geared toward social change. Right from the beginning, researchers and former-mayor Tubbs alike framed it as an attempt to know more on the role basic income could play in poverty alleviation and social inclusion in a community that has been hard-hit by the financial and housing crisis and globalization in recent years. However, the initial goal did not stop analysis of the public discussion of the results to be focused mostly on labor market participation. In the first interviews to the media, then-mayor Tubbs focused on how the SEED program gave people "the dignity to make their own choices, the ability to live up to their potential and improved economic stability going into the turmoil of the pandemic".[2] However, he also subsequently focused on the employment and productivity results in later interviews, namely that the additional money had not tampered with people's existing work ethics. In discussing findings in the press and with other politicians, it was mostly these results that were considered, despite the broad moral ends the experiment wished to contribute to,[3] echoing existing discussions on work ethic, reciprocity, and basic income (White 2003; Widerquist 2018; Neves 2021). Of course, this could have been a result of the way media portrayed the interview, or which questions were posed to ex-mayor Tubbs. Nonetheless, the focus was still on labor market activation when it came to publicly discussing the findings, as opposed to other salient results (e.g., well-being and health). Moreover, it also seems to indicate that the political agenda changed according to the context, whereas the research agenda apparently was unchanged throughout the

[2] See NPR report on the findings, available at: https://www.npr.org/2021/03/04/973653719/california-program-giving-500-no-strings-attached-stipends-pays-off-study-finds, accessed on May 2021.

[3] The SEED program, implemented in Stockton, released its preliminary findings in first semester of 2021, focusing on key variables: namely income volatility, employment and productivity, well-being and mental health and also autonomy and consumption patterns. In later interviews, ex-mayor Tubbs focused much more on the employment and productivity results, namely that the additional money had not tampered with people's existing work ethics. See Insider report on the findings at: https://www.businessinsider.com/stockton-basic-income-experiment-success-employment-wellbeing-2021-3, accessed on June 2021, or at PBS report, at: https://www.pbs.org/newshour/show/stockton-ca-gave-residents-a-guaranteed-income-heres-what-happened, accessed on June 2021.

experiment. These cases help illustrate the hypothesis that scientists and politicians, albeit honest most of the time, are usually moved by different concerns, which leads to an inherent tension between scientific and political interests. However, they also allow us to conclude that the distinction between "moral" and "instrumental" aims might be misguided.

Firstly, this is case because experiments serve both scientific (e.g., provide evidence, confirm hypotheses) and political purposes (e.g., stimulate a social movement around a topic, serve as a flagship program, stalling mechanism, etc.). As we saw in Chapter 6, all of our cases studies are a result of a political process (except the GiveDirectly experiment, where the political process played a smaller role) and were influenced by it (e.g., Ontario's case, where the experiment was cut short when a new party took office). Hence, even under the "instrumental" umbrella—the Utrecht experiment, the B-MINCOME, or the Finnish case—it seems we cannot find UBI experiments or pilots that are fully motivated by "scientific reasons", but we rather have cases where both agendas interplay or in some cases collide, and are manifest in their design, implementation, and interpretation. This is also perhaps the reason why experiments are failing to answer the "bottom-line questions" as Widerquist points out (2018). Not only might experiments not have adequate tools to do so (given the inherent limitations of most social experiments), but perhaps also because they are conditioned by political processes; they must accommodate political interests and concerns, making it more difficult to be able to answer the general bottom-line questions on basic income. As we saw in some of our case studies, experiments and pilots have at times included concerns from the political agenda (e.g., whether an unconditional cash grant will improve social inclusion or labor market activation, as in the experiments in Barcelona and Finland; can an unconditional cash lead to increased alcohol consumption, a concern in the Namibia pilot). Moreover, an experiment or pilot might also be influenced by changes in office, which might translate to different concerns or agendas (e.g., in Ontario, this led to the dismantling of the experiment). Because the context is key in any experiment, the political and institutional context are strong variables that influence what is going to be tested and how in most experiments and pilots, or even policies. Therefore, framing an experiment to answer the "bottom-line questions" might be more difficult when very particular and context-specific issues are on top of the concerns of those who are engaging in the experiment or influence it, such as politicians.

Additionally, we should not forget part of our discussion in Chapter 4, and again in Sect. 7.1: our case studies possess an inescapable combination between these instrumental goals—political or scientific—and moral principles (usually also linked to ideological views). These factors play into how politicians and citizens perceive UBI experiments, pilots, and policies, not only influencing how they are conducted (especially if politicians are the ones initiating them) but also how results are interpreted, since most of the time discussions are not on whether basic income *will lead to job loss* but whether *it should* (Widerquist 2021). Take again the case of Stockton: ex-mayor Tubbs' focus on labor market outcomes when discussing the results is a political strategy which is morally charged. He is responding to a concern about whether people should work, instead of using a basic income to become full-time unemployed.

Considering the inherent landscape, and the existing interplay between moral goals and instrumental ones—both scientific and political agendas alike—which stance should basic income experiments take? We discussed how using experiments as research tools is useful; they could grant us much evidence on impacts of cash transfers, namely unconditional ones, and we contend, with Widerquist (2018), that if framed to answer the "bottom-line" questions, they could advance our general knowledge on basic income. Hence, should we look to have "purely" scientifically driven experiments and pilots? There are some calls to do so, namely by using lab experiments or microsimulation studies as tools that can allow for more objective results and higher internal robustness standards, but also avoid being prey to the influence and even tampering of the design and goals of experiments by the political process (Noguera and De Wispelaere 2006). But at least three critical objections can be raised regarding the use of microsimulations studies. One is that they are limited. Simulations are only valid considering existing assumptions and caveats in the model. Then they tend to lack external validity and hence are also inadequate in dealing with important outcomes, namely community-level impacts, and as such their results will be as limited as social experiments (Widerquist 2018). Therefore, not only will they not necessarily provide more robust findings to what the impact of a UBI could be if implemented in each community, but the fact that their design and the subsequent results are limited will also open the possibility for misuse and misinterpretation of results by politicians. This is especially true if we consider that simulation studies can become quite complex; their results may be difficult to communicate, especially considering all their caveats and assumptions

(Neves 2021). Hence, and considering our discussion on how moral and instrumental ends are tightly linked in our case studies, the second objection is that one should expect that results from simulation studies will also possibly be prey to political manipulation, as much and as often as the results of social experiments and pilots. Thirdly, although scientists are not politicians, they are not "black boxes" empty of agendas and motivations. Researchers, namely the ones engaged in basic income experiments, also carry out their own agendas and perspectives when designing and implementing an experiment (Neves 2021; Laín 2021), even if they were trained to reduce their "subjectivity". In fact, doing so might be permissible, in certain cases, to understand the best possible design given inherent limitations, political agendas, and a certain context. Inasmuch as politicians are influenced by their agendas (which might tamper with scientific robustness), scientists are also influenced by context, their beliefs and demands from different stakeholders. But even if they could avoid such considerations, researchers are usually at least influenced by the "streetlight effect", defined as "research that focuses on questions that are easier to answer but less important rather than on questions that are more important but harder to answer" (Widerquist 2018, 32). This will be true both for social experiments but also for lab and microsimulation studies, hence the latter will probably not solve such issues, even if one would like them to.

Hence, looking for truly "scientific" and "objective" experiments and findings might be futile, given we will most likely not be able to have such experiments, and even if we were, the evidence collected will be much less important in settling the debate than the ethical discussions on such findings. Moreover, not accounting for the role of political processes, or how experiments derive from them, might result in increased frustration for both researchers and politicians. On the one hand, researchers might feel the experiment failed to answer their questions because of political tampering, as in the Finnish or Ontario experiments. Moreover, they might also find that results are poorly communicated, or worse, manipulated or misinterpreted to accommodate existing political agendas, as the case of Finland is again an example (Wispelaere et al. 2018). But politicians might also be frustrated: they might feel an experiment is too difficult to communicate, given their complex caveats and assumptions, or their results. Or maybe they might feel an experiment fails to be both morally and instrumentally relevant by not answering questions and challenges of a given community which were politically salient. Finally, we should also keep in mind how a third group of stakeholders might see their expectations unmet, namely the basic income movement, by considering that a given experiment might either be misinterpreted or not taken into account by politicians, or whose scientific design might fail to answer questions such as whether basic income is feasible and why, or how it might help solve local or global problems connected with some groups within the movement (e.g., the transition to more ecologically sustainable societies).

So, if scientifically driven experiments are not the answer, but existing social experiments have led to unmet expectations and frustrations from some of the key stakeholders around the basic income debate, how can we work around such shortcomings?

Our interviews provided different strategies to help mitigate this phenomenon, which go in line with some of the advice Karl Widerquist provides when recommending that we should "tailor the research to the empirical questions at issue; do not tailor the questions to the answers research techniques are good at finding" (Widerquist 2018, 136). Hence, a first strategy to consider involves collecting empirical inputs from communities before implementing a basic income experiment or pilot: we should know what questions a representative sample of the community would like to see answered with a basic income experiment. But these questions should be formed with the political process and agenda in mind. When discussing the Madhya Pradesh pilot in India, it was clear from our interview how the political process was fundamental in building momentum for a pilot to take place. First, the debate on basic income in the country was framed on an efficiency basis: to increase overall efficiency and decrease corruption vis-a-vis the existing food and commodities subsidies the government granted to the poor. But as the debate progressed, and the Madhya Pradesh pilot and several other experiments in the country took off, the debate shifted and started focusing more on basic income itself, instead of how it could solve the existing subsidies issue. The current COVID-19 pandemic shifted the debate again, focusing on how basic income can be an economic instrument to boost post-pandemic recovery, and therefore, our interviewee Sarath Davala believes such a context will most likely mean that a new experiment or policy will have to be framed as an economic instrument to help solve the current economic crisis in the country. As such, he considered this as having clearly shown how experiments need to fit within existing claims from the population and challenges of given social assistance mechanisms, which also means one needs to consider what key characteristics of basic income (e.g., universal, or unconditional nature) are most attractive for both the population and politicians. In India, for example, it seemed the unconditional nature of basic income was the most attractive political characteristic, since a nation-wide unconditional cash transfer for farmers was implemented. This means that the pre-requisite of being unconditional has become less of a moral principle, and more of an instrumental argument, namely for politicians, who perceive it as a chance to win over their electorate.

Hence, acknowledging the context is key. On the one hand, understanding which pillars of basic income are attractive and relevant for communities and politicians, and why, can help advance the debate and promote discussion toward implementing either a basic income policy or an experiment or pilot. On the other hand, acknowledging the concerns and topics that are on the agenda of both politicians and a representative sample of the community, and what they would like to see answered in a UBI experiment or pilot might be key to its success. This is partly what has been happening in some of the experiments taking place in the USA, and which has resulted in the MGI initiative. In the SEED experiment, the community had a hand in designing the experiment, but also in what results would be collected and published. For example, the community decided that the experiment should not be fully targeted, but rather should allow for most people in the community to have the chance to receive it. They also decided that each household should decide who would be the recipient of the SEED money (since the money was attributed to households, and not individuals), instead of the initial proposal of researchers to give it to women. The community also decided that spending patterns should be reported, an outcome which was not deemed critical by the researchers in the initial designing phases of the experiment. The surge in locally based UBI experiments in the country and the current MGI initiative are moves toward this direction. The initiative is not only collecting insights from existing and former experiments when designing and implementing new ones but is also looking to aggregate and relate findings to answer some local and nation-wide concerns.

Designing experiments, pilots, and even policies with inputs from political stakeholders and a representative sample from the local community will allow them to be better accommodated within the political process from the onset, and likely reduce the possibility for results to be misinterpreted or manipulated. It will also perhaps resonate more with the challenges and claims of communities, hence increasing community empowerment, belonging, and self-determination and most likely contribute toward the acceptance and ownership of the experiment, pilot, or policy by the community. Hence, it will likely help everyone in the community to better understand findings, and how they can be relevant (or not) to their concerns and aspirations. Finally, context-specific experiments might also increase the likelihood of the experiment, pilot, or policy resulting in new and more engaged advocates of basic income in case experiments do indeed help solve issues they find relevant. If this is the case, they might be the most effective tool to fuel local movements and collective action for basic income, hence becoming a strong advocacy tool.

Despite considering this the best way moving forward, it is important to be aware of how this strategy will enhance limitations of the debate on UBI experiments, pilots, and policies. On the one hand, connecting experiments with existing contexts and framing research questions to local concerns and challenges might result in very different research designs and clusters of impacts. In fact, this is what is happening in the current wave of experiments in the USA, where after Stockton several other experiments are taking place within and outside the MGI initiative. In fact, some are targeted toward groups, while others are more general in their targets, for example (Baker and Martin-West 2020). This will reinforce the already existing limitation of scalability and comparability between experiments and their findings, which we discussed in Chapter 2. The more locally tailored experiments we have, the less we might be able to compare experiments, and especially findings, limiting the possibility of concluding which results might be attributed to basic income as an instrument and policy. On the other hand, tailoring experiments, their questions, and their designs, might also move us far from a basic income. Hence, the more we tailor experiments to local contexts, the further we might move from basic income.

Although the limitations presented above will make the researchers' job more difficult, acknowledging the role of context, incorporating it in the experiment, pilot, or policy design, implementation and aftermath seems to be the necessary step toward more meaningful and clear experiments for communities. It might also be the best way to reduce their vulnerability to misinterpretation and manipulation. Hence, acknowledging the role played by welfare states, political agendas, and the values and concerns of the communities is key. Are they concerned about paternalism, namely whether the money will be spent on items which are deemed unhealthy or morally wrong? Or are they concerned with how basic income can jeopardize individuals' work ethic, which might lead to exploitation? Maybe they simply feel receiving money no strings attached is wrong, echoing concerns with reciprocity? These are all relevant questions for communities, and experiments, pilots, and policies should engage with them and others which might be deemed relevant by stakeholders. As discussed in Sect. 7.1, engaging with such normative questions head-on is critical for the basic income debate, but also as mentioned, for the success of a UBI experiment, pilot and policy. Moreover, even if more locally tailored experiments reduce the scope for comparison and universalization of findings, they might just be enough to fuel local movements for basic income. If that is the case, they might contribute more to a given community or even an entire country adopting a UBI, than what a robust and universal set of findings might be able to do. Finally, the push for countries or communities to adopt a UBI might come more from one real-life and relatable example, and their subsequent results, than from attempts to have universal findings on the impact basic income had across different experiments, pilots, and policies. As such, and despite the challenges, we should acknowledge the limitations of social experiments, but also how they are influenced by the context. Doing so should allow us to use the insights and concerns stemming from context to the advantage of the key players engaged in a basic income experiment, pilot, or policy, namely researchers, politicians, the basic income movement, and particularly the communities impacted by such experiments.

7.3 Toward a Pandemic Basic Income?

The COVID-19 pandemic has caused one of the most dramatic economic crises of the last decades. While most European and OECD countries were experiencing a period of prosperity and economic growth when the pandemic hit, they were still recovering from the austerity measures adopted by many of them since the financial crisis of 2008 (OECD 2021). As a result of these measures and the pandemic, many countries now have a large part of their populations living in precariousness and in constant economic uncertainty. Obviously, worse economic and labor conditions lead to a more vulnerable life-situation. Therefore, and beyond the dramatic impact on public health and the loss of human lives, hundreds of millions of people are now struggling to cope with the current economic situation.

Most governments across the ideological spectrum have endorsed some economic measures that would have been unimaginable in 2008 and even just a few weeks before the COVID-19 pandemic, including increasing public investments and macro-stimulus packages like the NextGeneration package at the European level (ILO 2021). As early as May 2020, 168 countries reinforced or implemented new social programs, such as anticipating payments of in-cash benefits, increasing the coverage rates of already-existing policies, as well as the amount and conditions of some means-tested benefits, extending health insurance for temporary workers, subsidizing social protection contributions for at-risk workers and companies, or reinforcing child protection programs, among others measures (UN 2018). In particular, 130 new cash transfer programs have been implemented in 88 countries (Gentilini et al. 2020).

In Latin America, various cash transfer policies have been implemented while most of those already in place have also been reinforced or substantially redesigned.[4] Argentina and Colombia, for example, have increased the amount and the coverage of their already existing means-tested benefits. Mexico is testing different modalities of cash transfer schemas and reinforcing unconditional policies like non-contributory retirement pensions, while also redesigning other pre-existing programs such as in-poverty workers' benefits, student allowances, and micro-credit for individuals and families (CEPAL 2020). Massive popular mobilization in Brazil forced conservative president Jair Bolsonaro to implement what could be called an "emergency basic income" for three months (which was extended to four), which granted 595 *reais* (about 115 US dollars) to all adult Brazilians living with a monthly income below half the minimum wage, and thus covering about 60 million direct beneficiaries, plus 120 million indirectly (Lavinas 2020).

In the USA, the Coronavirus Aid, Relief, and Economic Security Act—an emergency package of about 2 trillion US dollars—was rapidly rolled out, including extended coverage and larger unemployment benefits, along with direct cash transfers without any other condition than having a gross income below 99,000 US dollars for individuals (the threshold was increased by 10,000 US dollars for each child under 17).

[4] See for instance: https://dds.cepal.org/observatorio/socialcovid19/listamedidas.php?id_tmedida=1.

The USA, perhaps due to the weakness of its welfare model and social policies, opted to grant people cash rapidly and directly through different in-cash mechanisms, whereas European governments seem to have prioritized providing public support by subsidizing companies and strategic sectors while meliorating some other in-kind social policies. Despite these two different strategies and the debate on their differing efficiencies,[5] the COVID-19 pandemic has potentiated in-cash measures in Europe too. Although a European basic income schema to help citizens cope with the COVID-19 pandemic has been proposed (Neves and Merrill 2020), many European countries have opted to reinforce their already-in-place means-tested schemas or by implementing new ones, such as the *Ingreso Minimo Vital* in Spain. However, most of these programs were either temporary or based on a single cash transfer. Others targeted only workers in poverty, or only those temporary unemployed due to the transitory lockdown of their companies. Some of the pitfalls and administrative limitations of these kinds of mechanisms in addressing poverty and inequality are well-known, including stigmatization, low coverage rates and non-take-ups, which end up excluding many people who need those programs (EESC 2013). These and other administrative, bureaucratic, and moral problems associated with these traditional cash benefits have potentiated the interest for more efficient, rapid and simple solutions, such as the UBI proposal. Illustratively, the *Financial Times* even stated that "policies until recently considered eccentric, such as basic income and wealth taxes, will have to be in the mix".[6]

In places as different as Barcelona, Iran, India, Kenya, and Germany, the pandemic has stimulated the pre-existing debate among the population and governments. The interview from Stockton, for example, revealed how the pandemic exposed the already-existing fragilities and

[5] A recent article by the *Financial Times*, for example, asks whether the US stimulus payments sent to each American are reducing the incentive to go back to work. In some US states with unconditional grants, companies are facing challenges in hiring, now that economies are opening up due to vaccination roll-outs. It is doubtful whether this can be entirely attributed to these cash grants, but nonetheless raises the familiar issue of the impact basic income can have on labor market participation. See the article of the *Financial Times*: "Why pandemic benefits spell trouble for universal basic income" available at: https://www.ft.com/content/51ed65c0-44fa-4e70-801e-1eaa3fdc2bae (accessed 5 May 2021).

[6] See the article of the Financial Times: https://www.ft.com/content/7eff769a-74dd-11ea-95fe-fcd274e920ca.

inequalities in the USA and its social assistance system, thus leading to more political and individual support for a policy such as basic income. For our interviewees, COVID-19 acted as a catalyst for a surge of interest in basic income. According to both Djavad Salehi-Isfahani from the Iran experiment and Wayne Lewchuk from Ontario, the pandemic has made the unions and other political actors' opinions much more positive toward basic income, understanding it as way to promote a more comprehensive and robust social safety net. Jamie Cooke from Scotland also believed the pandemic has promoted a more positive conception of the idea of a basic income and that has "leapfrogged the basic income discussion up to three or five years". As we were told, it seems that Scotland is now on the verge of deciding whether an experiment or full-fledged national implementation is best—especially since the political window for implementation now appears wide open, particularly since Scottish first minister Nicola Sturgeon stated that due to COVID-19 and its economic consequences, the "time has come [for universal basic income]".[7]

However, the impact of COVID-19 has not always helped advance the idea of basic income, and it might have negatively affected the interpretation of results from already-conducted experiments and basic income-related policies. For example, as we were told by both Timo Verlaat and Roger van Loon on the Utrecht case, the pandemic has reinforced the idea of targeting the neediest members of society and thus has devaluated the unconditionality framework behind some of the treatment groups in their basic income experiment. This is also partly a result of the government's position which, according to our interview, prioritizes a more conservative spending pattern, looking to direct money to specific targeted policies instead of an idea like basic income. In other places, such as Macau, the cash transfer policy might be under threat since it is entirely dependent on casino revenues, which have decreased significantly since the start of the pandemic. Since the benefit is annual, rather than a monthly cash transfer, and dependent on an industry currently under pressure, José Luís de Sales Marques told us in our interview he felt it could be more vulnerable to dismantling or severe cutbacks, hence COVID-19 could reduce popular support for that policy. Therefore, popular opinion might now be less enthusiastic than before due to use of a temporarily vulnerable financing model. Hence, while in some

[7] See the article in *The Independent*: https://www.independent.co.uk/news/uk/home-news/universal-basic-income-ubi-scotland-uk-nicola-sturgeon-coronavirus-a9498076.html.

cases the COVID-19 pandemic has validated the results of experiments and paved the way for further advancements in this sense, in other cases, its socioeconomic consequences and the reaction of governments seem to favor more traditional solutions based on targeted and means-tested benefits. In this way, and although our case studies' results seem quite relevant for informing the possible implementation of a full basic income scheme, the need for emergency remedies seems to have been driving many governments' recent decisions.

Of course, our research was conducted during this global pandemic, which affected everyone's perspectives on the present moment as well as their perception of the basic income idea. Moreover, it also affected the debates on the current and the planned UBI experiments (or related programs) and their role in fighting the most salient and urgent effects of the pandemic. In the media, the number of articles on basic income increased, discussing the history of the idea,[8] while interest from the political sphere grew as well. Finally, it has also fueled the local and global debates on the feasibility and viability of basic income in many ways. For example, as we were told during the interviews, there is an increasing amount of people and social, political and advocacy organizations in Barcelona demanding an "emergency basic income". The current scenario has also made the demand for unconditional cash policies much more salient in Iran. Similarly, the pandemic and its consequences have invigorated the debate in India, particularly on basic income's potential role as an instrument to boost the economic recovery of the country. Although the debate on basic income has been quite persistent in Germany for many years, the team involved in the experiment there is fearful that the actual discussion will turn toward the necessity of adopting a temporary measure instead of a permanent one. In Ontario, as we were told during our interview with Wayne Lewchuk, the pandemic made the idea of basic income even "more plausible than it used to be before the experiment". In this case, even some important labor unions, traditional opponents of basic income in many countries, are now advocating for it. Undoubtedly, COVID-19 has opened the window for political discussion on basic income, yet it is too soon to determine whether it will bring increased

[8] Such as several articles in *The Guardian*, *Vice*, and an endorsement by The Word Economic Forum: by April 2020, major media, and institutions were discussing the possibilities of the idea of basic income or "helicopter money" to tackle the economic and social challenges of the pandemic.

pressure for more experimentation or reduce it in favor of a political adoption of basic income.

Despite this "opened window" and growing interest, our interviewees identified different opinions regarding the basic income idea. Two main, persistent ideological positions within mass media, public opinion, governments, and policymakers seem to stand out. On the one hand are those defending the reinforcement of social policies already in place within the framework of means-tested and conditional cash transfer mechanisms. This view is sometimes characterized by an "incrementalist" logic, which usually prioritizes targeting narrow segments of the population considered most vulnerable (the poorest, the elderly, single mothers, etc.), as a "first step" toward a more universal coverage. On the other hand, and because of the far-reaching impacts of the pandemic, many people, as well as more political parties, labor unions, NGOs, grassroot organizations, and different regional and international institutions turned to the idea of "just giving money to people", creating a strong push for the universalistic and unconditional logic behind UBI. Against this universalistic and unconditional view, three main objections usually emerge (Alabao et al. 2020). First, the *conditioned defense* states that cash transfer policies must not be universal but targeted only to neediest members of society and exclude those above a certain economic threshold, or those who fail to fulfill features or behavioral requirements. Second, the *economic opportunity cost* assures that a basic income would be extraordinarily expensive and disproportionally dominate budgetary allocations that may have been used to fund other public policies, such as public health and education, which would be morally inadmissible, especially during a global calamity, such as a pandemic. Third, the *inability criticism* sustains that basic income would not be an appropriate measure to fix all (or enough) problems related to the pandemic and might be less effective in doing so than measures already in place.

Why not prioritize those most in need as the first *conditioned defense* sustains? When an economic threshold is established as a requirement to receive a benefit, governments create "false positive" and "false negative" cases. The "false positive" is an individual who becomes eligible but in fact should not be so because he has committed some sort of fraud. In contrast, the "false negative" is an individual who must be eligible (because they are in need) but is excluded because the benefit's features may be overly strict, thus excluding them, or because of other administrative reasons (lack of information, difficulties in applying, stigmatization, etc.). Both mistakes similarly distort and affect the efficiency of welfare mechanisms and social policies, but in moral terms, the latter is more problematic than the former. Two additional, related comments are worth stressing here. First, as already observed (Kosec and Mo 2019), satisfaction with the government by individuals receiving means-tested benefits (because they are considered "eligible") increases 0.6% in comparison with those who are not receiving these benefits (those considered "ineligible") decreases by about 10.5%. This means that the negative evaluation of the government is 17.5 times greater than the positive. Governments and politicians in general should worry about this. The second comment is related to the *economic opportunity cost* objection to basic income. If a UBI was financed through a progressive tax model, the people in the position of "false positives", that is those who "do not deserve" a UBI, will end up paying for it in their annual income taxes. The most important thing is that those really in need do not end up without it. By implementing a full unconditional cash transfer, governments would eliminate this situation and consequently would remove the prejudice suffered by the individuals in the "false negative" position.

Why not first finance other social policies such as health services, as the *economic opportunity cost* criticism asserts? Economic resources to finance a UBI should not be taken away from other fundamental social services such as health systems or public education. Indeed, our position is that a UBI must coexist with other services and indirect income distributive mechanisms such as health care, education, pensions, and housing, which in many countries are constitutional rights, and hence cannot (and rightly so, in our perspective) be dismantled. Although most of the existing basic income financing models are usually based on personal income tax (Andrade et al. 2019; Arcarons et al. 2014; Pena Miguel et al. 2017; Torry 2016; Widerquist and Arndt 2020), other additional financing sources are available which would assure no funds would be allocated away from these measures. Tax havens might be eliminated, a sort of Tobin tax might be implemented on fiscal and speculative transactions, robots might pay social security taxes, 0.5% of the super-rich's wealth might be taxed, or new green taxes might be introduced, among other financing sources (Ortiz et al. 2018). Moreover, in line with Piketty's *Capital and Ideology*, a "progressive property and income tax" could also be rolled out, according to which those owning a hundred times the average wealth would pay a ten percent effective tax rate; those worth a thousand times the average would be taxed at 60%; and those ten thousand times wealthier than the average citizen would end up paying 90% (Piketty 2020, 982). A basic income might be financed by "taxing wealth, corporate profits, and income, thus shifting the tax burden toward the rich and the higher-income strata and resulting in strong redistribution" (Lapavitsas et al. 2020). But beyond the exact numbers and calculations, the point is that, particularly during a global pandemic and its disastrous economic consequences, "private ownership cannot count as legitimate where a few own everything and the rest nothing" (Dorfman 2014, 359). In sum, there are several funding sources to finance a UBI; the point is the need of political determination to implement them.

But what if a UBI is not able to solve all the problems caused by the pandemic, not to mention pre-existing ones, as the *inability criticism* posits? Obviously, a measure like a UBI would not be able to solve all the problems posed by COVID-19 nor many of the additional ones such as gender inequalities, the climate emergency, or political corruption, to mention just a few. Nobody can seriously ascribe such a capacity to a UBI. A government's economic policy is based on several complex and interrelated measures, including different fiscal designs, monetary policies, labor programs, social policies, etc. Basic income is *just a single* economic measure among others, although its redistributive impact would be tremendous. Likewise, social protection and welfare systems would not have to end simply because cash would be granted to individuals. Moreover, a UBI would have to be implemented alongside other policies and programs tackling gender inequalities, assuring affordable housing, caring for the elderly and young populations, providing quality public education, granting full access to public health services, and so on. After all, this is precisely what makes a particular model of basic income progressive, namely, the previously mentioned funding model with a progressive taxation on the one hand, and on the other, which other social policies should be implemented present in parallel. We are not defending a UBI as a mechanism to cope with all the problems posed by the current pandemic, nor all other additional socioeconomic challenges, but it cannot be denied that it could entail profound improvements on existing and future, post-pandemic welfare models.

Until now, we have addressed and briefly refuted the three main criticisms the proposal of a basic income usually receives: the *conditioned defense*, the *economic opportunity cost*, and the *inability criticism*. Despite our (and others') counterarguments, it is hardly imaginable someone opposed to basic income will suddenly shift their opinion, since most of the time our opinions are neither based upon available experimental evidence nor upon rational, systematic, and convincing argumentation, but largely on basic ideological assumptions. However, this should not lead us to a dead-end street. The fact that someone does not agree with a basic income does not necessarily entail that he or she cannot accept its implementation just as a temporary, extraordinary measure to cope with the most dramatic consequences of a pandemic or a national emergency. Therefore, both positions might agree on implementing a so-called emergency basic income (EBI), that is, a basic income with a duration limited to the most desperate moment. For example, in the Netherlands, the government introduced the "temporary bridging" measure for self-employed professionals (TOZO in Dutch), an emergency benefit with no-strings attached and free from taxes for self-employed people with an income below the considered "social minimum" (1,239 euros for individuals aged 21 years or older, or 1,701 euros for a two-adult households), amounts which were certainly higher than the benefit offered by the municipal experiments. In Namibia, the Emergency Income Grant (EIG) was also implemented. The EIG was unconditional, and near universal, since all Namibians between 18 and 59 years old who had lost their jobs or had seen their situation worsened because of the lockdown restrictions were entitled to receive a single payment of about 50 US dollars.

Although this is an acceptable *mid-term solution*, it is important to note the downsides and weaknesses of this type of emergency basic income. Jamie Cooke and Jurgen De Wispelaere (2020) have noted two of these problems. The first is precisely its temporary character designed to face the most severe impacts of quarantines and lockdowns and the subsequent general economic shutdown. Indeed, this EBI would be a very efficient and rapid response in the form of a temporary social policy. There would be those who might be able to maintain their previous living standard thanks to an EBI, but in contrast, there would also be those who might not, whose economic situation might end up even worse once the EBI finished. What would have been implemented to support the most affected members of society might have paradoxically ended up worsening their situation in contrast with their better-off fellow citizens. The second pitfall of this EBI is that it must "face both practical and political hurdles at a time when immediate remedies are required as a matter of urgency". Even in a moment of an emergency which requires rapid responses, politicians still reject supporting people unconditionally, by prioritizing and even reinforcing workfare-based programs and means-tested benefits which are much less efficient and more time-consuming and demanding in administrative and bureaucratic terms. Once again, a measure that was supposedly implemented in order to support the entire population would likely end up excluding those most in need, precisely those who were already unemployed or excluded from labor markets even before the pandemic, that is, single mothers, precarious young people, migrants, long-term unemployed people, etc.

Again, as a *mid-term solution* and despite these two (and other possible) limitations, an EBI might seem an adequate measure during pandemic times. Nevertheless, most governments persist in prioritizing strictly conditional, means-tested, and workfare targeted programs, whose efficiency in reducing poverty and social exclusion has been largely criticized (Dwyer 2004; Fletcher and Wright 2020; Gustman et al. 2014; Hanna and Olken 2018; Neuert et al. 2019). However, a basic income must not only be "an emergency policy response to the current pandemic, but also a tool for building resilience into the economic and social fabric of societies that are likely to face further pandemic events in the near future" (De Wispelaere and Morales 2021). Accordingly, we should think of long-term, anticipatory policies which can bring about this resilience in the face of a wide range of potential future crises, such as economic, health, and climate. A full, permanent, universal, and unconditional basic income seems much better equipped to cope with these. As Guy Standing (2020) recommends, this basic income might be initially implemented by only granting a small amount of money, though unconditionally, to all members of society with no strings attached.

Note the difference: Standing's proposal seems quite convincing and strategically superior to the EBI for at least two main reasons. On the one hand, it would remove the necessity to discuss in a confusing and improvised way the convenience of implementing such a measure every time there is a pandemic or an emergency and hence providing a more rapid, stable, and efficient societal safeguard. On the other hand, as it has been defended elsewhere (Standing 2020; Cooke and De Wispelaere 2020; Lapavitsas et al. 2020), its small amount might permit a large and permanent political support. A small amount might also permit rapid adjustment to a dynamic scenario as the emergency context transforms itself. So, this variability of the amount would then work as an "automatic economic stabilizer" maintaining or even boosting internal aggregate demand. This way, the whole economy would resist and recover faster and then the government might reduce the amount until finding a permanent, more stable funding source. Otherwise, if the pandemic or the emergency worsens, the government might easily raise the quantity and adapt to the circumstances.

This seems to be what has occurred in Maricá according to the news released by the program's webpage. Although the plans were to expand the policy to include more recipients in the city, Brazil's legislation did not allow that since it prohibits the introduction of new benefits during an electoral year (as was the case in 2020). However, COVID-19 has potentiated an innovative solution in this case, as the amount of the existing basic income was increased from 130 to 300 reais (46 euros). As reported, COVID-19 deaths and infection rates were lower in Maricá which, as revealed in our interview, might be partly attributed to this change. Because the previous basic income policy turned into this new (more generous) EBI policy, "people could choose to stay at home, to protect themselves instead of having to go to work, regardless of their personal health". The response from the local municipality was much quicker, hence more efficient, and effective than the federal one, since it took just one week to send out the "extra money" to everyone simply because the infrastructure of the cash transfer schema was already in place. In South Korea too, according to the data offered by the Gyeonggi Research Institute, due to the poverty and unemployment caused by COVID-19, the pre-existing Youth Dividend Program implemented in 2019 across all of Gyeonggi Province extended its coverage to all citizens regardless of their age and increased the amount of the grant to 250,000 won (about 220 US dollars). In Barcelona, the city council revived the former B-MINCOME's cash transfer by expanding its coverage beyond its former beneficiaries to reach 34.000 households in need across the whole city. This new "temporary pandemic benefit" unified the previous B-MINCOME grant with other municipal benefits, and it was in place during the first seven months of the pandemic. It was a monthly payment between 250 and 475 euros according to the households' composition and income. It was set up upon the previous B-MINCOME structure since the payments were done through the debit card the pilot project launched in 2017.[9] As discussed above, these examples would support

[9] This and other anti-COVID measures implemented by the city council can be found at: https://ajuntament.barcelona.cat/serveissocials/es/canal/prestacio-economica-durgencia-social-persones-i-families-en-el-context-de-la-covid-19.

the hypothesis according to which, once the cash schema is already in place, the political debate is easily reduced and shifts to the technicalities, which again would make this proposal—a small though permanent basic income, instead of a temporary one—much more efficient and able to rapidly cope with any new crisis or emergency.

Nevertheless, and beyond this debate, it seems the results gathered by UBI experiments have contributed to enhancing scientific and popular understanding of the hypothetical effects of a basic income. Many more people than ever now seem more informed about what basic income is and, probably due to the consequences of COVID-19, they are now less reticent than they used to be when considering unconditionality and universality attached to the welfare state and to social policies. In contrast, these very same socioeconomic impacts have forced our governments to implement urgent measures which are often not consistent with (or even opposed to) the experiments' findings. In doing so, support from governments for this emerging unconditional and universal logic seems more hesitant than support from the general population. Accordingly, in just a very few cases have quasi-basic income measures been adopted, though always under the auspices of emergency responses rather than as a permanent or structural mechanism. The economic and political tensions created by the pandemic and the pressing need for urgent solutions will surely affect the prospects of future basic income experiments and related policies. Therefore, it is not yet clear enough whether the pandemic will contribute to expanding actual interest in experimenting with basic income or, on the contrary, result in prioritizing targeted and focused policies supporting those most in need.

In sum, the COVID-19 pandemic has boosted the debate about the convenience of a universal and unconditional basic income enormously. Although there are those who oppose it because they consider (a) its unconditionality unjust and inefficient, (b) it too costly, or (c) it would not be able to solve all socioeconomic challenges, the so-called emergency basic income is worth considering precisely because both basic income detractors and supporters might agree on it, due to its limited duration and amount. As suggested, this EBI seems to be a well-equipped measure to rapidly cope with the most severe consequences of the COVID-19 pandemic. Nevertheless, the empirical evidence gathered from the interviewed cases and the existent scientific literature discussed above suggest that a permanent, though small, universal, and unconditional basic income might be a superior, more efficient, and stable solution if our concern is not merely restricted to the current pandemic. We need our governments to establish background conditions which enable us to survive this pandemic, but also to build stronger and more resilient societies able to cope with other potential challenges, including other pandemics and ecological crises. In a nutshell, by introducing a permanent, though small, universal, and unconditional basic income now, rather than improvising partial solutions, we would be anticipating future challenges by establishing a stable, robust long-standing tool for a more resilient and decent present and future.

References

Alabao, Núria, Bru Laín, and Daniel Raventós. "Per una renda bàsica universal i incondicional més enllà de la situació actual: una proposta per a un món que s'acaba." *Journal on Social Knowledge and Analysis* 26 (2020): 1–7.

Andrade, Julio, Geoff Crocker, and Stewart Lansley. "Alternative Funding Methods." In *The Palgrave International Handbook of Basic Income*, de Malcom Torry (ed.), 175–190. Cham, Switzerland: Palgrave Macmillan, 2019.

Arcarons, Jordi, Daniel Raventós, and Lluís Torrens. "Feasibility of Financing a Basic Income." *Basic Income Studies* 9, no. 1–2 (2014): 79–93.

Baker, Amy Castro, and Stacia Martin-West. Learning Agenda. The Center for Guaranteed Income Research. The University of Pennsylvania School of Social Policy and Practice, 2020.

Calnistsky, David. "'More Normal than Welfare': The Mincome Experiment, Stigma and Community Experience." *Canadian Sociological Association/La Soci'et'e canadienne de sociologie*, 2016: 26–71.

CEPAL. Comisión Económica para América Latina y el Caribe. *Construir un nuevo futuro. Una recuperación transformadora con igualdad y sostenibilidad.* Santiago de Chile: CEPAL, 2020.

Cooke, Jamie, and Jurgen De Wispelaere. "Basic Income and Pandemic Preparedness." *Green European Journal*, May 18 2020.

de la Brière, Bénédicte, and Laura B. Rawlings. "Examining Conditional Cash Transfers Programmes: A Role for Increased Social Inclusion." In *Social Protection and Inclusion: Experiences and Policy Issues*, 9–32. Geneva: International Labour Office, 2006.

De Wispelaere, Jurgen, and Leticia Morales. "Emergency Basic Income during the Pandemic." *Cambridge Quarterly of Healthcare Ethics* 30, no. 2 (2021): 248–254.

Dorfman, Avihay. "On Trust and Transubstantiation: Mitigating the Excesses of Ownership." In *Philosophical Foundations of Fiduciary Law*, de Andrew S.

Gold and Paul B. Mille (eds.), 339–362. Oxford: Oxford University Press, 2014.

Dwyer, Peter. "Creeping Conditionality in the UK: From Welfare Rights to Conditional Entitlements?" *The Canadian Journal of Sociology* 29, no. 2 (2004): 265–287.

EESC—European Economic and Social Committee. *European Minimum Income and Poverty Indicators*. Brussels: EESC, 2013.

Fletcher, Del Roy, and Sharon Wright. "International Perspectives on the Theories and Practices of Welfare Conditionality." *Social Policy & Administration* 54, no. 2 (2020): 185–326.

Forget, Evelyn. "The Town with No Poverty: The Health Effects of a Canadian Guaranteed Annual Income Field Experiment." *Canadian Public Policy* 37, no. 3 (2011): 283–305.

Gentilini, Ugo, Mohamed Bubaker, Alsafi Almenfi, Pamela Dale, and Vanessa Santos Gustavo C. Indhira. *Social Protection and Jobs Responses to COVID-19: A Real-Time Review of Country Measures*. Washington, DC: World Bank, 2020.

Gertler, Paul J., and Sarah L. Barber. "Empowering Women: How Mexico's Conditional Cash Transfer Programme Raised Prenatal Care Quality and Birth Weight." *Journal of Development Effectiveness* 2 (2010): 51–73.

Gustman, Alan, Thomas Steinmeier, and Nahid Tabatabai. "Distributional Effects of Means Testing Social Security: An Exploratory Analysis." NBER Working Paper n. 20546, 2014.

Hanna, Rema, and Benjamin A. Olken. "Universal Basic Incomes vs. Targeted Transfers: Anti-Poverty Programs in Developing Countries." NBER Working Paper n. 24939, 2018.

ILO—International Labour Organization. *World Employment and Social Outlook: Trends*. Geneva: International Labour Office, 2021.

Kosec, Katrina, and Cecilia Hyunjung Mo. "Does Relative Deprivation Condition the Effects of Social Protection Programs on Political Attitudes?" International Food Policy Research Institute—Discussion Paper , 2019.

Laín, Bru. "Report on the Preliminary Results of the B-MINCOME Project (2017–2018)." Ajuntament de Barcelona, 2019.

Laín, Bru. "Basic Income Experiments: Limits, Constraints and Opportunities." *Ethical Perspectives* 28, no. 1 (2021): 89–101.

Laín, Bru, and Roberto Merrill. "Why Do We Run Basic Income Experiments? From Empirical Evidence to Collective Debate." *Basic Income Studies* 16, no. 1 (2021): 27–38.

Lapavitsas, Costas, Lluís Torrens, Sergi Cutillas, and Pablo Cotarelo. "A Pandemic Basic Income to Confront the Crisis: Evidence from Spain." Rosa-Luxemburg-Stiftung Policy Paper n. 3/2020, 2020.

Lavinas, Lena. "Brazil: COVID-19 and Universal Basic Income under Ultra-liberalism." CIEPP Serie Análisis de Coyuntura, no. 26 (2020).
Merrill, Roberto, and Catarina Neves. 2021. "Unconditional Basic Income and State as an Employer of Last Resort: A Reply to Alan Thomas." *Basic Income Studies*.
Neves, Catarina. "Basic Income Experiments: Expanding the Debate on UBI and Reciprocity." *Basic Income Studies* 16, no. 1 (2021): 55–74.
Neuert, Harrison, Eleni Fischer, Matthew Darling, and Anthony Barrows. Work Requirements Don't Work. A Behavioral Science Perspective. Ideas 42, 2019.
Neves, Catarina, and Roberto Merrill. "Encouraging European Solidarity: An Unconditional Basic Income." Social Europe, 2020.
Noguera, José A., and Jurgen De Wispelaere. "A Plea for the Use of Laboratory Experiments in Basic Income Research." *Basic Income Studies*, 2006: 1–6.
OEC—Organisation for Economic Co-operation and Development. *OECD Economic Outlook*. Paris: OECD Publishing, 2021.
Ortiz, Isabel, Christina Behrendt, Andrés Acuna-Ulate, and Quynh Anh Nguyen. "Universal Basic Income Proposals in Light of ILO Standards: Key Issues and Global Costing." International Labour Office Working Paper n. 62, 2018.
Pena Miguel, Noemi, J. Iñaki De la Peña Esteban, and Ana Isabel Fernandez-Sainz. "Financial Model for Universal Minimum Benefit for Spain." *Basic Income Studies* 12, no. 1 (2017): 1–16.
Piketty, Thomas. *Capital and Ideology*. Cambridge, MA: The Belknap Press of Harvard University Press, 2020.
Standing, Guy, Coronavirus, crisis económica y renta básica, *El País*. 2020. Available at: https://elpais.com/elpais/2020/03/11/opinion/1583929510_196303.html
Torry, Malcom. *The Feasibility of Citizen's Income*. Cham, Switzerland: Palgrave Macmillan, 2016.
UN—United Nations. *Some Lessons from Microfinance and Basic Income*. United Nations Conference on Trade and Development, Geneva: United Nations, 2018.
White, Stuart. *The Civic Minimum: On the Rights and Obligations of Economic Citizenship*. Oxford: Oxford University Press, 2003.
Widerquist, Karl. *A Critical Analysis of Basic Income Experiments for Researchers, Policymakers and Citizens*. Parlgrave Macmillan, 2018.
Widerquist, Karl. "Possibilities and Pitfalls of UBI Experiments." Symposium on Karl Widerquist's book, 2021.
Widerquist, Karl, and Georg Arndt. "The Cost of Basic Income in the United Kingdom: A Microsimulation Analysis." BasicIncome.org. 2020. https://basicincome.org/wp-content/uploads/2020/07/Cost-of-BI-in-the-UK-A-Microsimulation-ForPosting.pdf.

Wispelaere, Jurgen De, Antti Halmetoja, and Ville-Veikko Pulkka. "The Rise (and Fall) of the Basic Income Experiment in Finland." CESifo Forum, 2018: 15–18.

World Bank Group. *Exploring Universal Basic Income: A Guide to Navigating Concepts, Evidence and Practices*. Washington: International Bank for Reconstruction and Development/The World Bank, 2020.

CHAPTER 8

Conclusion: Why Should We Conduct Basic Income Experiments, Pilots, or Policies?

The main goal of this book is to inform students, researchers, practitioners, and policymakers about the main philosophical, epistemological, and sociological questions stemming from UBI experiments, pilots and policies past, present, and future. To do so, we believe we should engage with those who have been involved in bringing about or evaluating such experiments, pilots, and policies. Therefore, we interviewed 18 stakeholders—mostly researchers, but also politicians, advocates, and one beneficiary—to understand how the cases in which they have been involved provide interesting information on the goals, contexts, methodologies and of course implementation and aftermath of UBI experiments, pilots, and policies. Based on their comprehensive answers, and the literature on UBI and cash grants, we aimed to provide a set of findings and discussions that contribute to the ongoing debate on the benefits, hurdles, and legitimacy of conducting basic income experiments and pilots, but also in the assessment of basic income policies that have been implemented.

Such a project involved acknowledging our limited sample: not only in terms of the scope of our interviewees (mostly researchers) but most importantly of our case studies. Hence, in Chapter 2 we highlighted the critical aspects from our interviews which illustrate how so-called UBI experiments, pilots, and policies often bear little resemblance to

R. Merrill et al., *Basic Income Experiments*, Exploring the Basic Income Guarantee,
https://doi.org/10.1007/978-3-030-89120-6_8

the definition of basic income. Moreover, they are a result of methodological decisions—in terms of research design and data collected and analyzed—which led to distinctive outcomes among our case studies. Finally, as any other social experiment, their goals, designs, implementations, and outcomes are all results of their context: the political and institutional context, cultural norms or even the scientific design and purpose, particularly when discussing pilots and experiments. Specifically, we discussed how scientific rigor influences experiments and policies, but perhaps most importantly, how political processes and the national and international debates on basic income influence these experiments. This led to a challenging conclusion: our fifteen case studies, their findings, and their results share very little. Inasmuch as they are representative of UBI in general—which is quite a leap, as we discussed in subsection 2.1 of Chapter 2—they also tell us how difficult it is to compare and generalize findings from these experiments and transpose them to our general knowledge of basic income. This is not new, but rather an acknowledgment of how much the experimental cases of basic income have divested into differing design methodologies and goals, an ongoing discussion when it comes to experimenting with basic income (Torry 2019; Widerquist 2018).

Despite these limitations, it's important to acknowledge another important piece of evidence from both our case studies and interviews, but also from the ongoing literature on cash transfers and basic income (World Bank Group 2020): the fact that we have significant evidence on the impact of *giving money to people*. Some cash transfer experiments investigated the impact of unconditional and universal cash grants, while others looked at varying degrees of targeting, (un)conditionality, and coverage. Besides such evidence, in Chapter 3 we highlighted how our case studies provide additional evidence that unconditional cash transfers have significant positive effects on well-being, happiness, health or promoting trust, autonomy, and social participation, among other qualitative dimensions. Their impact in stimulating economic activity or the role women play in enabling many of the positive results is also highlighted. However, despite such evidence, we still have many important gaps in our knowledge on basic income, namely when it comes to labor market participation, but also other results such as migration or consumer behaviors. As such, we looked at our interviews to try to sketch out a general impression on what role UBI experiments can and or even should play: gathering additional evidence, acting as a tool for advocacy, expanding the debate, promoting political implementation of basic income, or contributing to the normative debate on basic income.

Chapter 4 elaborated on the role of the context, briefly discussed in Chapter 2, by going deeper into what our interviewees told us about the motivations to implement a UBI experiment, pilot, or policy. For some, instrumental and strategic motivations were key, while for others, moral reasons were behind the decision to implement a UBI experiment, pilot, or even policy. Such an apparent dichotomy might not be so relevant: most of our case studies were motivated by both (even when one is able to identify one as dominant). Hence, understanding how an experiment might have different scientific and political goals, and result from competing motivations (or not), is perhaps more important to make sense of the results and aftermath. Next, we discussed the role researchers and politicians play in framing the discussion, and how the latter are not the former, and vice versa. Finally, we considered how one of the defining contextual features that shape UBI experiments, pilots, and policies is the welfare state or existing mechanisms for social security. Each of these factors combines to create a unique situation in each of our case studies.

Chapter 5 also builds on part one but extends our discussion to the findings of our case studies. It begins by discussing how results tend to be interpreted. Specifically, it discusses how national and international media have a tremendous influence in how a given experiment's results might be interpreted. This in turn creates long-lasting impressions on the experiment, pilot, or policy, or even on basic income as an idea. As we mentioned, we have a lot of evidence on UBI experiments, and on cash grants in general. However, such findings are scattered, usually highly influenced by the context, by a narrow definition of the goals of experiments, pilots, and policies and by the "mainstream" interpretation of the experiments' success and results. This, combined with the limitations in testing many of these outcomes, results in important gaps in our understanding, most notably on labor market participation, as discussed in Chapter 2, but also in findings such as trust, shifts in power relations, or even impacts on migration.

Chapter 6 discusses some of the challenges in moving from experimentation to political implementation. This was a key concern for most of our interviewees. It was also a puzzling problem to many of the stakeholders we engaged with, particularly those who were involved in experiments or pilots that have ended with positive results. In Sect. 6.1 we discuss how experiments are both tools for political mobilization, but also research tools. The problem is that most of the time, politicians and researchers do not share the same language, tools, or motivations. Hence, mismatched expectations and differences in their aims and methods can lead to frustration and conflict between all parties, which is an additional challenge to navigate when experimenting with basic income and related concepts. Moreover, experiments and pilots can also be prey to political manipulation, namely of the results. This seemed a looming concern to some of the stakeholders we interviewed: basic income is controversial, but can also be attractive, as a transformative idea. It can, in a way, become the ultimate populistic idea, and hence be used as such. Finally, our case studies also highlighted the need to discuss experimentation versus lobbying as mechanisms for the implementation of a basic income. For some, experiments and pilots are legitimate because of their research purpose, but also for what they can do in terms of promoting the support for a basic income. Some of our interviewees highlighted the need to consider the policy window for basic income implementation: if such a window is opened, pushing for experiments or pilots might undermine, rather than lead to, implementing a nation-wide or regional basic income.

Building on the discussions on the goals, contexts, methods, results, and advocacy claims we had in parts one and two, we started part three by providing normative claims to different questions:

In Sect. 7.1, we wondered whether we should legitimize UBI experiments on the grounds of needing more empirical data. We asked the following: should we focus on trying to understand the gaps in our knowledge on basic income, based on the insights from experiments? Our answer was ambiguous: we believe evidence won't settle the debate on basic income. However, empirical data gathered from experiments can indeed contribute to the advocacy movement and to the ethical discussion on the role basic income can play in solving current societal challenges. Doing so involves trying not to generalize findings, but rather to acknowledge the pieces of evidence we have from different UBI experiments, and understand how they relate to their particular context, but also to the idea of basic income.

In Sect. 7.2, we discussed the role of different stakeholders' motivations and goals, and how they can influence a UBI experiment. Instead of arguing against the possibility of tampering with an experiment, and claiming the need for self-contained experiments, we reinforce the need to acknowledge and also consider the context. Many gaps in our knowledge can't be answered by self-contained experimentation. Moreover, experiments can also possibly become prey to misinterpretation and manipulation, especially if the language, design, and communication of the results is geared toward discussing their scientific nature (e.g., caveats and assumptions), rather than making sense of results for critical stakeholders (e.g., communities or even the media). Therefore, we believe we should soften the call for self-contained experiments, and argue for context-meaningful experiments, pilots, and policies. Doing so means understanding which features of basic income are of relevance for researchers, politicians, communities, and other stakeholders, but also framing the experiment's goals in accordance with the concerns and challenges faced by the same set of stakeholders. This will increase the likelihood of communities and politicians having ownership of the experiments, pilots, and policies, but also make them clearer and reduce their vulnerability to misinterpretation.

Finally, in Sect. 7.3, we discussed the role the COVID-19 pandemic has in the current debate on basic income. Our interviewees discussed the role the pandemic has had in accelerating the debate in their countries. In some cases, it has led to a push for UBI experiments (e.g., the USA), whereas in others, it seems to be contributing to widespread support for a nation-wide roll-out of a basic income (e.g., in the Netherlands, or Namibia). There are also places where the pandemic inspired countries to consider short-term quasi-basic income programs (e.g., Spain). We discussed the different recent outcomes of these quasi-basic income programs and questioned whether an external shock such as the COVID-19 pandemic should encourage basic income advocates to argue for short-term quasi-basic income policies or whether we should push for UBI experiments. We argued that an emergency basic income is arguably a much needed and likely more efficient measure to cope with vulnerabilities exposed by the pandemic, but is inferior to what a modest, permanent, universal, and unconditional basic income could do. Hence, we argue that instead of focusing on using the pandemic to justify short-term, targeted unconditional transfers, we should rather focus on permanent universal and unconditional cash grants, even if the amount for now would have to be lower than what most basic income advocates would like to see implemented.

Considering the information and discussions in part one, two, and three, it is important to summarize our main lessons, before finally addressing the key question of our book: Why should we have basic income experiments? What is the role of basic income experiments, pilots, and policies as political, research or advocacy tools?

The first, and one of the key conclusions is the role played by the context. Our case studies cannot escape their context. Their historical, cultural, institutional, and scientific context influenced the process of the experiment, pilot, or policy from its ideation up until its aftermath.

The impossibility of escaping their context means that generalizing findings is a very difficult task. Hence, what we have is a set of evidence from different experimental and non-experimental contexts, that might offer us some information on the impact of unconditional cash grants on issues such as labor market participation, community empowerment, trust or economic activity. However, this set of findings will most likely not be robust enough in aggregate to allow a general conclusion on the impact of UBI on any of these variables. Basic income advocates or researchers, but also politicians and media, should all be more prudent when looking at the findings from these case studies as sources for universal knowledge on basic income and its potential impacts.

This was also a struggle we faced throughout the book: the impossibility of having a tidy conclusion on the impact of basic income on any particular result. Not being able to escape the context of our case studies also meant we could not aim to generalize any of our presumptive hypotheses (e.g., the role media or politicians might have in framing an experiment or policy goal, or the role of institutional welfare mechanisms have on the design of a given experiment or policy). Therefore, during the book we do not provide one single narrative on basic income or even on basic income experiments, pilots, or policies. However, we encourage you, the reader, to consider this one valuable contribution: we offer fifteen different narratives of how basic income can be framed differently, according to the context where each of our case studies took place, but also according to the perspective of each of our stakeholders. As Anna Tsing points out in her book on matsutake mushrooms: "A rush of stories cannot be neatly summed up. Its scales do not nest neatly; they draw attention to interrupting geographies and tempos. These interruptions elicit more stories. This is the rush of stories' power as a science" (Tsing 2015, 43). Hence, while the fifteen narratives we provide cannot offer generalization, they can highlight discontinuities, similarities and how particular features of each context play a significant role in how each case study was implemented and interpreted by various stakeholders.

The second conclusion is about the nature of our case studies. In fact, they share two features: (1) they are all social science experiments or policies which are being evaluated as such, which means they inherit the limitations of the methodologies employed in such experiments; and (2) they all differ from the definition of what a UBI is. In that sense, they should probably be called quasi-basic income experiments, pilots, or policies.

Such a conclusion will seem obvious by now, but it should be a second reminder of how our case studies do not allow much generalization and are even limited in what they can tell us about the impacts of unconditional basic income as a policy. Hence, when surveying the results of our fifteen case studies, we were able to highlight impacts that seem to be significant in all of them (e.g., happiness, well-being and health impacts) but we were mostly left with questions about how a UBI could impact consumer choices, migration, labor market participation, or trust. The fact we cannot answer these questions stems from two critical limitations faced by all our case studies.

The first limitation is about how we assess results. The experimental cohort of our case studies (which includes experiments and pilots) fits into the definition of social science experiments, which try to understand the impact of given policies on particular groups of the population or communities. Because they are not self-contained experiments (e.g., laboratory experiments, where we have more control over the treatment variables), it is very difficult to establish causality between the treatment and the results obtained. Hence, in most of our case studies, it was not possible to say that the increases or decreases in labor market participation are solely attributable to the unconditional cash grant implemented during the experiment. Our case studies tried to answer these limitations using different methodologies (saturation studies or RCTs) and combining different methods to collect data (quantitative, qualitative or both). However, in all of them escaping the complexity of the context made such causality very difficult to obtain, hence making any strong claim on the impact of unconditional grant very difficult to assert.

The second limitation is about their similarity with what unconditional basic income is, according to the definition we provided in our introduction. All our case studies differ in some respect to this definition. Hence, even if we could attribute results to the cash grant implemented, we would still have to be very careful in relating those results to basic income. Hence, we should most likely call our case studies quasi-basic income experiments, pilots, or policies, and acknowledge such limitations when discussing how their contexts and findings might help us make sense of basic income as an idea and potential policy.

The third limitation is that none of our case studies has directly led to political implementation. However, they all have been influenced by political processes and agendas.

In all our interviews, particularly those related with past experiments or pilots, one of the key questions that came up was: why has not basic income been implemented in any of the places where an experiment, pilot, or policy has proven to be successful? We have seen positive results across variables such as well-being or health in most cases, and there does not seem to be any sign of major labor withdraw that could scare off widespread support for basic income. Then why haven't we seen a basic income implemented in places such as Namibia or Finland?

One possible answer might be that results are limited and cannot be entirely related to basic income as an idea. As we have seen, we cannot truly attribute results (positive or negative) to basic income, hence a political party or politician might not want to commit to implementing a basic income based on existing evidence. Another alternative explanation might be that evidence is in fact not that useful to settle the debate on basic income. Maybe basic income as an idea would have to fit within political and ideological agendas, instead of using evidence to explain why basic income could help solve a given issue. Finally, it might be a combination of both: maybe experiments and pilots can be helpful to push for political implementation, but only if the political window for basic income is open. Hence, if there is some political support for basic income as an idea, evidence (from that specific context or elsewhere) might be helpful as an additional push.

Hence, and even considering these three possible alternative explanations, what our case studies seem to show is that basic income experiments, pilots, or small-scale policies per se will not lead to political implementation of basic income. Hence, arguing for them solely on the grounds of political implementation might not be the best possible route for basic income advocates.

These critical conclusions all point toward understanding that:

1. Experiments and pilots are limited, and hence, they will most likely not be able to answer our questions on knowledge gaps regarding basic income.

2. Even if they were, the influence of the context makes generalization and scalability difficult or impossible. Moreover, the difference between experiments and pilots and what a basic income actually is makes attributing their results to a basic income a very difficult task. And lastly,
3. None of the experiments or pilots seem to have led to political implementation, at least in the places where experiments took place.

Hence, it follows that experiments and pilots are not entirely useful as research tools: they cannot answer our knowledge gaps, and findings are not universal or cannot be generalized. But they don't seem to be useful as political or advocacy tools either: experiments do not seem to lead to implementation. Then how can we justify having more basic income experiments or pilots?

We believe experiments can be justified as research, political and advocacy tools if we take all these limitations and considerations into account, and include them in the way we design, implement, and evaluate experiments. To do so, we propose seven general principles that experiments and pilots (and even small scale, quasi-basic income policies) should try to respect, to be justified as meaningful research, political and advocacy mechanisms.

Principle one: Experiments or pilots should be designed and implemented in a way that allows for scientifically robust collection of empirical data (looking to be able to attribute certain results to the policy implemented). Even policies should be evaluated having such concerns in mind.

Principle two: Experiments and pilots should have sound ethical designs (and policy evaluation should also incorporate such concerns). Before conducting an experiment or pilot, or implementing any evaluation mechanism, the stakeholders behind the initiative should consider whether testing an unconditional grant in a particular population for a short period of time is ethically reasonable and what are its ethical downsides. Adequate compensation, methodological changes, or even withdrawing from the experiment should be considered. Moreover, engaging the communities in the ideation and design process should also be considered from the start to mitigate some of the possible ethical downsides of the initiative.

Principle three: Any experiment, pilot, or policy should engage different stakeholders throughout its different stages: ideation, design, implementation, evaluation, and aftermath. Stakeholders should not only be informed, but also depending on their degree of influence, power and how they might be affected, should also be asked to provide insights and their concerns should be taken into consideration as much as possible in the framing and design the initiative.

Principle four: The empirical data collected according to principle one should be relevant for local stakeholders, which means it should be relatable with existing challenges in the context where it's being implemented, and which led to the experiment in the first place.

Principle five: To generate meaningful and relatable data, the researchers involved in the experiment, pilot, or policy need to be capable of informing other stakeholders (e.g., politicians, media, other researchers, and communities) about the purpose, design, and results of the experiment, pilot, or policy. Providing quality and clear information for the main stakeholders should be a key concern in any of these cases.

Principle six: Whenever possible, experiments, pilots, and policies should look to engage with the normative debates on basic income. Basic income is at least as much a discussion on values as it is on empirical data. Therefore, relatable evidence collected should be discussed in light not only of local challenges, but also local normative debates: is working preferable? Should we aim to increase institutional or interpersonal trust or why not? Do we want to attempt to influence migration fluxes, or not? Should we aim to increase individual autonomy or not?

Principle seven: The political window for basic income should always be considered before, during, and after an experiment, pilot, or policy. It is important to understand whether the political climate favors implementing a basic income, in which case an experiment might stall or derail such impetus or whether gathering relatable data through an experiment might be the decisive ingredient for a political movement favoring basic income. In the first case, an experiment or pilot might be detrimental, whereas in the second, it might be essential. But this also means that an unfavorable policy window might mean an experiment won't be able to lead to political implementation, in which case its justification would have to lie elsewhere, or it may not be legitimate to argue for an experiment at all.

These seven principles provide guiding recommendations for those who wish to engage in basic income experiments, pilots, and policies, considering all the limitations and hurdles we mentioned throughout the book. Moreover, they also tell us that there is not one single justification for deciding to have a basic income experiment, pilot, or policy. In fact, if these seven principles are met, we might find that a given case is legitimate on the grounds of its benefits as a research, advocacy, or policy tool. In some cases, principle seven might not be applied, meaning that political window for basic income favors adoption rather than experimentation. In that case, an experiment or pilot would only be justified as a research tool, provided that all other principles were to be met. Arguing this is a sufficient justification, given the costs and the ethical compromises of an experiment or pilot, should probably be a case-by-case analysis. In most of our experimental case studies (much less in the policy ones) a mix of research, policy, and advocacy-related motivations seem to have been present in the framing of the experiment or pilot. Hence, we believe these principles provide a good starting point to contribute to the achievement of all these motivations.

We believe that the fifteen narratives contained in this book provide a rich overview of the context-specific nature of basic income experiments, pilots, and policies, allowing us to compare them and highlight their differences and features. These learnings are also significant to understand not only the context and limitations of experimenting of basic income, but also to know more of UBI as a policy. One such conclusions is the need to disregard a view of UBI as a standalone policy. The evidence on our case studies seems to demonstrate the importance of socially inclusive policies or social activities and involvement, especially for those who are worst-off. The idea of UBI as a mechanism to expand real freedom is a critical normative claim. Our case studies highlight the potential role a basic income can have in advancing such a clame, particularly to those who are worst-off in society, and to whom the potential impacts of maximizing real freedom would be tremendous. However, the several interviews we had also seem to indicate that such a promise—of expanding real freedom—might in some cases come solely from a UBI, whereas in most times it might probably only come as a result of combining a UBI with other policies such as social inclusion ones, or state as employer of last resort, for example (Merrill and Neves 2021).

Hence, the exercise conducted in this book is not only helpful to understand the limitations involved in experimenting with basic income, but also contributes to debates moving forward about how these initiatives can help both normative debates on basic income and research on the topic, and the political movement pushing for its implementation. As such, we believe the findings provided in this book are helpful for the various stakeholders—researchers, politicians, advocates, media, and communities—who are interested or have been engaged in basic income experiments, pilots, and policies throughout the world.

References

Merrill, Roberto, and Catarina Neves. 2021. "Unconditional Basic Income and State as an Employer of Last Resort: A Reply to Alan Thomas." Basic Income Studies.

Torry, Malcom (ed.). *The Palgrave International Handbook of Basic Income.* London: Palgrave Macmillan, 2019.

Tsing, Anna Lowenhaupt. *The Mushroom at the End of the World: On the Possibility of Life in Capistalist Ruins.* Princeton: Princeton University Press, 2015.

Widerquist, Karl. *A Critical Analysis of Basic Income Experiments for Researchers, Policymakers and Citizens*. Parlgrave Macmillan, 2018.

World Bank Group. *Exploring Universal Basic Income. A Guide to Navigating Concepts, Evidence and Practices.* Washington: International Bank for Reconstruction and Development/The World Bank, 2020.

Exhibits

Exhibit 1

Name of the Experiment/Policy	*Stakeholder*	*Description*	*Status*
Basic Income Experiment (Finland)	Minna Ylikännö	Senior Specialist, Ministry of Economic Affairs and Employment At the time of the experiment, worked at the Research Unit of Kela as head of the research team	Finished
Utrecht Experiment (The Netherlands)	Roger van Loon	Utrecht Municipality (one of the institutions behind the experiment)	Finished
Utrecht Experiment (The Netherlands)	Timo Verlaat	PhD candidate at Utrecht University School of Economics, involved in the Utrecht experiment	Finished

(continued)

R. Merrill et al., *Basic Income Experiments*, Exploring the Basic Income Guarantee, https://doi.org/10.1007/978-3-030-89120-6

(continued)

Name of the Experiment/Policy	*Stakeholder*	*Description*	*Status*
B-MINCOME—Barcelona experiment (Spain)	Lluís Torrens	Director of social innovation at Barcelona city council and one of the researchers responsible for the B-MINCOME experiment	Finished
Ontario's Experiment (Canada)	Wayne Lewchuk	Researcher involved in the Ontario experiment, from McMaster University	Finished
Basic Income Grant Coalition experiment in Namibia)	Dirk Haarmann	Claudia and Dirk Harmann coordinated the Basic Income Grant Coalition in Namibia (2004–2009), implemented the BIG Pilot Project in Otjivero (Namibia) and led its impact assessment	Finished
Madhya Pradesh experiment (India)	Sarath Davala	One of the lead researchers involved in the design and implementation of the experiment	Finished
SEED—The Stockton Economic Empowerment Demonstration (USA)	Stacia West	Co-Principal Investigator of the Stockton experiment in California, USA. Co-Founder of the Center for Guaranteed Income Research at The University of Pennsylvania	Ongoing
SEED—The Stockton Economic Empowerment Demonstration (USA)	Amy Castro	Co-Principal Investigator of the Stockton experiment in California, USA. Co-Founder of the Center for Guaranteed Income Research at The University of Pennsylvania	Ongoing
GiveDirectly experiments in Kenya	Caroline Teti	Works for GiveDirectly, involved in the experiment happening in Kenya	Ongoing

(continued)

(continued)

Name of the Experiment/Policy	*Stakeholder*	*Description*	*Status*
Renda Básica da Cidadania in Maricá (Brazil)	Fábio Waltenberg	Lead researcher from Universidade Federal Fluminense hired to assess some of the results of the Maricá experiment	Ongoing
Renda Básica da Cidadania in Maricá (Brazil)	Fernando Freitas	Researcher in the team hired to assess the results of Maricá experiment	Ongoing
Macau's Wealth Partaking Scheme	José Luís de Sales Marques	President of the Institute of European Studies; Member of the Board of Directors at Portuguese School Foundation-Macau	Ongoing
Eastern Band of Cherokee Indians' Dividend	Randall Akee	Public policy researcher at UCLA Luskin School of Public Affairs	Ongoing policy
Youth Basic Income Project in South Korea	Hyosang Ahn	Executive director of BIKN – Basic Income Korea Network	Ongoing
Iran	Djavad Salehi-Isfahani	Professor of Economics at Virginia Tech and Nonresident Senior Fellow, Brookings Institute	Ongoing
Scotland	Jamie Cooke	Head of RSA Scotland	Planned
Berlin	Maheba Goedeke Tort	Conception and research coordination of the UBI experiment	Planned

Exhibit 2

General script of the interviews for the book project
On the experiment's design:

1. Which was/is the main goal of your experiment (e.g., reduce poverty or social exclusion, reduce sanctions of actual social policies, etc.)?
2. Who is the targeted population and why?
3. How is the experiment funded? Which is the main funding source?

4. Which is the department, office, or institution in charge of your experiment? Who is designing, implementing, and evaluating the experiment?
5. Which results are you interested in the most? Which effects do you expect to find out? How was the evaluation process designed (qualitative, quantitative, ethnographic, crisscross methods, etc.)?
6. Did your experiment attract the media interest? And if so, how was their coverage?
7. Did other collectives/groups react to your experiment? If so, which ones (practitioners, political groups, scholars, etc.) and in which manner did they react?

On the experiment's context:

8. Why and how did you test a UBI experiment? Which were the main reasons to start an experiment?
9. Which were (if any) the political and social forces claiming for a UBI experiment, there were any political coalition pushing for?
10. Did you negotiate among multiple actors to run the experiment, and if so which were those actors?
11. What is the actual state of the debate on UBI in your country? Did you receive critics for advancing/claiming for a UBI experiment?
12. Did/Does your national/regional legal framework affect your experiment? Did/Will your experiment entail any kind of legal/juridical modification?

On the experiment's results:

13. You already have some preliminary results. Can you explain them briefly to us?
14. Did the results surprise you? If so, why? What were the most important results in your view and why?
15. Do you find differences in the results in terms of gender or minorities?
16. Considering the results of other experiments, do you think these results are like the results from these experiments or not?

Future:

17. How has the COVID-19 pandemic changed the experiment?

Index

R. Merrill et al., *Basic Income Experiments*, Exploring the Basic Income Guarantee,
https://doi.org/10.1007/978-3-030-89120-6

The manufacturer's authorised representative in the EU is Springer Nature Customer Service Centre GmbH, Europaplatz 3, 69115 Heidelberg, Germany. If you have any concerns regarding our products, please contact ProductSafety@springernature.com

Printed and bound by CPI Group (UK) Ltd, Croydon, CR0 4YY
22/09/2026
02221067-0003